D1196457

MUSLIM-CHRISTIAN DIALOGUE:

Promise and Problems

First Edition, 1998
Published in the United States by

Paragon House
2700 University Ave. W.
St. Paul, Minnesota 55114

Library of Congress Cataloging-in-Publication Data

Muslim-Christian dialogue : promise and problems / edited by M.
Darrol Bryant and S. A. Ali. -- 1st ed.
    286 p.   cm.
   Includes index.
   ISBN 1-55778-764-6 (pbk.)
   1. Islam--Relations--Christianity. 2. Christianity and other
religions--Islam. I. Bryant, M. Darrol. II. Ali, S. A., 1933-
BP172.M8215   1998
297.2'83--dc21   98-26383
                                          CIP

Manufactured in the United States of America

A-1

MUSLIM-CHRISTIAN DIALOGUE:

Promise and Problems

EDITED BY
M. DARROL BRYANT & S. A. ALI

PARAGON HOUSE
ST. PAUL, MINNESOTA

Table of Contents

PART IV: PROSPECTS

Acknowledgments

THE PREPARATION of a book is always a collaborative effort, especially when it is, as here, a volume of collected essays. Thus we want to name and thank those who participated in making this contribution to dialogue between Muslims and Christians possible. The conference on "Muslim Christian Dialogue: Problems and Possibilities" where most of these essays were first presented was initiated and supported by the Inter-Religious Federation for World Peace (IRFWP) based in New York City. We are grateful for their support and for their continuing efforts to initiate dialogue among believers of all traditions. We are also thankful for the support of the Department of Islamic Learning in the University of Karachi, Pakistan, a co-sponsor of the conference, and the generous role played by Renison College in the University of Waterloo, Canada, the third co-sponsor of the event. Moreover, the staff at Renison College, especially Karen Sanderson, Andy Vasileas, Kathy Henke and Barbara Checketts were most helpful during the conference in providing the amenities for the conference participants. We are grateful to you all.

As the principal editor for the volume, I also wanted to thank my co-editor, S. A. Ali, for his counsel and support. He has kept me from mistakes in relation to the faith of Islam, and I am grateful to him for that. His access through his daughter, Muna, and her e-mail is what made this long-distance co-editing possible. The role of Susan Hodges Bryant in improving the grammatical and literary quality of these essays must also be acknowledged. She improved, as always, not only my contributions, but also worked her literary skills on all the essays to good effect. When the writers of the essays come from such diverse cultural backgrounds, there is always an issue about the proper role and limits of an editor. Here, we have resisted the temptation to standardize the essays in terms of the voice more characteristic of the western academic world. Instead, we have simply sought to edit the essays for clarity within the context of their own distinctive voice and mode of expression. Consequently, one encounters a range of personal and cultural modes in the following essays, and I consider this diversity essential to the process of dialogue: that is, that we not only allow people to speak in their own voices but that we strive to hear those different voices in their own terms. We must also thank Louise Perlowitz who did the inputting of the essays and graciously handled the many revisions. Finally, to the authors of each essay, thank you for your contributions and your cooperation.

M. Darrol Bryant, April 20, 1998

Muslims, Christians, and Dialogue: An Introduction

M. Darrol Bryant and S. A. Ali

Muslim and Christian/Christian and Muslim

OVER SIXTY PERCENT of the believing world is Christian and Muslim. Christians constitute over thirty percent of the believing world, and they are internally divided into Catholic, Orthodox, and Protestant streams. Just under thirty percent of the believing world is Muslim, and they are divided into Sunni and Shiite streams. Both traditions are referred to by scholars of religion as "Abrahamic" and "monotheistic" faiths, which suggests that there are things held in common by both faiths. Yet ever since the emergence of Islam in the seventh century of the common era, the relations between these traditions have been marked more by misunderstanding and hostility than by mutual respect. There have been rare moments in that history when more positive relations between these two remarkable world faiths have been the order of the day, but those moments have been rare. Here, in this introduction, we want to say something about each of these traditions as background for the essays in Muslim-Christian dialogue that follow.

Christianity emerged out of a Jewish matrix in the first century of our era. It revolved around the figure of Jesus of Nazareth, his life, teachings, and resurrection. The scripture of the early Christians was the Hebrew Bible or "Tanakh" which the Christians read in light of their belief that Jesus was the long-awaited Messiah. The early Christian community was initially confined to the Jewish community. Jesus was crucified c. 30. And in the 40s, Paul, the Apostle who did not know Jesus of Nazareth, began to gain converts among the Gentiles, the non-Jewish population outside Israel. His letters to his newly founded communities are the oldest documents in what came to be the Christian scriptures. The Gospels came later, in the 50s and 60s. By the end of the first century, small Christian communities had emerged across the Roman empire. Christians, however, were often persecuted for their refusal to acknowledge the civil religion of Rome.

In this new faith that gradually separated from its Jewish matrix, Jesus was increasingly central. He was called the "Lord" and at the heart of the developing rituals and beliefs of the early Christian community. In the 4th century, the status of Christians in the ancient Roman world was dramatically altered when Christianity was first tolerated under Constantine and then made the religion of the Empire in 383. In 325, Christians held their first "ecumenical" council at Nicea, Constantine's summer residence. Here began to emerge the orthodox confessions that characterize the Christian tradition, the Nicean Creed wherein Jesus is considered the Logos or Second Person of the Trinity.

For the next thousand years, Christianity was inextricably linked to the dominant political forces of the West and in much of the Orthodox eastern world as well. In the year 1054, the long simmering hostility between Western or Roman Christianity and Eastern or Orthodox Christianity erupted in a split between the Western bishop of Rome and the Eastern bishop of Constantinople. Western Christianity further fragmented in the period of the Reformation, the 1500s, when the Protestant denominations emerged. The Protestant denominations were often linked to emergent nation states so that the English became Anglicans, the Norwegians, Swedes, Finns and Northern Germans became Lutherans, some of the Swiss and later Scots became Calvinists and Presbyterians, etc. The French and southern Europe remained Roman Catholic.

Christianity also spread to the so-called "New World," with Latin America becoming Roman Catholic and North America becoming largely Protestant. In the centuries following the Reformation, a missionary movement sought to spread the Christian message in the colonized lands of Africa and Asia. Only in the 20th century did there emerge an ecumenical movement to bring unity again to a divided Christianity.

While most of the Christian churches affirm the Nicean Creed, there is considerable doctrinal diversity within the Christian world, as well as different emphases within different strands of the Christian world.

There are also differences that arise due to the different cultural settings in which Christianity has been accepted. Thus it is not possible to speak about Christianity in the singular. Moreover, it is always necessary to acknowledge that dialogue is between Christians and persons of other faiths rather than between a disembodied Christianity and other equally abstracted entities.

The Muslim faith, known as Islam, emerged around the figure of Muhammad in the 7th century of the Common Era. Muhammad was born in Mecca in the Arabian Peninsula in 571; he was orphaned, and when he was forty he began to receive revelations from the angel Gabriel. He was urged to "Recite" what was given to him in visions. A small group of followers gathered around this Prophet, and from his visionary experience there emerged the Qur'an, the sacred scripture of the Muslim community. Muslims believe that the words of the Qur'an are the words of Allah. The Muslim conviction becomes: There is no god but Allah and Muhammad is his Messenger. Thus, the Way of Islam, the peace that comes from surrender to Allah, "the Gracious, the Merciful, the Beneficent," was born out of a profound revelation to the Prophet Muhammad.

Initially, this proclamation brought Muhammad and his followers into conflict with their polytheistic countrymen and there were attempts to end his life. In 622, Muhammad went from Mecca to Medina and founded the Muslim *umma* (community), and this event, the Hijra, marks the beginning of the Muslim calendar. At Medina, Muhammad is at once prophet and political ruler. In 630, Muhammad returns triumphantly to Mecca. Two years later, Muhammad dies. But Islam continues to grow and spread so that by 635, Islam is established in Damascus and by 650 across North Africa.

A century of phenomenal growth follows so that by 750, Islam reaches from Spain across North Africa through the Middle East to the eastern edges of the Persian empire or modern day India. Baghdad is the center of this Islamic civilization for the next 500 years.

In the decades following Muhammad's death, there were internal difficulties that later led to the division into the Sunni and Shiite traditions, with the Sunni being the largest. About ninety percent of the Muslim world is Sunni. This faith centers in faith in Allah, the Messenger Muhammad, and the Qur'an. Muslims were enjoined to pray five times daily, and prayer was established as the heart of the Muslim Way. The Qur'anic revelation led to the view of a community fashioned on the guidance given by the Qur'an—it affects the whole of life and not just a religious sphere. As this community spread, it created a remarkable civilization.

Within the emergent Muslim world, Christians and Jews in the lands where Muslims ruled were mostly treated with respect. However, in Christian Europe, the Muslim armies were met by force. In the early Middle Ages, the Catholic Church launched a number of crusades to recapture the "Holy Land" from the "heathen." The so-called "heathen" were Muslims, and the fighting that took place during the Crusades was horrendous. Many Muslims still consider this hostility and violence as typical of the Christian response to Muslim people. Following the decline of the Muslim civilization, many formerly Muslim lands were colonized by European powers. These developments further antagonized relations between Muslims and Christians. It was only in the twentieth century that many Muslim lands regained their independence. It is, in part, the legacy of this conflictual history of Muslim-Christian relations that needs to be addressed and overcome in the dialogue of Muslims and Christians.

Dialogue Between Faiths

The possibilities, problems and prospects of dialogue between Muslims and Christians is the subject of this volume. Thus the inevitable question arises: what is dialogue? And what is dialogue between Muslims and Christians? While these questions cannot be addressed exhaustively, it might prove helpful to share with you the understandings of dialogue and Muslim-Christian dialogue that emerged from those meeting at Renison College in June of 1995 where most of the papers in this volume were first presented. When we met, we wanted both to engage in dialogue and to explore the possibilities and problems of dialogue among Muslims and Christians. The six features of dialogue listed below are not exhaustive, but they are, we believe, essential for Muslim-Christian dialogue.

1. Dialogue between people of different faiths, in an environment of mutual respect, is a process that has emerged only in the second half of our century. There have been isolated moments of dialogue between Muslims and Christians over the centuries, but it is only in our century that we can speak of a movement of interfaith dialogue that aims at understanding between the different traditions of faith.

2. Dialogue aims first at mutual understanding. In the case of Muslim-Christian dialogue, this involves understanding a Muslim as a

Muslim and a Christian as a Christian. It seeks to explore our respective faiths, coming to know what we as Muslims or as Christians believe and hold dear, what we practice as peoples of prayer and spiritual discipline, how we live our lives and the role of religious and moral guidance in that living, the way we hold our sacred books, the worries that we have as Muslims and Christians about our children, the life of our communities, the life we live as peoples of faith. That mutual exploration does not proceed in a spirit of debate or even of apology. It seeks to proceed in a spirit of dialogue—of honest, open and frank exchange—that leads to mutual understanding.

3. Dialogue is not just talking together but may also involve praying in each other's presence and being silent together. It may involve observing and/or participating in something of each other's spiritual disciplines, rituals and festival life. Such participation in the life of the other faith is not to be done flippantly or in a spirit of syncretism. It is rather a way to become more aware of the faith and practice that characterizes our respective traditions. It may involve reading the Scripture of the other and seeking the help of the other to understand its message.

4. Dialogue can proceed only if we allow the dialogue partners to define themselves, their beliefs and practices. This self-definition (and self-revelation) is essential in dialogue. We often find in dialogue in general and especially in dialogue between Muslims and Christians that we carry, often unconsciously, very curious stereotypes of and unconscious prejudices about the other. And thus it becomes essential that we listen to our partners in dialogue **deeply** and **in their own terms**. Only then can we genuinely encounter one another and our mutual dialogue proceed. This quality of listening offers a special challenge for Muslims and Christians. Many Christians feel that their faith requires them to be hostile to what many Christians still call "Mohammadanism" [sic]. And many Muslims believe that the Qur'an teaches them all they need to know about the Christian faith. But both attitudes fail to meet this essential requirement of dialogue, namely, allowing the dialogue partners to define themselves **in their own terms**. We believe that it is essential for Christians to listen to Muslims and to hear how Muslims define their own faith. It is equally essential that Muslims listen to Christians and hear how Christians define their faith. Only in this way can we begin to move beyond the polemics and stereotypes that have too often characterized the meeting of Muslims and Christians.

5. Dialogue is a way of meeting one another across the similarities

and differences of our religious faiths and communities. But such meeting is not easy. All of us come to dialogue burdened by a host of factors—historical, economic, and cultural—that profoundly affect how we hear and understand one another. Many Muslims are understandably dubious about the possibilities of dialogue with Christians because they believe it is just another ruse for continuing the aggressive conversionism that has been so characteristic of Christian attitudes towards Muslims. Some other Muslims believe that it is just the latest phase of Western imperialism and colonialism. Christians have also been burdened in their attitudes towards Islam by factors arising from the past. Christian literature on Islam, from the very beginning, has been laced with pejorative images of the Muslim and of the Islamic world, and such attitudes remain prevalent in the contemporary world.

6. Dialogue is often initiated between scholars and religious leaders of different religious traditions. But it is an activity that may unfold wherever Muslims and Christians meet. Increasingly, dialogue takes place as Muslims and Christians meet not only in the academy or in conferences, but in the factory or at school or in the neighborhood, as they do in many Western societies. The essential experience of dialogue can occur here too. In this process, religious leaders have an important role to play in portraying the other faiths as honorable and worthy of respect.

The Renison Conference

As we already indicated, most of the essays in this volume were first presented at a conference of Muslim and Christian scholars and religious leaders at Renison College in Canada. There, one of the participants, noting the long history of antagonism between these two faiths, remarked that "we have come together to explore the possibility of a new beginning in that relationship."

The Conference was a co-sponsored event of the Inter-Religious Federation for World Peace (IRFWP) of New York, New York, the Department of Islamic Learning at the University of Karachi, Karachi, Pakistan, and Renison College at the University of Waterloo. Though the Council of the World's Religions (CWR) and the International Religious Foundation (IRF), sister organizations of the IRFWP have sponsored intra-Muslim, intra-Christian, and multi-faith conferences, this was the first the focused exclusively on Muslim-Christian dialogue. The four days of our meeting revolved around sixteen papers that had been circulated prior to our meeting at Waterloo. As one might expect, the topics ranged broadly. In this volume, we have grouped the papers under four headings. Part I is entitled "Contexts," Part II is called "Perspectives," Part III is "Issues," and Part IV is "Prospects." Each section needs some further words of introduction.

Part I: Contexts

The essays in this section provide some overarching contexts for dialogue between Muslims and Christians. The remarkable essay by H.G. Dr. Paulos Mar Gregorios, retired Bishop of Delhi and the North and an IRFWP President, was the plenary address of the conference. In considering "Liberalism and Fundamentalism in Islam and Christianity," it focuses on Christian and Muslim responses to modernity. In the claim of "modernity" to complete autonomy of the human from Transcendence, we have, Gregorios argued, a challenge to all religious traditions. How can we, as believers in different traditions, affirm our commitment to Transcendence in the face of a modern culture that rejects the fundamental claims of religion? He then outlined some Christian and some Muslim responses to the culture of the Western Enlightenment. His essay set the tone and direction of the conference. It is also the fitting beginning of this volume.

It is coupled with important essays by Dr. 'Izz al-din Ibrahim and Dr. M. Darrol Bryant. In Dr. Ibrahim's view, Muslim dialogue with Christianity has been part of Islam from the beginning, but it has been "renewed" in the past forty years. Dialogue, Ibrahim observes, must be distinguished from "syncretism," and the participants in dialogue must be carefully chosen. Dialogue, Ibrahim hopes, will "lead to the spread of friendship and a spirit of conciliation between the followers of the two religions." Professor Bryant's essay provides a larger overview on the necessity for dialogue between Christians and Muslims. He acknowledges the many failures of Christians to rightly understand the faith of Islam, beginning with their failure to rightly name this faith tradition. For Bryant, there is a need for Muslims and Christians to overcome the history of hurt that still colors our views of each other.

Part II: Perspectives

The next section of the volume, entitled "Perspectives," contains essays that bring varying perspectives to the question of Muslim-Christian dialogue. It opens, for example, with two irenic statements by Dr. S. A. Ali and Dr. A. M. Khattab. While they highlighted the positive possibilities for dialogue, they also present some of the problems that confront dialogue between Muslims and Christians. These essays note the doctrinal/theological obstacles to dialogue between Muslims and Christians in relation to Christian doctrines of the Trinity and the Incarnation. Dr. Badru Kateregga focuses our attention on Muslim-Christian relations in Africa as he outlines the unhappy encounter of Muslim and Christians in Africa. Dr. Siddiqui's essay looks at the "Problems and Challenges" to Muslim Christian dialogue that have arisen in the context of dialogues initiated by the Geneva-based World Council of Churches (WCC) over the past three decades. While providing an excellent overview of WCC dialogue efforts, Siddiqui rightly observes that there is often an overlapping of evangelization with dialogue, an overlap that calls into question the motives of some Christians engaged in dialogue. Such confusion of motives partly explains the unease felt in Muslim circles about Christian initiatives at dialogue.

Further perspectives emerge in the important essay by Saba Risalludin which makes us acutely aware of the need to attend to the language we use in dialogue, especially its hidden associations and assumptions. She also makes us aware of the need to challenge and redress the negative image of Islam that is so pervasive in the West, a theme that is also underlined by Dr. Sheik Abdullah Durkee. While Durkee notes that there are real theological differences between the two traditions and no easy common ground, he nonetheless affirms the value of dialogue. Within the context of the Renison conference, these papers provoked intense discussion of the purposes of dialogue, leading us to affirm that the goal of dialogue is not to blur differences in the name of commonality, but to understand the other tradition in its integrity, with a sense of mutual respect.

Part III: Issues

The section entitled "Issues" is the largest in the volume, containing eight essays that deal with a variety of issues that arise in the dialogue of Muslims and Christians. Dr. Khan's expresses some of the anguish and anger felt by Muslims in the face of contemporary challenges and the conviction that more faithful adherence to the Qur'an provides a way to address these challenges. Dr. Martin Forward writes about the issue of Westerners studying the Muslim tradition. Some recent critiques of Western scholarship of Islam, especially that of Edward Said, call into question all attempts by Westerners to study Islam. Dr. Forward examines the work of Geoffrey Parrinder, a Western scholar, in order to see how justified those critiques might be. Dr. Reza Shah-Kazemi's essay leads us into a dimension of Muslim life that is little known and little understood by Christians, the role of the Prophet Muhammad in Muslim piety. It allows the Christian reader insight into this important dimension of Muslim piety where the Prophet is the exemplar of submission to Allah. Here we see something of the depth of Muslim feeling and regard for Muhammad.

Dr. M. Darrol Bryant and Dr. Muhib. Opeloye explore from different angles the very controversial issue of dialogue concerning Jesus/Isa. Dr. Bryant lays out the developing Christian views of Jesus from the prophet from Nazareth to the incarnate Word of God at Nicea. He acknowledges that Christians have often failed to make clear their confession of Jesus as the Christ in His relation to God. He also explores the Muslim view of Isa and calls for both Muslims and Christians to listen more deeply to the others' view of Jesus/Isa. Dr. Muhib. Opeloye continues this discussion with a Muslim view of Isa/Jesus and a review of Biblical material from a Muslim perspective. Dr. Opeloye's essay allows Christians to see the different way that Muslims interpret the Christian scripture in light of their own commitments to the Qur'an. Again, we are led to see that there are profound differences in the traditions, a fact belied by terms such as "prophet" which are common to both traditions, but mean such profoundly different things.

Dr. Riffat Hassan's masterful essay reveals some of the internal ferment in the Muslim world concerning the issue of women in Muslim culture. Her essay echoes parallel critiques in the Christian world of Christian theologies that have played a negative role in relation to women, but here she also challenges many readings of the Qur'an found in the Muslim world. Her voice is often difficult for other Muslims—and Christians—to hear, but it is important both to intra-Muslim discussions and to the dialogue of Muslims and Christians. Similarly, the essay by Raficq Abdullah opens an area of Muslim life that is surrounded by controversy and misunderstanding. Mr. Abdullah observes that "fundamentalism" is a Western term often inadequate to what is happening in parts of the Muslim world. Indeed, as Abdullah remarks, "All Muslims are fundamentalists insofar as they believe that the Qur'an is the literal word of God and therefore infallible" but not in the sense of a fundamentalist as "a type of person who uses religion as an all-encompassing ideology." Christians need to be more nuanced in their reading of the Muslim world. Finally, Dr. Thomas Walsh offers a comparative exploration of Muslim and Christian ethics in relation to the family. The merit of Walsh's essay is the way it allows us to see both similarities and differences in each community's regard for the family. While both traditions affirm the family, Muslims, for example, have been more generous than Catholic Christians in relation to the issue of divorce. In exploring these various issues, we are led into a deeper understanding of each tradition including our differences.

Part IV: Prospects

The final section of this volume is entitled "Prospects" and contains three essays that explore the prospects for future dialogue between Muslim and Christians. The first, by Dr. Frederick Denny, author of a widely used textbook on Islam, explores some of the "Boundaries and Gateways in the Social, Cultural and Religious Landscapes of Muslim-Christian Relations." His stimulating essay again reveals both the problems that confront us in our joint efforts at dialogue as well as the possibilities for that dialogue that are emerging. Dr. Abdul Rashid turns to Jesus' Sermon on the Mount and Muhammad's Farewell Sermon to find a basis for Muslim-Christian dialogue and cooperative effort. The last essay in the volume by Dr. Jane Smith—"Christian-Muslim-Jewish Dialogue in Denver"—points to the need for such local initiatives to be multiplied around the world if we are to build the bridges of understanding so profoundly needed.

Concluding Comments

The Renison conference, where most of these essays were first presented, was a living event in Muslim-Christian dialogue. We began each day with a response to a paper from another participant, then a word from the paper writer, and then a general discussion. Those discussions were often heated, sometimes difficult, but always useful. Indeed, they were essential to dialogue. As one conference participant remarked, "There was a remarkable spirit of charity that prevailed in the midst of our honest and frank exchanges." But our time together was not confined to discussion. We also shared meals, went for walks together, shared sleeping quarters, and lived together over four days. Two mornings began with prayer and meditation. Imam A. Khattab from the Islamic Center of Greater Toledo, Ohio, whose members include fourth-generation Muslims born in the USA, led us in prayer and meditation one morning, and Rev. Dr. Martin Forward, Director of Interfaith Relations for the Methodist Church of the U.K. led another morning. We did not attempt to create an interfaith service. Rather, we simply asked that we gather for prayer and meditation in Muslim forms to which Christians might be present and then in Christian forms to which Muslims might be present. These were important moments in the conference and in the dialogue that we sought to pursue.

When we met on the final afternoon to consider our meeting, there was agreement that we had all learned a great deal. One of the participants summarized the feelings of most: "Before I came, I wondered if this would be worthwhile, but I found it immensely helpful in understanding another tradition and my own." It was agreed that we should seek to communicate our dialogue to a wider audience. Thus the essays in this volume were revised in the light of our dialogue and, together with some additional material, we offer them to a wider audience in the hope that they will contribute to that dialogue within the hearts and minds of Muslims and Christians that can lead to mutual understanding of these two great communities of faith.

M. Darrol Bryant and S. A. Ali

PART I

CONTEXTS

1

LIBERALISM AND FUNDAMENTALISM IN ISLAM AND CHRISTIANITY:

HOW TWO TRADITIONS HAVE HANDLED MODERNITY

Paulos Mar Gregorios

THE PARALLELS BETWEEN the noticeably different ways in which two great world religious systems, namely Islam and Western Christianity, have handled the problems posed by the modern period and its secular civilization are indeed striking. This essay seeks only to have a cursory look at these parallels and differences. A more adequate study, undertaken jointly by competent scholars on both sides, could be highly productive and useful for both religions in clarifying and correcting their own self-understanding and improving their mutual relations.

Let me at this point state clearly that there is a great difference between the way Western Christianity, i.e. the Roman Catholic Church and the Protestant Reformation churches on the one hand, and the Eastern and Oriental Orthodox churches on the other, have handled this issue. Of the latter, i.e. the Orthodox, it can be said that as a church it has made no major effort to encounter the challenges posed by modernity. It has, by and large, left the problem to be handled by the believers, in their personal freedom. As far as the central issues of the faith were concerned, the Orthodox have chosen to live in conflict with modernity rather than come to terms with it through any particular intellectual approach.

One reason for this difference between the attitude and approach of the Western and the Eastern churches may be that while modernity was predominantly a Western phenomenon, and endemic to its culture, the Eastern Orthodox officially looked upon modernity as a disease of the West and preferred to ignore it as a matter of no moment to itself, or at best as something to be resisted rather than reconciled with. Clearly the ostrich attitude of the East has been rather counterproductive in the outcome, resulting in the loss of millions of followers who preferred to adapt to modernity even at the risk of abandoning their faith. Those who have remained faithful have, however, done better than many in the West in holding on to the essentials of their faith. But I am not suggesting that the Eastern Orthodox attitude to modernity is the model to be emulated by all.

What Is Modernity? Where Is the Conflict?

Naturally, neither the word nor the concept "modern" is of classical or ancient provenance. Both the word and the concept were created in the modern period, i.e., in the post-Industrial Revolution era. Its roots seem to be in the Latin word "modo" which means "current" or "in fashion." Of the writing of books on modernity, there has been up to now no end. Peter Berger, in his *Facing up to Modernity*, suggested five phenomena as characteristic of modernity: abstraction, futurity, individualism, liberation, and secularization.[1] These may indeed be its marks, but its essence lies elsewhere. Max Weber was closer to the target when he identified the central feature of cultural modernity as *the shift from religion to human rationality, as the unifying framework for integrating our experience of the sum total of reality.*

By human rationality Weber means more than the instrumental reason which we use in our science and technology; he calls it "substantive reason," more or less what others call "ontological reason" as distinguished from technological reason. This substantive reason was previously expressed in religion and metaphysics. In modernity, this substantive reason is divorced from all religion and tradition, and domesticated within an autonomous human rationality, subsumed in three autonomous realms—science, morality and art—free from all religion or revelation, metaphysics or tradition, totally freed from all dependence on any external authority outside of human reason. Weber's intuition about the central feature of cultural modernity seems basically correct. In giving below my own basic intuition about the nature of cultural modernity, I acknowledge my indebtedess to Weber.

To be "modern" is fundamentally and primarily to affirm the freedom, autonomy, and sovereignty of the adult human person; hence, secondarily it is to repudiate totally all dependence on external authority—on God or the creator, religion or revelation, scripture or tradition, metaphysics or theology. The human person, in modernity, acknowledges no authority above oneself, and one's rationality is totally sovereign. Humanity owes its existence to no one else, and the autonomy of the human is not based on any divine gift or mandate; it is by virtue of being human that the human person is self-sufficient, free and sovereign. There is no judge above human reason; if it is to be questioned or criticized, it can only be by that same reason—not by something higher than it or transcendent to it. The human reason alone lays down norms for itself—for action, for knowledge, for political economy; free human persons legislate for themselves, and will not submit themselves to other people's laws or religious laws.

Private property is an essential condition of this freedom of the modern person; for if one is economically dependent on others, one is not free, as Immanuel Kant, one of the fathers of modernity, pointed out. My modern readers, with their highly developed critical rationality, should be able by now to recognize modernity for what it is—the ideology of the newly emerging burgher, the bourgeoisie as the new ruling class of the industrial revolution, anxious to overthrow the authority of church and priest, of feudal baron and the traditional aristocracy; of the past as such with the dominance of church and theology, of sacrament and priesthood, of the feudal Lord, and his traditional or past-derived authority. As one whose critical rationality is still rather underdeveloped despite years of western training, one never ceases to wonder about the historical fact that marxism, which was supposed to be the ideology of the working class as opposed to the bourgeoisie, remained basically within the structures of this bourgeois ideology of the Enlightenment and its secularism. Dialectical materialism is also a rationally derived ideology, a product of the same enthronement of the human and its rationality in place of God, sometimes calling this God either history or nature. At this point, both liberalism and marxism, the two aspects of cultural-intellectual modernity, are equally unscientific; their foundations are in human desire and speculation, not in any kind of scientific objectivity. The basic assumptions of both liberalism and marxism can neither be scientifically proved or philosophically justified.

It is this modernity that came in head-on conflict with all forms of religion, especially the West Asian traditions of Judaism, Christianity and Islam, all of which affirmed the total authority of God and regarded as the height of impiety to attribute to humanity such absolute sovereignty or unquestioned autonomy. That, I believe, is still the issue.

The compromises which religion has made with modernism in the last two hundred years will need substantive reconsideration in the light of what we, today, understand as the essence of modernity and our questions about its philosophical justification. Religions were too easily bedazzled by the dramatic achievements of science and technology, and wrongly took them as validation for the secular ideology, and the unproved and arbitrary assumptions behind that ideology which created modern science and the technology based on it.

Neither modernity nor its enthronement of critical reason has any philosophical validity. These were unphilosopical affirmations of a ruling class which wanted to establish its authority over all. There is absolutely no philosophical or scientific justification for the claim that the human being is self-derived, autonomous and sovereign, recognizing no obligation to any higher authority. But this claim has been often uncritically accepted even by religious thinkers and leaders. The end result has been that instead of directly exposing the fallacies in these ideologies, religions have made compromises with them, in a misguided attempt to salvage themselves.

It is in the light of the above understanding of the relation between religions and modernity that we seek to take a quick look at the historical developments in their relationships.

Liberalism and Modernism

Both liberalism and modernism are primarily nineteenth-century creations of the Christian churches of Europe, later adopted by others. In the beginning, liberalism had a pejorative sense, as reflected in the writings of Cardinal John Henry Newman, who called it tainted with the spirit of "Anti-Christ." Writing in 1841, Newman spoke of "the most serious thinkers among us" as regarding "the spirit of liberalism as characteristic of the destined Anti-Christ." Twenty-three years later, in 1864, Newman stigmatized liberalism as "false liberty of thought, or the exercise of thought upon matters in which, from the constitution of the human mind, thought cannot be brought to any successful issue, and therefore is out of place."[2]

But Newman's view was regarded as reactionary by many of his contemporaries; others, like Edward Irving (1826) saw the issue thus: "Religion is the very name of obligation. . . Liberalism is the very name of want of obligation."[3]

By the time we come to T. S. Eliot in the twentieth century, the more positive approach to liberalism seems to have taken root everywhere: "liberalist" being opposed to "traditionalist, dogmatist, and obscurantist"—all three very pejorative terms now. Eliot wrote: "Liberalism is something which tends to release energy rather than accumulate it, to release rather than to fortify. It is a movement not so much defined by its end, as by its starting point; away from, rather than towards, something definite."[4] The characteristic feature of liberalism now becomes unfettered freedom for enquiry and research, without fear or inhibition.

In the German Protestant tradition, F. C. Baur (1792-1860) and Albrecht Ritschl (1822-1889) may be regarded as Fathers of what came to be called "Modern Critical Theology"—based on an unquestioning acceptance of the claims of modernity and on the unexamined acceptance of the canons of the now absolute authority of liberalism's critical rationality. For Ritschl, religious doctrines are merely human value judgments—*Werturteile*—on humanity's attitude to the world. Roman Catholic modernism was deeply affected by Baur and Ritschl; they were one reason why the Pope's Syllabus of Errors roundly condemned modernism and liberalism. The Roman Catholic Church refused to bow before the totalitarianism of the Enlightenment which, so to speak, excommunicated as obscurantist and reactionary all those who did not accept its canons.

One German thinker who saw through the pretensions of modernism in the nineteenth century was Friedrich Nietzsche (1860-1900). In his *Untimely Observations—On the Advantage and Disadvantage of History for Life*, Nietzsche said an unqualified and angry "no" to modernism's attempt to unify all experience through the dialectics of the Enlightenment—in particular to the historicist deformation of the modern consciousness, which is "full of junk details and empty of what matters." Nietzsche doubted whether modernity could fashion its criteria out of itself, "for from ourselves we moderns have nothing at all."[5]

The second major internal critique of modernity and the claims of the Enlightenment, again in Germany, came from the Frankfurt School of Social Research. *Dialectic of Enlightenment* by Max Horkheimer and Theodor Adorno proclaimed loudly and clearly, "The Enlightenment is totalitarian," and again, "The fully enlightened earth radiates disaster triumphant."[6]

Horkheimer and Adorno lampoon the European Enlightenment, and its rationality-based modernity, as setting out to master reality within its own categories: "From now on, matter would at last be mastered without any illusion of ruling or inherent powers, of hidden qualities. For the Enlightenment, whatever does not conform to the rules of computation and utility is suspect."[7] They accuse Marx of having tried to reduce human reason to the mere instrumental reason of science and technology, ignoring the higher functions of ontological or substantial reason which seeks emancipation and fulfilment.

The third and most recent European assault on modernity has come from the Post-Moderns and Deconstructionists—Jacques Derrida, Michel Foucault, Jean-Francois Lyotard, George Bataille, and all the rest. Their contention is that the project of modernity to capture and present truth through language, logic, discourse and critical rationality has totally and dismally failed.

But none of these critiques of modernity touch its basic core—the affirmations about the total self-sufficiency, autonomy and sovereignty of the human person. Even post-modernity stays within that basic affirmation of modernity—the patricidal denial of the transcendent, and the consequent absolutization of the secular, with its totalitarian project for taking over all the universe and all knowledge as subject to it. This is the point at which the battle should have been joined long ago between religion and modernity. And it is about time that battle actually began.

Islam and Modernism

I know so little of the cultural history of Islam that I have to ask my Muslim brothers and sisters ahead of time to correct me on any bloopers I am likely to make on the subject. Islam, battered and beleaguered by the technological superiority of the West and under the onslaught of its relentless imperialism, seemed to react to Western modernity in spurts and spasms. The first wave had already begun in the sixteenth century, especially in the Indian sub-continent, where Islam had to contend both with other religions and with the strident culture of the Portuguese. Shaikh Ahmad Sirhindi (1564-1625) and Shah Wali Allah (1703-1762) represent this first attempt of Islam to come to terms with industrial culture and its incipient modernity.

The second wave, beginning in the nineteenth century and spreading into the twentieth, was more widespread and embraced the Indian Sub-continent (Sayyid Ahmad Khan - 1817-1898; Ameer Ali - 1849-1928; Sir Muhammad Iqbal - 1877-1938); the Maghreb (Abd al-Hamid Ibn Badis - 1889-1940; Abd al-Kadir al-Maghrubi - 1867-1907; Abu Shu-'Ayb al-Dukhali - 1878-1937); the Fertile Crescent (Abd al-Rahman al-Kawakabi - 1854-1902; Mohammad Kurd 'Ali - 1876-1952; Shakib Arslan - 1869-1962; Muhammad Rashid-Rida - 1865-1935) and Egypt (Muhammad Farid Wagdi - 1875-1954; Ahmad Amin - 1886-1954) and also Iran (Muhammad Hussayn Na'ini - 1860-1936).

The Islamic *Ummah* was under brutal aggression, not only from Enlightenment rationality, but also from the aggressively imperialist military-technological imperialism out to destroy Islam. Egypt, Syria and Persia, the heartland of Islam, had already been conquered and subdued. Along with successive military defeats, Islam suffered also from internal dissensions. The new plea was for Islamic solidarity and resistance to the aggressor. Jamal al-Din al-Afghani, the Persian (1839-1897), urged mutual toleration among Muslims for the sake of the *Ummah*. To this end he advocated the adoption of Western science and technology, while at the same time preserving Islamic values. As a political agitator, he went to Afghanistan, Iran, Egypt, Paris, London and Istanbul seeking to spread his views. Shaikh Muhammad Abdu of Egypt (1849-1905) was his disciple, a good bourgeois who underlined the congruity between Islam and modernity. Drawing again from the rich treasures of bourgeois individualism, he taught the principle of *Ijtihad* or *the privilege of individual interpretation of the Scriptures.* This gave one the freedom to violate some of the traditional inter-pretations of Islam without violating its fundamentals.

Both Al Afghani and his disciple Shaikh Abdu were Islamic repre-sentatives of the new bourgeoisie, and as such felt that modernism would be advantageous to his class, and derivatively to all. Modernism would, they expected, dissolve all old theological conflicts created by the Mullahs and unite the *Ummah* to resist the imperialist aggressors like Britain and France. They did not reckon with the possibility that the whole of Islam might not accept Enlightenment rationality and the secular modernity based on it. They did not envisage a new conflict within Islam, created by the introduction of modernism into it. They were rather simplistic in their over-optimistic assumption that Islam and modernity can be so easily fitted to each other. We need not agree with Lord Cromer's dictum that Islam Reformed is Islam no longer.

Islamic modernism wanted to make Islam relevant to contemporary issues and responsive to modern problems, without having to imitate the West. The idea of an indigenous ideology of development not copied from the West, faithful to the fundamentals of Islam, yet rational and successful, has been the driving motif behind what is today attempted in some Muslim countries like the United Arab Emirates. And, compared to certain other less disciplined Islamic communities, the achievements of the U.A.E. are indeed impressive when measured by the usual parameters of crime rate, alcoholism, drug addiction, suicide rate, homelessness, unemployment, labor strikes, ethnic conflict and so on. Of course there is the question whether more populous Islamic countries like Pakistan or Bangladesh could ever achieve that level of efficiency, discipline and social control.

Three basic tenets of Islamic modernism seem to be these:

a. Purify Islam from accrued superstitions and malpractices, whether introduced by Sufi orders or drawn from rigid Koranic interpretations. Follow faithful but rational reinterpretation of the Holy Qur'an and the Sunnah;

b. Exercise *Ijtihad,* or the principle of individual reinterpretation, stressing the rational and universal elements; and

c. Emphasize the social and moral aspects of Islam rather than its philosophical and metaphysical ideas, since these are what the people need now in modern society.

Fundamentalism in Christianity and Islam

The history of Western Protestant fundamentalism is rather easy to trace. The "Conference on Christian Fundamentals" took place in California in 1908, and the Report of the Conference was published by the Moody Bible Institute in 20 volumes from 1909-1912. It was, in fact, a defiance of Protestant liberalism and its "Critical Theology" which lampooned what evangelical Christians believed to be the basics of the Christian faith: the verbal inspiration and inerrancy of the Bible, salvation by the blood of Christ alone (liberals called it slaughterhouse theology), the substitutionary theory of the Atonement, the Virgin birth of Christ, Christ's physical resurrection from the dead, the need to be born again, and so on—precisely the targets of attack by the rising critical theology claiming to be modern and liberal. The two most offensive phenomena were the Darwinian theory of evolution, which went against the biblical account of creation, and the German higher criticism, which denied all the miraculous or supernatural elements in the Bible. Behind this American Protestant fundamentalism, so different from Islamic fundamentalism, were "The Great (Religious) Awakening" in 18th-century New England (the powerful hellfire preaching of Jonathan Edwards), the Puritanism also of New England, as well as the European Pietism that prevailed in the immigrant communities. The American fundamentalists believed that what they stood for was the essence of Christianity. It was also for them the traditional religion of America which was attacked by modernism, liberalism and scientism. The new scientific ideology of modern culture was, according to them, sweeping away the spiritual foundations of America—God's Own Country. These pernicious "Moderns" are thus enemies of God and of America. So are the Communists. Protestant Christian fundamentalists thus take on the task of defending the Christian faith, as they understood it, while defending America as well. Later, many of the fundamentalists became more open to science and technology and to Christian social responsibility; thus they called themselves "Evangelicals" rather than "Fundamentalists" (National Association of Evangelicals, USA, for example). Neither group had much of a political program beyond getting as many of their number as possible into key positions in church, society and state.

The situation is quite different in Islamic "Fundamentalism." In fact, it can be argued that the term "fundamentalism" cannot be applied to the phenomenon of anti-modernism in Islam. We need to invent a new name for it—something like "strident anti-modern resurgence."

The earlier movement, often called Wahhabi fundamentalism, was more of an Islamic renewal movement, advocating a more strict interpretation of the Qur'an and the Sunnah than most modernists were willing to accept. Muhammad Ibn 'Abd al-Wahhab, the founder, died in 1792. Theirs was a mission for the Oneness of Islam—the *dawat al-Tawhid*; the great teachers of the Wahhabis had a science of their own: *ilm al-Tawhid*, or the science of the oneness of God and the unity of the Qur'anic law, rationality and mystical intuition. By the beginning of the nineteenth century, the Saudi Wahhabis had gained control of Mecca and Medina, the two holy centers of Islam. In 1812, they lost it to the Egyptian Turkish Sultan. The Wahhabi family mustered its resources and recaptured the capital, Riyadh, soon to lose it again to other Arab chieftains. What we have today is the Third Wahhabi state, established by Ibn Saud ('Abd al-Aziz ibn 'Abd al-Rahman - 1879-1953), through some bold military and diplomatic measures.

Wahhabi fundamentalism, if it can be called that, is not what people today call Islamic fundamentalism. In fact, I would like to contend that there is no such entity as Islamic fundamentalism. The Christian fundamentalists were proud to be called by that name. In Islam, I know of no movement which expressly calls itself fundamentalist. Islamic fundamentalism is a creation of the Western media more than anything else. The media wanted to identify a new enemy for Western society, now that Communism no longer serves that purpose. There is a spectre haunting the end of our millennium—the cooked-up version of something called Islamic fundamentalism. By very subtle means, the Western media associate it with terrorism and violence and make its image quite spooky. I propose that we stop using the expression "Islamic Fundamentalism" and ask those who use the term to pinpoint the main elements of it.

Christian fundamentalism was basically a strong reaction against the arrogance of modernity. Many Muslims may be antagonistic to modernity and may regard the highly educated modern secular Muslim as a betrayer of the faith. There may have been some attempts at affirming strict faithfulness to the Qur'an and the Sunnah, but even such Muslims often accepted modernist principles like *Ijtihad* and some freedom of reinterpreting inconvenient traditional interpretations of the Qur'an and the Sunnah.

But the fact of the matter is that there is a great deal of resentment among Muslims—resentment against the West's political-economic and technocratic as well as legal domination of the world in which Muslims live. The West's secular, godless culture is imposed upon Muslim children through the school. Without secular Western education, the Muslim cannot rise on the social or economic ladder. But the education in the schools is always a god-denying or god-ignoring one, a faith-destroying false ideology imposed by the state on the people. Many Muslims deplore the fact that the noble Islamic civilization of the medieval period has now been superseded by a soul-less, secular civilization.

Many Muslims feel that the so-called Christian nations of the West are now ganged up together against the renaissance of Islam. The refusal to give adequate moral and economic support to the Bosnian struggle for independence and autonomy is often interpreted as caused by the Christian West's desire to prevent the emergence of an Islamic state again in Europe after Islam was vanquished in Spain.

The resentment has many sources. In many countries, Muslims are still socially and economically backward, and the reason given is that the educational level is low, particularly among the women. Many Muslims are reluctant to send their daughters to schools run by the state. They know that the strength of Islam is in the women who keep the faith and teach it to their children. If Muslim women are also to be secularized, Islam itself may become weak.

In a country like India, those Muslims who opted for Indian citizenship at the moment of partition in 1947, with a guarantee of equality of all citizens, now feel that they are treated as second-class citizens, and the law of the land is flagrantly violated, seemingly with the concurrence of a democratic government, and Muslim holy places are humiliatingly destroyed or desecrated in full limelight.

It is this resentment, rising from a sense of outrage, on the part of Muslims, that the authorities are now afraid of and the media would like to taint with associations of violence and terrorism. Islamic fundamentalism is not the issue. The smoldering resentment of Muslims as victims of injustice is a problem indeed. That matter, I suggest, good Muslims and good Christians should jointly investigate.

NOTES

1. See Peter Berger, *Facing Up to Modernity* (New York: Basic Books, 1977).
2. See John Henry Newman, *Tracts for the Times* (New York: AMS Press, 1969) and *Apologia Pro Vita Sua* (London: Oxford University Press, 1931).
3. Edward Irving, 1826.
4. T. S. Eliot, *After Strange Gods: A Primer of Modern Heresy* (New York: Harcourt Brace, 1931).
5. Friedrich Nietzsche, *Untimely Observations—On the Advantage and Disadvantage of History for Life* (Cambridge: ET, 1980), p. 24.
6. M. Horkheimer and T. Adorno, *Dialectic of Enlightenment* (Cambridge: ET, 1944), p. 6.
7. *Ibid.*

2

ISLAMIC-CHRISTIAN DIALOGUE:

A MUSLIM VIEW

'Izz al-din Ibrahim[1]

I.

THE DIALOGUE BETWEEN Islam and Christianity is as old as Islam itself. The holy Qur'an is full of verses directed towards Christians, at times confirming the truths shared between the two religions, at others indicating their clearly attested differences of belief, and at others calling for a meeting on "common terms" between them. The Prophet (God's blessing and peace be upon him) held discussions with the priests and monks of Najrān for three days in Medina when they stayed as his guests in the mosque. He also wrote to the Coptic Patriarch in Egypt, to the Negus, king of Abyssinia, to Heraclius, the ruler of the Byzantines, to Jabala b. al-Ayham, one of the kings of the Ghassanids, to Bishop Daghātir of Constantinople and to Abū Hārith b. 'Alqama, bishop of Najrān.[2] Muslims have continued this dialogue both orally and in writing almost without cease, except in the periods of the regrettable clashes between followers of the two religions, and then during the Crusades and the period of Western colonialism.

Although dialogue between the followers of the two religions has

not always been palatable, and at times there have been harsh exchanges arising from the zeal with which each side has held its beliefs,
nevertheless the teachings of Islam themselves have remained true to
three important qualities: that debate with the People of the Book
should be "in a way that is better"; that Muslims should remember that
Christians are "nearest in affection"; and that relations with those who
do not take part in attacks upon Muslims should follow the way of
kindness and justice. For God Almighty has said, "And argue not with
the People of the Scripture unless it be in a way that is better" (*Sūra*
29.46), and "Thou wilt find the nearest of them in affection to those
who believe to be those who say: Lo! We are Christians. That is because there are among them priests and monks, and because they are
not proud" (*Sūra* 5.82), and "Allah forbiddeth you not those who
warred not against you on account of religion and drove you not from
your homes, that ye should show them kindness and deal justly with
them. Lo! Allah loveth the just dealers" (*Sūra* 60.8).

II.

At the present time, and for forty years to be exact, Islamic-
Christian dialogue has been given new vigour. Regular meetings and
gatherings have been held in Broumana, Riyadh, the Vatican, Tripoli,
Geneva, Paris, Salzburg, Cairo, Beirut, Lagos, Tunis, Hong Kong,
Cordova and elsewhere. The result has been declarations, recom-
mendations and clarifications, as well as a great many books.[3]

The initiative in contemporary dialogue was taken by Pope Paul VI,
who promulgated *Ecclesiam Suam*, his encyclical calling for dialogue,
on 6 August 1964.[4] This was shortly after the appearance of the well-
known Second Vatican Council statement which mentioned the Islamic
religion with approval on account of its call to the worship of the one
God and its teachings concerning acts of devotion and moral values,
and which called for past conflicts to be forgotten.[5]

Following this, two offices appeared in the Christian world, both
specialising in organising dialogue. These were the Secretariat for non-
Christian Affairs in the Vatican, direction for which was first entrusted
to the late Cardinal Pignedoli, a man for whose person and wide-
ranging activities all parties involved felt unanimous respect, and the
Sub-Unit for Dialogue with People of Living Faiths and Ideologies of
the World Council of Churches in Geneva, among the staff of which
Dr. Samartha and Dr. John Taylor must not be overlooked. In the

Islamic world, no equivalent unit concerned with matters of dialogue has appeared, except for the initiative from the Muslim World League in Mecca under the direction of the late Shaykh Muḥammad al-Ḥarkān and Dr. Maʿrūf al-Dawālībī, and similarly *Jamʿiyya al-Daʿwa al-Islāmiyya* in Tripoli under the direction of Dr. Maḥmūd al-Sharīf.

Without doubt, dialogue meetings have produced an atmosphere of optimism and positive understanding between the Islamic and Christian worlds, and have helped to remove mistaken perceptions about the two religions. They have encouraged commendable cooperation in the struggle against attitudes and tendencies which the two religions reject, in the fields of thought, action, community and politics. They have helped to develop individual friendships between intellectuals and educated followers of the two religions, fostering potential growth in understanding and cooperation, and the spread of friendship and peace in the world.

However, participants in these dialogue meetings—and I myself have been one on many occasions—have noticed a number of weak points and shortcomings in this process. These should be mentioned and confronted frankly and faithfully if we wish the current of dialogue to continue successfully. This is particularly pertinent when the call to dialogue has been renewed in recent years at the highest level at both international and Arab conferences.[6]

III.

Perhaps the first weak point in these dialogue meetings is their lack of a clear, declared statement of intention agreed upon by all sides. It is not enough for such a statement to be a vague spiritual call to mutual understanding and love without establishing the basic principles and putting aside the hidden intentions that may surround it. These will eventually emerge and stir up doubts and evil suspicions that may abort the dialogue and empty it of its most important elements of frankness, trustworthiness and clarity.

In view of the fact that the initiative in the contemporary dialogue movement has come from the Christian world, the documents available for study on the subject of its definition, purposes and related intentions are necessarily Christian. If the Islamic world had ever found itself able to produce documents on this subject, then the two sides might have been in the same unfortunate position of regarding dialogue as a veiled means of evangelization. Those who wish may find information about dialogue in the following Christian documents:

1. the well-known encyclical *Ecclesiam Suam* of Pope Paul VI, published in 1964;

2. the publication *Reflections and Orientations on Dialogue and Mission* issued by the Vatican Secretariat for Non-Christian Affairs in 1984, in connection with the twentieth anniversary of the beginning of contemporary dialogue;

3. the report of the consultative seminar organised by the World Council of Churches in Zurich in May 1970.

For the sake of brevity, I will content myself with these three documents, the first and second issued by the Catholic Church, and the third by the other churches together. I should also mention the detailed study published by Dr. Hallencreutz,[7] a Norwegian theologian, in which he states that dialogue is the second development in the movement of Christian evangelization, the first being that from evangelization to witness, and the second from witness to dialogue; these three phases are different in degree but with one purpose as regards their substance, which is evangelization.

I have no intention in making these references to embarrass my Christian colleagues, who believe in Christian evangelization as part of their creed. I myself as a Muslim stand for mission, and I recognize this concern both in myself and in my companions in mission, for each of us is engaged in mission for his own religion. Rather, I want the purpose of dialogue to be perfectly clear to both sides. If the aim is evangelization, then so be it, let them be Christian evangelists and us Muslim missionaries. But if the aim of dialogue is some other shared interests with no evangelization involved, then let us be honest and give it a definition which is free from the will to evangelise, and let us all keep sincerely to it.

To this end, the large dialogue meeting held in Tripoli in February 1976, which more than five hundred scholars attended under the presidency of Cardinal Pignedoli and Dr. Maḥmūd al-Sharīf, agreed to adopt the following definition:

> The aim of dialogue is for participants from the two religions to exchange information, thinking, and factual knowledge, which increases the understanding on each side of the other's religion, history, culture and further concerns, in order to clarify matters of convergence and divergence between them sincerely and objectively, while allowing each

side to maintain its beliefs, obligations and commitments, in an atmosphere of friendship and mutual esteem.

This definition can be described as precautionary rather than comprehensive, because it guards against the inclusion of evangelization as a component of dialogue and sets out the available possibilities for dialogue in general terms. Still, it seems that the very nature of the meeting from which the definition emerged could not have produced any more than this. But the good it did was sufficient, because excising the harmful is more urgent than promoting the beneficial, as our legal scholars say.

IV.

One of the weaknesses which must be avoided is that of confusing dialogue with syncretism, whether explicitly or implicitly. Explicit syncretism occurs, for example, when a participant in a dialogue meeting proposes agreement on a declaration of faith composed of seven points which he has selected from the teachings of Islam and Christianity. While these seven points may be acceptable to Muslims and Christians when taken separately, their presentation as a seven-part formula can be mistaken as a replacement for the existing Islamic declaration of faith with its two parts (the declaration that there is no god but God, and that Muḥammad is his servant and messenger), and will be unknown to Christians in this form. So even though the proposal might arise from pure motives, it turns out for this reason to be explicit syncretism. An example of implicit syncretism occurred in the dialogue meeting which was held in Beirut, when participants attended two services, in a mosque and in a church; and in another session, meetings were opened with prayers made up from passages out of the Holy Qur'an, the Psalms and the New Testament. This was abandoned, and everyone agreed with complete consent and approval to a straightforward reading from the Holy Qur'an alone followed by a reading from the New Testament alone.

If participants made concessions to syncretism, there would be opened for them "a gate of extreme punishment," and dialogue would be changed into something resembling the search for the middle formula which politicians try to arrive at in their compromises. Yet there is a difference between revealed religious injunctions and devised political positions.

V.

Lack of care in choosing participants properly must be considered a weakness in any dialogue. It is assumed that the participant will be a specialist in the subject and be able to express the viewpoint of his people on the issue presented for discussion. It has been noted in past dialogue meetings that our Christian brothers have attended as representatives of specific churches or specialist university departments. This has allowed them access to research material and given them the responsibility to speak in the name they represent. But the Islamic participants, for the most part guests, have been invited as individuals, and none of them has previously attended a dialogue session more than once. This has not been conducive to good preparation or follow-up, nor to their being representatives of the bodies which specialize in and are accredited for this work.

In the Islamic world, representatives should be invited from Islamic universities, such as al-Azhar, the Imām Muḥammad Ibn Saʿūd University, and the Jāmiʿa Nadwa al-ʿUlamāʾ Lucknow, or international assemblies such as the Assembly for Islamic Research, the Assembly for Islamic Law, and the Assembly for Islamic Civilization, or major Islamic organizations such as the Muslim World League, etc. And in all situations, it is desirable to minimize language difficulties by providing appropriate translation facilities.

Related to the issue of choosing suitable participants is that we should keep our young people in the Islamic and Christian worlds away from dialogue. Young people need time, knowledge and experience to become intellectually and emotionally qualified for these difficult undertakings. It is not wise to expose them to discussions which might cause their faith to waver and leave them believing neither this nor that. If the intention is to establish ties of human friendship between children among the followers of the two religions, this can be accomplished by regular meetings between them in schools, cultural associations and sports teams. And provision can be made for them to learn about religious behaviour appropriate to the best kind of relations with followers of other religions without involving them in the trials of religious dialogue, which only the specially qualified should undertake.

VI.

Among the matters of chief importance in dialogue meetings is that of taking care in choosing topics and getting as far as possible away from the sensitive issues of the ancient theological disputes with which books on sects and denominations, on comparative religion and on the doctrines of different parties and their distinctions are filled. Such topics are concerned with technical details, and if necessary, they should be referred to the experts who can discuss the matters pertaining to them.

A pressing topic on which our Christian brothers expect us to explain the position of Islam is the legal and civil position of non-Muslims in the Islamic community. In Arab countries, there are differing proportions of followers of the two religions: in one community that of majority and minority, in another equality or almost so. Elsewhere, there are countries with Muslim inhabitants and Christian rulers, just as there are countries with Christian rule in which Muslim minorities have become established through immigration. All this requires words which are clear and precise in order to satisfy the general thirst: majority and minority, equals, immigrants, newcomers.

It is only fair to say that Islamic jurisprudence has dealt with these legal issues and has laid down just procedures for the treatment of non-Muslims in the Islamic community. These are discussed in a valuable book by Professor Dr. Yūsuf al-Qaradāwi, in which he sets out the laws concerning those who have protection, those who seek protection, and those who have temporary protection in the Islamic community. In addition to this book, there is much that can be referred to[8] in order to demonstrate the just treatment Islam offers non-Muslims, confirming their human rights and the benefits given to them, and granting them opportunities for a dignified life and worthy participation with citizens who are Muslims.

However, what our Christian brothers want to hear about is their position as fellow citizens, not as *Dhimmīs*, and equality with their Muslim brothers in a community in which all are equal due to shared origins, birth and history. The response to such questions is easy: the essence is fixed as fairness of treatment, and changes extend no further than contemporary legal formulations which the ancient experts of legal policy never met with nor considered. Their successors are required to offer opinions appropriate to the state of this issue, and to explain to their non-Muslim countrymen about their equality in the rights and responsibilities of citizenship, without this infringing on the Islamic character of the community in which Muslims form the majority. By the same token, Muslims would like to receive from their counterparts in foreign communities and from their legislators re-assurances about the practice of their devotions, the education of their children and the conduct of their personal affairs in accordance with their beliefs and their Islamic law, just as they would like to be treated in the country to which they have migrated as citizens and not as strangers.

Among the matters which deserve investigation, because it affects Muslims and Christians jointly, is the issue of aggression against communal life and attacks on places of worship. This is a regrettable issue which causes friction between the followers of the two religions in many places, such as Lebanon during the recent civil war, the south of Egypt during the brief period of religious disturbance, and Bosnia and Herzegovina in the period of struggle after the demise of former Yugoslavia and the Serb attempt to establish Greater Serbia. Aggres-sion is prohibited in both religions, and assaults on lives other than combatants', as well as on possessions, is prohibited even in time of war. The Prophet Muḥammad, may God bless him and give him peace, and his caliphs after him granted protection "to all who profess Christianity in the east of the land and the west," undertook to protect their sides and defend "their churches, synagogues and houses of worship, the places of monks and dwellings of hermits, whether mountain or valley, cave or construction," and to guard them "from all violation, imposition or encumbrance." This is all documented and well-known in the sources on the time of the Prophet and the Rightly Guided Caliphs,[9] and anyone who wishes can refer to it, Muslim or Christian; it requires no explanation, and it exposes every tendency to aggression as baseless and a violation of Islam and Christianity to-gether. Even though it is clear, dialogue about this matter brings into the light this resplendent feature of the history of friendship and observance of the covenant of protection between Muslims and Christians through the history of their long co-existence.

There is also the matter of school textbooks which are full of falsifications and prejudice, and which promote in young people attitudes of irrational hostility. These negative attitudes became established in the West following the Crusades, as many fair-minded scholars have shown.[10]

A major issue in Islamic-Christian dialogue, and in fact in Islamic-Christian cooperation, is that adherents of the two religions should help one another in resisting the evils, crimes and wickedness which manifest themselves in all places—unbelief, social injustice, unbridled materialism, moral corruption, dictatorship in government, the traces of military, political, economic and cultural colonialism, the bloody engagement between different races and nations, civil wars and the genocides which usually result, the indifference of the rich, affluent, developed world towards the third world which is sunk beneath the oppression of poverty, backwardness and disease, the disregard of human rights, and the abuse of the environment on earth and in space. These and their like are the great evils which confront humanity and which must be resisted by those who hear God's word in the Torah, the Gospel and the Qur'an, working together in mutual support.

It was said at the end of the Cold War that a meeting of experts from the two super powers of East and West in scientific cooperation, space exploration or humanitarian relief would be a means of assisting rapprochement. Such a recommendation applies even more appropriately to the followers of the religions, who prostrate themselves and tremble in awe of God. What can be better than their collaboration in combatting human wickedness against those who seek to come closer to the beneficent, merciful Deity?

VII.

Any projected Islamic-Christian dialogue will be successful if it is distinguished from what bears the name but is nothing of the kind in either its objectives, aims or conduct. Such dialogue has nothing more than a purely political intention. An example from the past was the dialogue meeting held in Moscow in 1978 entitled *Religions for World Peace*, which was attended by representatives from almost all the religions.

The manifest purpose of this meeting was the call to reduce tension between East and West and to eliminate the nuclear threat. The Soviet Union issued this call as a means of strengthening its position in the Cold War, and it would not have been objectionable if it had not been pursued at the meeting in an openly abusive manner. For among the discussions at the conference was a paper which accused the religions of being the causes of strife among humankind. The Muslim delegation expressed disapproval of this document and made its withdrawal a condition of their continuing presence. This forced the conference organisers to withdraw it, since their real purpose was to get the representatives of the religions to agree to the call to renounce the arms race between East and West and its dangers, and nothing else.

Another more recent example was the conference *The Unity of Religions* held at St. Catherine's Monastery, Sinai, in 1984 and 1986. It was clear that its real purpose from its inception was the call to normalize relations between the Arabs and Israel.

We do not disapprove of followers of religion expressing their views about political matters, or rather matters of human wrong which politics has brought about. But we think religions are too important to be the vehicles of political whims, and if they are to speak out, we would wish them to utter the truth, the whole truth and nothing but the truth, for the sake of God the One Truth, and not for the advantage of one group of people over another. For he has said: "And let not the hatred of others to you make you swerve to wrong and depart from justice; be just, that is next to piety." (*Sūra* 5.8)

In the same way, we find it strange that no meetings between Muslims and Christians have ever been called in order to condemn crimes of extermination, torture, rape and the ethnic cleansing which is going on in Bosnia and Herzegovina, particularly at the hands of the Serbs, who allege that the existence of an Islamic enclave in Europe is not right. This is an allegation without foundation, because the Muslims of Bosnia and Herzegovina claim, and have always done so, to have a dispersed presence throughout the whole of Bosnia and Herzegovina. Moreover, they have recently agreed upon the existence of a federal entity with the Croats, and they for the most part are not Muslims.

Concerning the situation in the Middle East and the legitimate rights of the Palestinians in the land of Palestine, we find the statements issued by the Eastern churches to be balanced, fair and inspired by a just religious spirit. But we stand dismayed before the many statements issued by other churches, which have spared no opportunity to condemn anti-Semitism and cast it as a religious offence, or to uphold the rights of Israel in the land which it is granted in the Bible. Yet their declarations about the rights of the Arabs and refugees show none of the same force or sympathy.[11]

In short, we would like Islamic-Christian dialogue to remain distant from political exploitation. And if it is called upon to speak about politics, it should be inspired by the spirit of religion and its sense of fairness.

VIII.

Among the forms of dialogue about which opinion varies, from approval if their conditions are fulfilled and disapproval if they degenerate into dispute (which is not "what is better"), is that which is called the open debate. These debates proliferated at the end of the eighteenth century in India thanks to English missionaries and others. One of the best known among them was the great debate which took place between the German priest C.G. Pfander and the Indian Shaykh Rahmat Allah al-Kayrānawī, in the year 1854. The views of Shaykh Rahmat Allah are recorded in his famous book *Iẓhār al-Ḥaqq*.[12]

Such debates have been revived in recent years between Shaykh Ahmad Deedat from South Africa and various missionaries, such as the American preacher Jimmy Swaggart and others, and broadcast on radio and television.

Some of those who are concerned for Islamic-Christian dialogue to succeed and not to veer from its course set for mutual understanding and harmony think that these debates should be restricted to specialists who will keep to the conditions of intellectual, objective and calm exchange. There is no objection to publishing them so that those who can understand the issues involved may study them. But releasing them in the manner generally followed can turn them into what the experts of the two religions regard as unwholesome quarrels and possible sources of harmful dissension.

IX.

In conclusion, I have tried in this article to keep to absolute clarity and not to conceal truth or cover up problems, though I have not intended to defame anyone or cause injuries in any way. I have only wanted to disclose the true facts to enable everyone to cooperate in conducting dialogue, so that meetings may be successful and friendship and mutual help secured.

What is to be concluded from this presentation is that Islamic-Christian dialogue can become useful, and in some situations even necessary, if the dangers are avoided and the safeguards for its success increased.

So if the intentions of both sides are good, and dialogue is free from the tendencies to sow doubt or evangelize, if it is reserved for those who are qualified for it, and the participants concentrate on exchange of information and cooperation over what can be agreed together, such as acts of charity, kindness, and those which relate to the general benefit of humankind, the support of clear right and condemnation of manifest wrong—then we may hope that it will lead to the spread of friendship and a spirit of conciliation between the followers of the two religions, especially in the countries where they live together, either continuing a long history of co-existence as in Egypt or Lebanon, or resulting from the waves of migration everywhere throughout the world.

Let the tune of peace be the slogan for all, for Muslims, who are summoned by the teachings of their religion to kindness, justice and conduct to others in "ways that are best," and similarly for Christians, to whom the appeal is made, "Blessed are the peacemakers." (Matthew 5:9) And peace be upon those who follow God's guidance.

NOTES

1. This translation of the Arabic original, which was made by Dr. David Thomas with help from Mr. Adnan Alamasi and the Reverend John Davies, first appeared in the *Christian-Muslim Reflections Papers*, No. 5, June, 1996, published by the Centre for the Study of Islam and Christian-Muslim Relations, Selly Oak Colleges, Birmingham, United Kingdom. This version has been slightly revised by the editors.
2. Muhammad Hamidullah, *Majmū'a al-wathāā'iq al-siyāsiyya li-al-'ahd al-nabawī wa-al-khilāfa al-rāshida*, 3rd edition, Beirut 1969, pp. 75ff.
3. See *Nadwāt 'ilmiyya hawla al-sharī'a al-islāmiyya wa-huqūq al-insān fi al-Islām*, Dār al-Kitāb al-Lubnānī, Beirut, 1973-4.
4. The address of His Holiness Pope John Paul II to the general meeting of the Secretariat for Non-Christians, 3 March 1984.
5. *The Documents of the Second Vatican Council,* ed. W.M. Abbott (London, 1966), p. 663.
6. For example, the Gulf Summit Conference 1991.
7. Karl Hallencreutz, *Dialogue in Ecumenical History*, Living Faith Series, Geneva, 1971, pp. 71-87.
8. Yūsuf al-Qaradāwī, *Ghayr al-Muslimīn fī al-mujtama' al-Islāmī*, Maktaba Wahba, Cairo.
9. See especially Hamidullah, *Majmū'a al-wathā'iq al-siyāsiyya*, pp. 153ff.
10. E.g., Dr. Marcel Boissard, a Swiss scholar, who wrote a detailed report on this subject for the conference *Islam and the West*, as yet unpublished. Among his writings is the book *The Humanism of Islam* which has been translated into Arabic.
11. See for example: the statement of the Consultative Group on the Problem of Palestinian Refugees, Nicosia, 1969, issued by the Eastern Churches—its

contents are fair and balanced; the statement of the World Council of Churches meeting in Amsterdam, 1948, on the issue of anti-Semitism; the statement of the World Council of Churches meeting in Canterbury in 1969, entitled *Statement on the Middle East*, which is fair in its references to Palestinian rights compared with those of others; the statement of the Catholic Church in April, 1973, and the study from the World Council of Churches and its appendix concerning the consultative seminar which met in Cartagena in January, 1974, entitled *Biblical Interpretation and its Bearing regarding the Situation in the Middle East*. Both give support to the right of Israel to the land, as stated in the Bible.

12. Raḥmat Allah b. Khalīl al-Raḥmān al-Kayrānawī al-Hindī, *Iẓhār al-Ḥaqq*, Riyādh edition, 1989 (among other impressions and translations).

3

OVERCOMING HISTORY:

ON THE POSSIBILITIES OF MUSLIM-CHRISTIAN DIALOGUE

M. Darrol Bryant

Introduction

IN THIS ESSAY, I want to explore the possibilities of Muslim-Christian dialogue. But I must begin with a few qualifications. First, I must acknowledge that I am not an expert in Islam. I have come to some knowledge of the Muslim faith and world through my involvement in interfaith dialogue. It is in this context that I have developed some living awareness of the power of faith in Allah and the acknowledgment of Muhammad as his prophet. Second, I must admit that I do not know Arabic, so I have not been able to recite the Qur'an in its proper language but only in translation. Third, I must acknowledge with gratitude the opportunity to spend part of an earlier sabbatical in the Indian Institute of Islamic Studies, whose Director, Syed Ausaf Ali, has helped me to understand something of the tradition of Islam

in India. One of the first things that often surprises a Western student
of religion is to discover that Islam is not confined to the Arab peoples
but embraces diverse racial and ethnic communities, from Indonesia
to India and the former Soviet Union through the Middle East and
down into Africa. It is also worth noting that Islam is now the fastest
growing religious community in both the USA and Canada.

But let me now turn to my essay and place over it two verses from
the Qur'an. First:

> Let there be no compulsion in religion. For this is the truth, which
> stands out from error. That whoever rejects evil and believes in God
> shall grasp the most dependable handle. It shall never break. . . (Surah
> 2:256) (Or A. Yusaf Ali's translation: "Let there be no compulsion in
> religion. Truth stands out clear from error: whoever rejects evil and
> believes in God hath grasped the most trustworthy handhold, that never
> breaks. . .")

And, second:

> O Believers, persevere patiently
> And be unwavering in your faith.
> Vie with one another in your devotion and
> fear of God so that you may prosper. (Surah 3:200)
> (Or A. Yusaf Ali's translation: "vie in such
> perseverance, strengthen each other;
> And fear God; that ye may prosper.)

Both are from the translation found in Rafiq Zakaria's *Muhammad
and the Qur'an*.[1] We shall return to them at the end of this essay, but
for now let them stand without comment.

I have entitled this essay "Overcoming History" for the simple
reason that in order for there to be a significant encounter and dialogue
between men and women of the Muslim and the Christian faiths, it is
necessary to overcome the long history of antagonism between these
two remarkable faiths. In his introduction to *The Concise Encyclopedia
of Islam*, Huston Smith says simply and directly, "During most of their
history, Muslims and Christians have been at odds. . ."[2] Albert
Hourani, in his *Islam in European Thought* writes, "From the time it
first appeared, the religion of Islam was a problem for Christian
Europe. Those who believed in it were the enemy on the frontier."[3]
Such statements could be multiplied by citing other authorities, but
these will suffice.

From the very beginning of the Muslim era, Christians, especially in the West, have misunderstood, misrepresented, and maligned the faith of those who regard Muhammad as "the Messenger of God." Albert Hourani characterizes the Christian attitude in this way: "They (Christians) knew that Muslims believed in one God. . .but they could not easily accept that Muhammad was an authentic prophet. . . .The teaching of Muhammad. . .was (perceived as) a denial of the central doctrines of Christianity."[4] Thus it is essential that the Christian world repent of its failure to adequately acknowledge the faith of Islam. The Christian stereotype of Islam begins with a mistake about its very name. Rather than recognizing Islam for what it is, namely, "the perfect peace which comes from surrender to Allah," for centuries Christians have referred to Islam as "Mohammadanism." You know, and I have learned, that this is an error which strikes at the very heart of Islamic faith in Allah. It is only recently that Western Christians have even begun to name aright the great tradition of Islam. The West is just beginning to learn the fundamentals of Islam: the Five Pillars, the Qur'an, and the Prophet, Muhammad.[5] (Occasionally there has been a glimmer of another view, as when Pope Gregory VII wrote to Prince al-Nasir in 1076, "There is a charity which we owe to each other more than the other peoples because we recognize and confess one sole God, although in different ways."[6])

But it is not Christians alone who have failed to grasp the faith of Muslims. If I may be so bold, Muslims have also often characterized the Christian faith in ways that would not be acceptable to authentic Christians. Again let me turn to Albert Hourani: "For Muslim thinkers, the status of Christianity was clear. Jesus was one of the line of authentic prophets which had culminated in Muhammad, the "Seal of the Prophets," and his authentic message was essentially the same as that of Muhammad. Christians had misunderstood their faith, however, as they thought of their prophet as god, and believed he had been crucified."[7] While Muslims have always, in their own terms, recognized Jesus, they have often been not very positive about Christianity.

It is this history, both Christian and Muslim, that must be overcome.

In this essay, then, I intend to do four things: (1) to unfold something of that history that must be overcome, (2) to point to a way of meeting between the two faiths, (3) to highlight some of the outstanding issues that Christians and Muslims must address, and (4) to conclude with some recommendations. (The more specific theological points of convergence and conflict between Christianity and Islam will not be addressed here though they are raised in other essays in this volume.)

I.

Let me explain why I begin with "history" and the sense in which I am here using the term. Early in 1993, at the University of Waterloo, I invited a Muslim woman from Waterloo (originally from India) to present to my class on "interreligious encounter and dialogue" something of the faith of Islam. She did a splendid job of outlining the major features of the Islamic faith. But in the discussion that followed, she made the following statement: "Christians have always been hostile to Islam. Look at what's happening in Bosnia: Christians are killing Muslims and everyone just stands by and watches. It's a continuation of the Crusades." I was shocked by her statement. Partly because I realize that there is some truth to it—it is probably true that many countries in Europe and North America are not as exercised by these events as they would be if Christians were being slaughtered —and that in itself is appalling. But her statement also made me realize that for many (both in the Muslim and Christian world) the "Crusades" is not just an event of medieval history. It continues to be a living sense of the ongoing relationship between Christians and Muslims. While it is perhaps understandable—given the depth of Christian misunderstanding of and antagonism towards Islam—that a Muslim would perceive Christianity as a hostile, aggressive force, it is also disconcerting.

What her comment makes clear is that we all, whether Christian or Muslim, come to the encounter and dialogue between Muslim and Christian burdened, for good and ill, by the legacy of the past. We are, as Eugen Rosenstock-Huessy saw so clearly, creatures who face four directions simultaneously.[8] Backward and forward in time, inward and outward in space. And here at the intersection of these four fronts—the crux where we live—we are confronted continuously with what from the past we need to let go of and what we need to retain, what from the future we must respond to and that to which we must say no. These are certainly questions that confront the Muslim and the Christian in the present situation.

The issue for us is not "overcoming history" in some specialized or professional sense, nor is it a task of rewriting history. Rather, it is the past that lives in the present and shapes our perception and response to the faith of the other that must be overcome. I cannot speak accurately about this perception in relation to the Muslim world (though some Muslim writers make it clear that their perception of the Christian faith is not what we might hope it to be), but there are some points that can be made about Christians in the USA and Canada.

The image of Islam in the contemporary West is not positive. Here are some of the images North Americans have of Muslims. Muslims are people who blow up the World Trade Center in New York City. They are terrorists in the Middle East or oil-rich Sheiks who live without regard for the everyday Muslim in their home country. They have no regard for the rights of women. They are led by fanatical leaders in North Africa and the Middle East. And I could go on and on. Writing in 1983, R. Marston Speight in *Christian-Muslim Relations*, wrote, "In general. . .the people of this country remain uninformed as to what Islam is and what Muslims are like. . . .The prejudices and stereotypes of the past still persist so that the image projected of Islam upon the imagination of the average American is one of intolerant, legalistic, and fatalistic religion practiced by backward, ferocious, and scheming people."[9] Little seems to change.

Occasionally, a voice does challenge these images. On Sept. 14, 1993, former U.S. President Jimmy Carter (and a devout Christian) commented on the American attitude towards the Muslim world in the following terms: "I think there is too much of an inclination in this country to look on Muslims as inherently terrorist or inherently against the West" (*Times* of India). I was very pleased to see this statement, and it needs to be made often in the current climate in North America.

Let me be very clear. I am not saying that any of these negative images are correct. But I am saying that they are the ones that dominate the public media and the public consciousness of Christians (and the secular or non-religious as well) in the USA and Canada. And they are all negative. They do not serve the cause of truth and understanding between Muslims and Christians but they do serve the cause of political and religious forces that would maintain the long legacy of bitter relations between these two communities of faith.

Thus both the contemporary situation and the historical record do not bode well for any significant encounter and dialogue between the Islamic and Christian worlds.

II.

Is there a way to overcome this past and move towards a new day in the history of Muslim-Christian relations? I believe that there is, and that is the way of interfaith encounter and dialogue.[10] This movement heralds a new day for relations between different faiths and faith communities. It has as its aim mutual understanding and mutual recognition.

In a meeting of faiths characterized by dialogue, it is essential that each community be allowed to define itself. This is the first rule of dialogue. Rather than insisting on our perception of the other, we must began with the other's understanding of its own faith and community. When Christians and Muslims meet in this way, then we can move beyond the stereotypes and misperceptions of the past and be open to the other in terms of its own self-understanding, its own faith. When people of the two faiths begin to truly meet, we will begin to confront the living past and we will experience some of the dissonance between our preconceptions and prejudices and the reality of the other faith. I remember with considerable embarrassment my own encounter with Muslims over the past twenty years. I recognize that I, too, was caught in some of the prejudices and misconceptions I mentioned earlier. I was so surprised to meet Indian and Indonesian and Saudi Muslims who did not fit my expectations. Through meeting in the spirit of dialogue, then, I had to confront my own "living past" and "overcome" it so that I might relate to the reality of the other.

In the encounter and dialogue between people of different faiths, the obligation is to listen to the other and attempt to understand them in their own terms. Rather then either assuming one knows the faith of the other, or attempting to force them into the stereotypes of the past, we need to meet in a freshness and openness of spirit, willing to allow ourselves to be surprised and moved by the faith in Allah and His Prophet Muhammad, or by the faith in Jesus as the Christ. This is the second rule of dialogue.

The third rule of dialogue is that when we meet in dialogue, we meet as fellow human beings and pilgrims in faith. Too often in the history of religion—not only in the history of Christians and Muslims—we have "demonized" those of other faiths. We in the Christian traditions have too often called all non-Christians "pagans" and acted as if God were not present to other peoples unless we Christians were there. This is an insufferable arrogance and a betrayal of faith in the God who is the Creator, Redeemer, and Sanctifier of humankind. There are parallels to this attitude in other religions. However, when we meet in dialogue, we quickly discover that we share a common humanity (although some follow the Christian way of being human and others the Muslim way of being human) and that we are fellow pilgrims in our respective journeys towards God. We do not have the same faith; we have our own distinctive faiths. But at the same time, we discover crucial things that are shared across tradition: beliefs in the Ultimate, values of compassion and virtue, concerns for the welfare of "all sentient beings" (as the Buddhists say), and so on. To come into dialogue and to recognize these commonalities, especially in the Abrahamic faiths, is illuminating and transforming. It can and will profoundly alter the relations between the faith communities.

The fourth rule of dialogue—and the last one I will mention here—is that in the meeting of Muslims and Christians, it is essential that the depths of the respective faiths come to expression. There is often a misconception of what occurs in dialogue. Many believe that it is a polite meeting where the depths of our respective faiths are set aside in the name of an easy tolerance. But this is a misconception. Genuine encounter and dialogue is a meeting of the deepest levels of our respective faiths, where we bear witness to what of the spirit and of God has been given to us. This we do not for the sake of persuading the other that we are right and they are wrong, but for the sake of bearing witness to what each has experienced and knows of the One who is beyond. When we meet in this way, when the dialogue goes this deeply, then both parties can grow not only in their own faith but in their recognition of the validity of the other.

A similar point was made by John Taylor and Muzammil Siddiqi in "Understanding and Experience of Christian-Muslim Dialogue" when they wrote, "Dialogue was essentially to be undertaken in a spirit of repentance wherein we turned our backs on past and present prejudice, wherein we turned to our neighbor in the spirit of love, wherein we turned to God, as He offered Himself to us."[11]

Through meeting in a spirit of dialogue—taking the other seriously on their own terms, listening profoundly and speaking truthfully, growing in appreciation of our shared humanity across tradition, and witnessing to the Ultimate who is the source and object of genuine faith—we can begin to overcome history and enter a new day in the relations between faiths.

III.

As I have already indicated, the first problem to be overcome is the appalling ignorance of the West concerning Islam. This can be achieved most powerfully and profoundly only through face-to-face meetings of Christians and Muslims. In such meetings, stereotypes and misconceptions quickly give way to an acknowledgment of the integrity and depth of each other's faith and path. The second way is through education. We need to include education about the many religious traditions of humankind in our schools. Such education should not serve the apologetic interests of a given religious community, but should be an account of the various faiths that a believer in a given tradition can recognize as valid. I say this because I believe it essential that the study of religion not only be accurate and historically sound, but also convey something of the living heart of the various traditions.[12] Such education about the different religious traditions should also be a critical education, that is, it should not fail to speak accurately and critically of the way in which each tradition has lived its faith or has failed to live its faith in history.

When we meet one another on the basis of mutual respect and some understanding of the faith of the other, then there will be other issues we must address. There will be complex theological issues to address: our understandings of the Divine, our differing understandings of Jesus/Isa, our differing views of the Bible and the Qur'an, and so on. Among other issues are two that I would highlight as crucial for consideration: fundamentalism and conversionism. I have stated them in this way deliberately, for I want you to understand each for what it is, namely, an "ideology," as indicated by the suffix "ism." Let me try to make this clearer.

One of the problems that faces both communities of faith is that of "fundamentalism." I know that many within the Muslim world do not like to use this term, since they rightly see it as having originated in the Christian world and as first defining a Christian phenomenon. But if we can move beyond these polemics to the reality, then we can see the issue. If the movement we call "fundamentalism" is a return to the fundamentals of faith, then it is legitimate, for it revitalizes the faith of the community. But this is not what the term usually connotes. The "fundamentalism" that must concern both communities is when faith is transformed into an ideology. The ideology then becomes a way to clothe or mask the fear and alienated consciousness of a group.

Studies of Christian fundamentalism in the United States have shown that it arises among sectors of the Christian population that have been marginalized and feel threatened by modern conditions of life. They react by articulating an ideological version of the Christian faith that is not open to question, but must simply be affirmed in the ideological terms of the group. This reaction and development can be found across many religious communities, and it needs to be addressed from within our respective religious communities. Such an ideology does not lead to a vital faith in Allah or God, but rather legitimizes the fears of the group. When, in the name of Islam or Christianity, one proclaims "death" to those who oppose one, this is neither authentic Islam nor authentic Christianity.

Another issue, especially of the Christian world, that must be addressed if we are to move towards dialogical mutuality and understanding is "conversionism." I mean here the attitude that the only way to relate to people of other faiths, Muslim or otherwise, is to seek their conversion. This assumption is based on a profound confusion. In the Christian faith, metanoia or conversion is what follows in response to hearing the command to "Follow Me." Thus it is a word directed towards the disciple, the follower, the Christian. It is the Christian who is called to "be turned around" to be "renewed in mind and spirit" which is the meaning of conversion. But far too often, Christians project this need onto someone else, the Other, whether Muslim or Hindu or Jew or Buddhist or even fellow Christian, rather than seeing it as their own deepest need. Parallel attitudes are to be found within the Muslim world. But the point is that such a mentality stands in the way of dialogue, in the way of authentic meeting where Muslim and Christian meet one another as brothers and sisters seeking to understand the One who is gracious and beneficent and beyond.

It would be better for Christians to follow the lead of Vatican II which said: "The church also regards with esteem the Muslims who worship the One, Subsistent, Merciful, and Almighty God, the Creator of Heaven and earth, who has spoken to man. . . .If in the course of centuries there has arisen not infrequent dissension and hostility between Christians and Muslims, this sacred Council now urges everyone to forget the past, to make sincere efforts at mutual understanding and to work together."[13] Can we move in this direction?

These are but two of the issues that will need to be addressed in the encounter and dialogue between Muslims and Christians. From this dialogue there will not always emerge agreement; but even in our differences, we will have a deeper understanding of one another.

IV.

If there is to be a future of dialogue between Islam and Christianity, then it will be necessary to overcome the bitter legacy of the past and present.

Caricatures and stereotypes of each other must give way to accurate understanding and mutual respect. This change can only happen as we learn about each other, study one another's faith and history, and seek to grasp our respective structures of belief and practice. It is imperative, for example, for the non-Muslim world to understand, as R. Zakaria has written, that "The Prophet is presented in the Qur'an as the best example of its teachings and a perfect model of human behaviour."[14] Similarly, it is imperative for Muslims to understand that when Christians affirm that Jesus is the Christ, they do not diminish the God who is One.

We will also have to come to understand that there is diversity within each tradition. While Christians from East and West share a common faith, they are also diverse not only in terms of Orthodox, Catholic, and Protestant, but also in terms of different cultural and ethnic settings. Likewise, in Islam there are Shiites and Sunnis, and just as Muslims from West and East share the faith of Islam, they live it in different and changing ways across the Muslim world. Studies in Islam in the Indian, Indonesian, and Central Asian contexts—as well as Nigerian—are making us all aware of the plurality within Islam itself.

As we begin to encounter and dialogue with one another, then the prejudices and misconceptions that have entered our respective literatures will begin to be overcome. While, for example, I welcome Rafiq Zakaria's exposition of Islam, it also saddens me to see him repeat statements about Christianity that are not accurate. We need to reach a day when Muslims understand aright the Christian texts and Christians understand aright the Qur'an and other writings of Muslims. We should all have the experience I have had reading the works of people such as Hossien Nasr, the great Sufi scholar now working in the United States, or my friend Syed Ausaf Ali, or Abdullah Durkee and many other Muslim writers: the experience of growing in understanding of and sympathy with the other faith.[15]

At the outset, I placed two Qur'anic verses over this essay. Please forgive my audacity in offering these comments on them. The first, I believe, states a truth that both Muslim and Christian should affirm, namely, that in matters of religion there should be "no compulsion." Instead, we need to respect all those who "reject evil" and "believe in God" since this is the "most dependable handle." But it is important to link this verse with the second verse which urges "believers"—a term which I understand globally, including believers in all traditions —to "vie" with one another in "devotion" and "fear of God." For it is important to understand that in the dialogue between religions, we are called not to reduce the intensity or depth of our own faith but to bear witness to it while respecting the faith of the other. So the proper contest between believers is not, I believe, in terms of the superiority of my faith over yours, but in the depth of our devotion to the One that Muslims call Allah and that Christians call God. For it is that One and that One alone who should be the object of our striving and our faith.

NOTES

1. Rafiz Zakaria, *Muhammad and the Qur'an* (New Delhi: Penguin Books India, 1991), pp. 105, 114.
2. Huston Smith, "Introduction," *The Concise Encyclopedia of Islam*, C. Glasse (London: Stacey International), p. 5. In this context it is also worth noting Smith's citation of Meg Greenfield writing in *Newsweek* in 1979: "We are heading into an expansion of that complex religion, culture, and geography known as Islam. There are two things to be said about this. One is that no part of the world is more important. . .for the foreseeable future. The other is that no part of the world is more hopelessly and systematically and stubbornly misunderstood by us." p. 5.
3. Albert Hourani, *Islam in European Thought* (Cambridge: Cambridge University Press, 1991), p. 6.
4. Hourani, p. 8. Another Christian attitude towards Islam, and one more acceptable, is that found in the writings of Kenneth Cragg beginning with *The Call of the Minaret* in 1957.
5. There are now several good introductions to Islam available in the West. But one of the most accessible is Huston Smith, *The World's Religions* (first published in 1957 as *The Religions of Man*) (San Francisco: Harper and Row, 1991).
6. This is cited in Hourani, p. 9.
7. Hourani, p. 8. This is again not simply a medieval attitude; it is still present in volumes like *Islam and Christianity*, Waqf Ikhlas Publications No.12, Istanbul, 1991.
8. See Eugen Rosenstock-Huessy, *Speech and Reality* (Norwich, VT: Argo

Books, 1968). For an introduction to this remarkable but little-known thinker, see M. Darrol Bryant and Hans Huessy, *Eugen Rosenstock-Huessy: Studies in His Life and Thought* (Lewiston, NY: Edwin Mellen Press, 1985).

9. R. Marston Speight, *Christian-Muslim Relations, An Introduction for Christians in the USA* (Hartford, CT: NCCUSA, 1983), p. 2.

10. For some of my own contributions to this movement, see M.D. Bryant and F. Flinn, eds., *Interreligious Dialogue: Voices from a New Frontier* (New York: Paragon House, 1985), and *Religion in A New Key* (New Delhi: Wiley Eastern Ltd., 1992). The movement for interreligious and/or interfaith understanding includes all the world's religious traditions, not simply Muslim and Christian. See Chapter II in my *Religion in a New Key*. But here I am focusing on Muslim-Christian dialogue.

11. J. Taylor and M. Siddiqi, "Understanding and Experience of Christian-Muslim Dialogue," in S. J. Samartha, *Dialogue Between Men of Living Faiths* (Geneva: WCC, 1971), p. 60. See also S.J. Samantha and J.B. Taylor, *Christian-Muslim Dialogue* (Geneva: WCC, 1973) and Ismail Raji al-Faruqi, ed., *Trialogue of the Abrahamic Faiths* (International Institute of Islamic Thought, 1982). It should be clear that the call for dialogue is not equivalent to the comparative study of religion or history of religion, though contemporary studies by historians of religion and comparativists have certainly contributed to understanding across tradition.

12. I should mention here the many contributions of Wilfrid Cantwell Smith to the understanding of Islam including his *On Understanding Islam* (Delhi: Idarah-i Adabiyat-i Delli, 1981). For Professor Smith, "to be a Muslim is to participate in the Islamic process in human history. . ." p. 229. Here Smith emphasizes his role as a student of comparative religion. His Christian as well as professional commitments are clearer in his important *Towards a World Theology* (Philadelphia: Westminster Press, 1981).

13. This text is cited in W.M. Watt, *Muslim-Christian Encounter* (London: Routledge, 1991), pp. 148-149. The Vatican II Council statement is cited for the simple reason that it reflects a new departure in the institutional life of the Christian tradition, not because it is fully adequate to what is being called for here.

14. Zakaria, p. 8. For example, Muhammad Ata ur-Rahim's *Jesus, Prophet of Islam* (Norfolk, UK: Diwan Press, 1977), is not helpful in Christian-Muslim relations. It takes seriously only some hints in the Qur'an and not the Qur'anic affirmation of Christians as a "people of the Book." A study that contributes to our understanding of Islam in diverse cultural setting is William R. Roff, ed., *Islam and the Political Economy of Meaning* (London: Croom Helm, 1987).

15. And now, following the Aligarh lecture where an earlier version of this lecture was presented, I can add the names of Iqtidar Husain Siddiqui and M. Athar Ali who gave me some of their work. I am especially appreciative of Prof. Siddiqui's *Islam and Muslims in South Asia: Historical Perspective* (Delhi: Adam Publishers, 1987). See also his three contributions on Sufi saints and dargahs in C.W. Troll, ed., *Muslim Shrines in India* (Delhi: Oxford University Press, 1989).

PART II

PERSPECTIVES

4

CHRISTIAN-MUSLIM RELATIONS:

USHERING IN A NEW ERA

S. A. Ali

And nearest among them in love to the Believers wilt thou find those
who say "We are Christians": because amongst these are men devoted
to learning men who have renounced the world, and they are not
arrogant.

Qur'an 5:82

DESPITE THE AFFIRMATION of the Qur'an that Jesus was a
prophet, born of the Virgin Mary, who received divine revelation, and
a sincere attempt by early Muslims to forge a strong bond between the
two communities, Christian-Muslim relations have seen many ups and
downs during the last 1400 years. The reasons lie both in certain
doctrinal differences and political ambitions.

The first major doctrinal difference is that of the Trinity which has
puzzled the Muslim mind and has all along been a subject of hot debate.
Some Muslims even think that this doctrine was invented three hundred
years after Jesus,[1] and quote Christian scholars like Prof. Johan B.
Hygen of the University of Oslo, who "recognize that this doctrine is
not found in the Bible."[2] Perhaps I would not be wrong in saying that
this doctrine has puzzled the Christian mind too. Various Christian

thinkers interpret this doctrine differently, and recently a whole issue of *Dialogue & Alliance*[3] was devoted to the subject of the Trinity. It contains a fine article entitled "Recovering the Trinitarian Foundations of Christian Experience," by my old and esteemed friend, Prof. Darrol Bryant. There he states that "the Trinitarian symbol has become for many within the very family of Christian traditions opaque" partly because of "a loss of awareness of the Trinitarian nature and structure of our Christian experience."[4] One of the earliest polemical works on this doctrine is al-Warraq's *Against the Trinity* which has recently been translated into English.[5] It was written in the early ninth century by a Shi'ite scholar who met the arguments of the Nestorians and the Melkites at great length. Since then, a very large number of treatises have been written by Muslim scholars refuting the doctrine of Trinity.

A well-known modern Christian thinker, Prof. Raimundo Panikkar, reinterprets the Trinity as a "cosmotheandric" myth. In this myth, the three elements or dimensions—the cosmic, the divine, and the human —reveal a triadic oneness existing at all levels of consciousness and reality. Some such interpretation of the Trinity may come closer to acceptance by the Muslims, but the idea of "Father, Son, and Holy Spirit" poses insuperable problems for the Muslim mind nurtured on the Qur'an. The Qur'an believes in strict monotheism and rejects the idea of both divine incarnation and procreation.

Professor John Hick in his new book *A Christian Theology of Religions* argues that the Trinity was originally a metaphor that was transformed into a metaphysical doctrine. Professor John W. Miller, who recently retired as a Professor of Biblical Studies at the University of Waterloo in Canada, and Sir Anthony Buzzard, who wrote *The Doctrine of Trinity: A Self-Inflicted Wound of Christianity*, are not comfortable with the idea of the Trinity.

The second major doctrinal difference is related to the conviction of the Qur'an that Jesus did not die on the Cross. Instead, the Qur'an affirms that someone who resembled him was crucified and that Jesus was lifted up to the heavens. Christians believe the last part—that Jesus was lifted up to the heavens—but would not accept the statement that Jesus did not died on the cross. This is a second major point of difference which the Muslims and Christians have often debated. One of the earliest debates on the subject took place towards the end of the eighth century between Caliph al-Mahdi and the leader of the Nestorian Church, Catholicos Timothy I.[6]

The doctrine of Atonement is the third major issue between the

Muslims and the Christians. While the Christians believe that with the crucifixion of Jesus all the sins of men were washed away except the original sin which taints every human being, the Muslims believe that man is not born in sin, that everyone will have to account for his deeds, or misdeeds, on the Day of Judgement, and sins will be forgiven by God as an act of mercy, and not because of someone dying for the sins of others. According to Islam, the strict rule of reward and punishment is the only way to make people behave with responsibility and cleanse society of evils. "No laden soul can bear another's load" (Qur'an 17:15).

The last major doctrinal difference between Muslims and Christians involves the Prophet of Islam, Muhammad (PBUH) and the Qur'an. The Muslims consider the Christians to be lacking in the principle of reciprocity. If Islam can bring within its fold not only Jesus, but many other prophets—Abraham, Moses and many, many others sent at different times in different lands—the Muslims wonder why the Christians cannot accept Prophet Muhammad as a true Prophet who brought the same message from the same divine source. The Qur'an states clearly that all the prophets have brought to their people essentially the same message, and that they all stand on the same footing. Very few Christians have accepted, or are willing to accept today, the Prophet Muhammad as a true Messenger. The Qur'an states that he was no different from ordinary mortals, except that he brought the divine message.

It is interesting to note that when the Prophet received the first verses of the Qur'an, he was taken aback. Two Christians testified that this was the divine revelation. The Prophet's wife Khadija took him to a Christian cousin of hers, Waraqa Ibn Nawfal, who had transcribed a part of the Gospel into Hebrew. He confirmed that the verses revealed to the Prophet were of divine origin. The second Christian, according to tradition, who testified that the Prophet had received a divine revelation was Monk Bahira in Syria. Muslim scholars have also found prediction about the coming of the Prophet of Islam in The Gospel of St. Barnabas[7] and Gospel of John.[8]

Among the outstanding living Western scholars of Islam who have a sympathetic approach to Muhammad as a Prophet and the Qur'an as a divine scripture are Prof. Annemarie Schimmel, Prof. Wilfred Cantwell Smith, Prof. Montgomery Watt and Prof. Willem A. Bijlefeld. Another well-known orientalist, Rev. Kenneth Cragg, suggests that "the Christian conscience must develop a faithful appreciation of the Qur'an and thereby participate with Muslims in Muhammad within that community of truth as to God and man, creation and nature, law and mercy, which they afford."[9]

The non-acceptance by the Christians of Muhammad led to the rift which went on widening and, coupled with the fear that votaries of the new religion might overrun the Christian lands, led to the Crusades which, starting in A.D. 1095, continued for about two centuries. These events left bitter memories which persist to this day. Accentuating this bitterness is the reality that for more than two centuries, several major European powers, like Great Britain, France, Italy, Holland, and Portugal, ruled the Muslim lands and were a drain on their economy. Bosnia, Chechnya, Libya and Iraq are other causes of bitterness today. The Muslims think that the Western world is resorting to double standards. The Western world speaks endlessly about enforcing human rights, but tramples them in Muslim lands where innocent civilians are brutally punished for the fault of the rulers. Bosnia is the worst example where more than 200,000 peace-loving men, women and children have been massacred only because of the Western powers' intolerance in seeing the birth of even a single Muslim country in the heart of Europe. It must be admitted, however, that large numbers of fair-minded Christians have given their moral support to the suffering people in Bosnia and elsewhere. The visit of the Pope to Bosnia was hailed by the Muslim world, and Jimmy Carter's efforts to stop the massacre have won wide admiration.

The first lesson to be learnt in forging a new and strong relationship between Christians and Muslims is that we must face the past in order to forgive and forget it and work for the present and the future. This is specially important in the present time when education has brought enlightenment to the world and people are learning the lesson of interdependence in a shrinking world.

Shying away from polemics, Christians and Muslims should adopt a more constructive approach and realize, first and foremost, how close their religions are to each other. "Islam," says Aziz-us-Samad, "is thus seen by its followers as the revival, restatement and final and complete version of the religion of Jesus."[10] That the churches, along with other places of worship, were protected even in the time of the Prophet and freedom of worship guaranteed is evident from the Qur'an:

> Had Allah not checked one set of people by means of another, surely the monasteries, churches, synagogues and mosques in which the name of

Allah is commemorated in abundant measure would have been pulled down.

Qur'an 22:40

Every Muslim is enjoined to affirm:

I believe in Allah, and His angels, and His books, and His prophets, in resurrection, in divine decree for good and evil and life after death.

These articles of faith will be easily acceptable to Christians and can form a firm basis for Christian-Muslim relationship. However, Christians must show liberality and tolerance by including Muhammad in the line of prophets.

The guidelines for improving relations between the Christians and Muslims have been well set,[11] and the two communities, instead of reviving the spirit of the Crusades, should try to revive the spirit of reconciliation as was witnessed in Baghdad, Damascus and Toledo. The Christian nations should stop thinking of Muslims as their enemy, and should appreciate the fact that a large number of Muslim countries are allies of the Western powers—from the most populous Indonesia to the Islamic State of Pakistan, from Turkey to many an oil-rich country in the Gulf. A community should not be judged by the misdeeds of a few.

It is heartening to see that serious attempts are now being made to bring about understanding and harmony between the Muslims and the Christians, a shining example of which is this Conference itself. Another example is the Conference being organized by the Swedish Government next week in Rinkeby, near Stockholm, "to achieve, through better knowledge, dialogue and understanding, a counter influence to the mutually reciprocative negative illusions of the respective religions: Islam and Christianity."

The efforts of the Pope are admired by the Muslim world. He sends a message every year all over the Muslim world warmly greeting the Muslims at the beginning of the fasting month of Ramadan. The Muslims should respond by participating warmly in the celebrations marking the nativity of Jesus who is revered by the Muslims, too. A message greeting the Christians at Christmas should go out from some reputed Muslim organization, like Al-Azhar in Cairo, or some Muslim world-figure.

Influential religious leaders can play a vital role by molding the thinking of their communities. To give an example: when the Muslims wanted to build a massive mosque in Rome, there was much opposition from the Christians, but finally the view of the Pope, who welcomed the idea of a mosque in Rome, prevailed, and today a beautiful, sprawling mosque in Rome stands testimony to the new spirit of tolerance and liberalism.

The Pope has also established a Secretariat for Dialogue with Non-Christians in Rome which, under my friend Cardinal Arinze, is doing good work in fostering greater understanding. The Protestants, working through the World Council of Churches and various other organizations, are also awakening the spirit of ecumenism through dialogues, seminars and conferences.

The present writer, too, inspired by Professor Wilfred Cantwell Smith, organized under the auspices of the Indian Institute of Islamic Studies in New Delhi a series of Christian-Muslim dialogues with very good results. It was 1963-64 when Professor Smith was in India studying Sanskrit and Indian religions before taking up the new position of Director of the Center for World Religions at Harvard University, that he suggested to me that a series of dialogues should be organized jointly with the Henry Martyn Institute of Islamic Studies and the newly founded Indian Institute of Islamic Studies. He suggested that the first topic should be "Faith and Works." I welcomed the idea, as it came from one whom I admired both as a fine scholar and a sincere, well-meaning person. I viewed him as "half Christian and half Muslim." I was impressed to discover that he fasted along with his Muslim colleagues and students during the month of Ramadan when he was at McGill. He was earlier Director of the Henry Martyn Institute of Islamic Studies in Lahore which, after the birth of Pakistan, was moved to Aligrah, then to Lucknow, then to Nagpur, and is now located in Hyderabad, India. It was in Nagpur and Dehra Dun that the great scholars of the two Institutes met—the late Bishop Subhau, the late Dr. Yusuf Husain Khan, the late Professor M. Ajmal Khan, the late Dr. Syed Abdul Lateef, the late Maulama Sajjad Husain, Hakeem Abdul Hameed, Present of the Indian Institute of Islamic Studies (now Chancellor of Aligarh Muslim University and Hamdard University), Dr. S. T. Lokhandivala, Professor S. A. I. Tirmizi, the late Mr. Athar Husain and others. Needless to say, the discussions were very fruitful and helped the participants to appreciate each other's point of view. But a few dialogues are not enough. We have to have thousands of them around the world at regular intervals to achieve the goal of real understanding between Muslims and Christians.

Doctrinal differences should be relegated to the rear and more important issues should be the focus of discussion. What is the meaning of life? What constitutes sin? What is the position of Islam and Christianity on moral issues like abortion, machine-assisted insemination and euthanasia? What are the social issues of our times and how to solve them? How can terrorism be combated and how to put a stop to the diversion of funds from development to the production of weapons of mass destruction? How to check pollution and improve the quality of life? how to secure for all men on earth the basic human rights, freedom from fear and equality and dignity? To do this, and much else, is the mission and goal of both Christianity and Islam. Should they not, then, join hands and change the world scenario, fulfilling Omar Khayyam's dream:

> Ah Love! Could thou and I with Fate conspire
> To change this sorry scheme of things entire?
> Would not we shatter it to bits, and then
> Remold it nearer to the heart's desire?

NOTES

1. Mrs. Ulfat Aziz-us-Samad, *A Comparative Study of Christianity and Islam* (Lahore: Sh. Muhammad Ashraf, 1976), p. 71.
2. See Johan Hygan, *Norsk Theologisk Tidsskrift*, No.1, 1967.
3. See *Dialogue & Alliance*, Fall 1990, Vol. 4, No. 3.
4. M.D. Bryant, "Recovering the Trinitarian Foundations of Christian Experience," *Dialogue & Alliance*, Fall 1990, Vol. 4, No. 3, p. 71.
5. David Thomas, trans., *Anti-Christian Polemic in Early Islam: Abu 'Isa al-Warraq's "Against the Trinity"* (Cambridge: Cambridge University Press, 1992).
6. Neal Robinson, *Christ in Islam and Christianity* (Albany: State University of New York Press, 1991), pp. 107-8.
7. See *The Gospel of Barnabas*, translated by Lonsdale and Ragg (Oxford: Clarendon Press, 1907).
8. See the Gospel of John 14:16; 15:26 and 16:7.
9. Kenneth Cragg, *Muhammad and the Christian: A Question of Response* (London: Darton, Longman and Todd Ltd., 1984), p. 141.
10. Mrs. Ulfat Aziz-us-Samad, *op. cit.*, p. x.
11. See, for example, two important works: *Guidelines for a Dialogue Between Muslims and Christians*, prepared by Secretariatus Pro Non-Christians (Cochin: K.C.M. Press, 1979); R. Marston Speight, *Christian-Muslim Relations: An Introduction for Christians in the United States of America* (Hartford, Connecticut: Office on Christian-Muslim Relations, The National Council of the Churches of Christ in the U.S.A., 1986).

5

THE MUSLIM-CHRISTIAN RELATIONSHIP:

A CHALLENGE AND A PROMISE

Abdelmoneim M. Khattab

Introduction

ISLAM IS AN ARABIC word adapted from the infinitive "SILM" which means "peace" in English. Peace is a total action which entails peace with God by being obedient to Him, peace with one's self and peace with the members of the human family at large. In a global context, the word Islam indicates a universal religion directed to all humankind since the creation of man on earth. This universal religion calls people to worship the one and only God. It gives humanity the Divine Law with clear rules and instructions. The followers of this religion are required to shape their behavior after these rules, and consequently are promised happiness in this life as well as in the Hereafter. Contrary to what many people understand, Islam encompasses all the heavenly messages revealed to humanity since the beginning of life on this planet.

The holy Qur'an emphasizes this fact in many verses:

The prophet Noah, peace be upon him, said to his people,

> But if you are averse, I have asked of you no wage. My wage is the
> concern of God only, and I am commanded to be one of the *MUSLIMS*.
>
> Qur'an: X: 72

About the prophet Lot, peace be upon him, the Qur'an says:

> Then we brought forth such believers as were there. But we found there
> but one house of the *MUSLIMS*.
>
> Qur'an: LI: 35-36

After rebuilding the Kaaba, (the sacred house in Makka) the prophet
Abraham and his son Ismail prayed:

> Our Lord: accept from us (this duty). Lo: You are the Hearer, the Knower.
> Our Lord: and make us *MUSLIMS* to you and of our seed a *MUSLIM*
> nation.
>
> Qur'an: II: 127-128

Abraham recommended to his sons, especially Jacob:

> O my sons! Allah has chosen for you the (true) religion; therefore die
> not save when you are *MUSLIMS*. Or were you present when death came
> to Jacob when he said to his sons: What will you worship after me?
> They said: We shall worship your God, the God of your father Abraham
> and Ismail and Isaac, one God and to him we are *MUSLIMS*.
>
> Qur'an: 11: 132-133

And Joseph, peace be on him, prayed to his Creator saying:

> O my God, you have given me (something) of the sovereignty and have
> taught me (something) of the interpretation of events - Creator of Heavens
> and the Earth, you are my protector in the world and the Hereafter,
> make me die *MUSLIM* and join me to the righteous.
>
> Qur'an: XII: 101

The letter of the prophet Solomon to the queen of Sheeba states:

> Exalt not yourselves against me, and come to me as *MUSLIM*.
>
> Qur'an: XXVII: 31

The queen of Sheeba responded to Solomon's request:

O my Lord! I have indeed wronged myself and now became *MUSLIM*
and with Solomon I submit unto Allah, the Lord of the Worlds.
Qur'an: XXVII: 44

Jesus, the messenger of God, called his followers thus:

Who will be my helpers in the cause of Allah? The disciples said: We
will be Allah's helpers, We believe in Allah and bear witness that we are
MUSLIMS.
Qur'an: III: 52

Finally, the chain of heavenly messages was sealed by the last
Qur'anic verse revealed to Muhammad, the prophet of Islam, which
states:

This day I have perfected your religion for you and completed my favor
unto you and have chosen for you *Al-ISLAM* as a religion.
Qur'an: V: 3[1]

The above quotations from the holy Qur'an clearly indicate that even
though the heavenly messages consisted of a series of revelations to
different messengers at different periods in time, the substance of these
messages was always the same. It is appropriate to indicate here that the
concept *ISLAM* means submission, and is the first step a person must
take to acknowledge the will of God, a belief shared and understood by
every follower of a heavenly religion.

Next, we must understand the Islamic concept *IMAN* which displays
a person's effort to move closer to God. Iman consists of both Islam
(which is a proclamation of the oneness of God and the messengerhood
of Muhammad) and action (which is the actual worship of God and
obedience of his rules).

The Islamic concept *IHSAN* is even more inclusive than *Islam* and
Iman and is the highest degree of faith. It is an individual's constant
awareness of the presence of God. The angel Gabriel defined *Ihsan* as
that stage in which an individual "worship(s) God as if you see Him. If
you do not see Him, then He is seeing you."

The aim of this essay is to clarify the views of each religion towards
the other, to spell out the points of agreement as well as the differences,
and finally, to predict the future of the relationship between the two faiths in
the light of the present dialogue, communication and understanding.

Islam as Viewed by Christians

Upon the advent of Islam, Greek Christian theologians at first dismissed it as Christian heresy. When their knowledge about the new faith increased, they treated it as a false religion and charged Muhammad with various moral weaknesses. Islam challenged the basic tenets of Christianity, hence they used to discredit the rival faith.

Western Christians had little contact with Muslims until the occupation of Spain by the Muslims in the early eighth century. Then they realized that on the southern coast of the Mediterranean, they had a formidable enemy who was culturally and militarily far superior to them. Some Christians became interested in learning more about Islam and the Muslims. Yet, although they had access to the Qur'an and other Muslim books, the image of Islam they presented to Western Europe was a distorted one. This might have resulted from the Christian scholars' feelings of cultural inferiority and their consequent need to display Islam as a religion inferior to Christianity. For this reason, some common misconceptions prevail in the West even today: for instance, that Islam asserts deliberate perversion of the truth; that Islam is a religion of violence; that Islam was spread by the sword; that it is a religion of self-indulgence, especially sexual; that Muhammad is the author of a false religion; that he is identified with the devil. Although many historians today do not accept these distortions, their continuous propagation still influences the Western understanding of this faith. Some events linked with the present revival of Islam may also be playing a role in this misunderstanding. As in other religions, Islam has good followers as well as deviant ones. Hence, an act of violence committed by a Muslim is widely publicized in the Western mass media as an *Islamic* act. For example, the explosion in the World Trade Center was publicized as an act of *Muslim terrorism* or *Muslim fundamentalists*. The bombing of the Oklahoma Federal Center was initially ascribed to *Muslim terrorists*. When the *Christian* criminal was arrested, the media never harped on the concept of *Christian terrorism*. It seems that the violent actions committed by some Muslims conveniently serves the purpose of the mass media in their propaganda against the Islamic faith.

Christianity as Viewed by Muslims

The propagation of the Islamic faith by its prophet in the seventh century CE was carried out in an area of the Arabian peninsula which had already been exposed to Christianity and Judaism. In Makka (Mecca) there were a few Christians while in Madina there were several Jewish tribes. When Muhammad received the revelation for the first time, his wife talked about it to her cousin (Waraqa Bin Noufal) who was well versed in the Christian scripture. Based on this knowledge contained in the scriptures, Waraqa confirmed to Muhammad's wife that her husband would be a prophet and would receive the same revelation as Moses. Because of this, Muslims regarded the Christians as good friends. This belief was further strengthened when the Qur'an was revealed to Muhammad, stating:

> Strongest among men in enmity to the believers, you will find the Jews and the Pagans, and nearest among them in love to the believers you will find those who say: We are Christians, because among these are men devoted to learning, and men who have renounced the world, and they are not arrogant.
>
> Qur'an: 5: 82

When Muhammad emigrated to Madina, he was faced with Jewish opposition to his faith. After Muhammad's death, Islam spread rapidly east and west, a matter which put the Christian scholars in a defensive position, especially since the Muslims propagated the belief that both the Old and the New Testaments were no longer in their original authentic texts and consequently, they would not be given consideration on those subjects in which they disagreed with the Qur'an. This same belief has led some Muslim scholars at the present time to preclude the study of other religions. However, attitudes have changed and are changing in the last decade or so.

Reconciliation of Views

One of the distinctive features of the present era is its religious pluralism. Before this century, contact between Muslims and Christians was very limited in spite of the Western Christian colonization of the Muslim world. With improved communication and international trade, greater contact has occurred. Since the 1950s, this process has further accelerated with the immigration of millions of Muslims to Western Europe and North America. The new demographics forced the representatives of both Islam and Christianity to sit and communicate with each other. When factory workers found themselves working side by side with Muslims on the assembly line and school children found Muslims sitting with them in the same classrooms, of necessity communication between the followers of the two religions on an informal level also occurred. This is what we may call the contemporary meeting between Islam and Christianity. When the relations between members of different religions is a friendly one, it is convenient to speak of "dialogue." The emergence of this situation has urged Christian scholars to study Islam and Muslim scholars to reflect upon the attitudes and beliefs of non-Muslims. This sort of openness between the members of Islam and Christianity has led the two parties to base their relations not upon enmity or defense, but upon seeking the plain truth which is the goal of all religions. The Muslim thinker Al-Ghazali emphasized this when he wrote:

> I have made an assault on every problem, I have plunged into every abyss, I have scrutinized the creed of every sect, I have tried to lay bare the inmost doctrines of every community; all this I have done with the aim of distinguishing between true and false, between sound traditions and heretical innovations.[2]

The current dialogues serve the common purpose of defending Islam and Christianity against the on-going trend of atheism which falsifies and propagates the abolishment of every religion. Nearly a century and a half ago, Thomas Carlyle, speaking about Muhammad in his lecture on "The Hero as Prophet," said that in order to get at Muhammad's secret he intended to say all the good he could about him. Along the same lines, more recently, Thomas Merton has said that the good Christian is not one who can refute other religions, but one who can affirm the truth in them and then go further.[3]

The above cited principle of Merton ought to be adopted not only by Christians but by members of other religions as well. With such an attitude, dialogue can become a process of mutual understanding. Neither party abandons the essential truth of his faith, but each gains a clear idea of what is truly essential. In the final analysis, both parties are caught up in a friendly rivalry to discover and show to the other the fullest and deepest truth.

Jesus in the Qur'an

The holy Qur'an or Muslim Scripture, which is the last Divine Book revealed by God to the last of His messengers, Muhammad (peace be upon him), is the source of the Muslims' knowledge about Jesus (peace be upon him). Some of this knowledge cannot be found in any other source and is not even known to the followers of the Christian faith. The Qur'an informs Muslims of Jesus and teaches them to love and respect him. The Qur'an also lays out a great deal of what Muslims need to know about the life and teachings of Jesus.

The Holy Qur'an does not cover the life of Jesus in detail, but it refers to the miracles and powers which he was given. It also refers to the revelation he received, namely, the INGEEL (Bible). However, the Qur'an is very specific as to his purpose, how he appeared on earth, who he was, and, equally important, who he was not, and how his mission ended. It has been stated again and again that Jesus was one of a long chain of God's messengers sent to the people of this earth; that he was a messenger whose guidance and teachings were a reaffirmation and extension of the guidance which the messengers before him had brought, and were a preparation for the guidance of the messenger who would come after him.[4] In this regard, the Qur'an states:

> And truly We gave to Moses the Book and We caused a train of messengers to follow after him, and We gave to Jesus, son of Mary, clear proofs and We supported him with the pure spirit.
>
> Qur'an: 2: 87

With regard to the chain of messengers of which Jesus is a part, the Qur'an states:

> And We bestowed on him Isaac and Jacob; each of them We guided; and Noah did We guide in an earlier time, and of his seed David and Solomon and Job and Joseph and Moses and Aaron. Thus do We reward the good. And Zachariah and John and Jesus and Elias, each one was of the righteous. And Ismail and Elisha and Jonah and Lot. Each one of them did We prefer above the other creatures.
>
> Qur'an: 6: 84-86

About the unity of the message which was given to all the messengers, the Holy Qur'an states:

> He has ordained for you that religion which He commanded to Noah, and that which We inspire in you (Muhammad), and that which We

commended to Abraham and Moses and Jesus, saying: Establish the religion and do not be divided in it.

Qur'an: 42:13

To emphasize that Jesus was not an isolated event, the Qur'an refers to him as a messenger who, like all the other messengers, was sent for his own time and age, a part of the ordered unfolding of the universe.

And We caused Jesus, Son of Mary, to follow in their Footsteps, confirming what was before him, and We Bestowed on him the Gospel wherein is guidance and a Light, confirming that which was before it the Torah—A guidance and an admonition to those who are careful.

Qur'an: 5:46

Furthermore, Jesus, according to the Qur'an, confirmed that another messenger would be sent after him:

Jesus, Son of Mary, said: O Children of Israel! See! I am the Messenger of God to you, confirming what was Before me in the Torah, and bringing good news of a Messenger who will come after me, whose name is the Praised One (Ahmad).

Qur'an: 61:6

In the light of the above verses, the writer would like to conclude this section with the words of Muzammil Siddiqui:

Jesus is the common link between Islam and Christianity. Muslims believe in Jesus as they believe in Muhammad and the other Prophets of God. Prophet Muhammad is not the only prophet in Islam, he is only one of the many prophets of God. Before him came many prophets who preached the same message of submission to God, that is, Islam. The uniqueness of Muhammad, according to Muslim belief, is that he is the final Prophet and Messenger of God. Islam does not recognize any prophet after Muhammad. Jesus is called Isa in the Qur'an. He is also known as Al-Masih (The Christ) and Ibn Marriam (Son of Mary). He has many other beautiful names and titles in the Qur'an. He is a highly respected religious figure. Outside the Christian Church, there is no religious community that has given Jesus as much honor, respect, esteem and love as Muslims have done.[5]

Muhammad in the Bible

The contrast between Islam and Christianity becomes obvious when we compare the Islamic attitude towards Jesus with the Christian attitude towards Muhammad. Muslims believe in Jesus as a great prophet of God, while Christians disbelieve in Muhammad as a prophet of God. Today, some Christian evangelists try to discredit Muhammad and falsify his call. An impartial study of the lives of both Jesus and Muhammad reveals that both were righteous and completely dedicated to the task of preaching God's religion.[6]

It is very interesting to note that many Muslims believe that Jesus, peace be upon him, prophesied the coming of Muhammad:

> I have yet many things to say unto you, but we cannot say them now. Howbeit, when he, the Spirit of Truth, is come, he will guide you into all truth.
>
> St. John, XVI, 12-13

> If you love me keep my commandments. And I will pray the Father, and He shall give you another comforter, that he may abide with you forever; even the spirit of truth.
>
> St. John, XIV, 15-17

That Jesus had foretold the coming of the prophet Muhammad by name becomes certain when we read the Gospel of Barnabas:

> Jesus went into the wilderness beyond Jordan with his disciples, and when the midday prayer was done, he sat near a palm tree, and under the shadow of the palm tree sat his Disciples. Then sayeth Jesus: So secret is predestination, brethren, that verily I say unto you, to none save one shall it be clearly manifest, he it is whom the nations look for, to whom the secrets of God are so manifest that, when he cometh into the world, blessed shall they be that shall listen to his words, because God shall overshadow them with His Mercy, even as this palm tree doth overshadow us. The Disciples asked: O Master! who shall that man be of whom thou speakest, who shall come into the world? Jesus answered: He is Muhammad, the Messenger of God.[7]

Muhammad the Messenger of God about whom Jesus has given the good news was born in Arabia in the year 571 A.D. when people were in dire need of a reformer to correct the distorted faith and to guide them to the straight way.

The Differences between Islam and Christianity

In the light of the above information, one may assume that there should be no difference in belief between Islam and Christianity.[8] The two faiths, as previously indicated, are monotheistic. But, in fact, there are some essential differences in belief between the two faiths. With the hope that these differences can be reconciled, or at least, understood through the on-going dialogues between Muslims and Christians, the writer would like to briefly cite these differences.

1. Christians relate Jesus to God as His son, and some even say that Jesus is God himself. In contrast, Muslims believe that Jesus is the son of the Virgin Mary. He was created with no father as Adam was created without a father or mother. He is not divine but a normal human being who was honored by being selected as a messenger of God.

2. The Trinity as understood in the Christian belief, "father, son, and holy spirit," are three in one. In the Muslim belief, father is referred to as Allah (God) the One and Only. Son is identified as Jesus, the Son of Mary. The holy spirit is known in Islam as the angel Gabriel who is the messenger of God to His human messengers. This means that the Muslims believe in the three as three separate identities, not as three in one.

3. The original sin as known in Christianity is the sin of Adam which is transferred to his offspring. Jesus died on the cross to redeem this sin and save the Christians. Muslims believe that the first sin committed by man is limited to Adam and cannot be transferred to his descendants; according to the Islamic principle, "no one bears the sins of the other." Consequently, Jesus was not crucified and was saved just as the other messengers of God such as Noah, Abraham and Moses (peace be upon them all) were saved.

4. There is no priesthood in Islam and, unlike Christianity, there is no hierarchical system.

Islam and Humanity

Islam considers all human beings as one family consisting of brothers and sisters, irrespective of race, nationality, sex, or creed. As a result, all peoples are equal before God. The only criterion for judging human beings is piety and good deeds. The Holy Qur'an states:

O Mankind, We have created you from a single (pair) of male and female, and made you into nations and tribes that you may know each

other (not that you may despise each other). Verily, the most honored
of you in the sight of Allah is (he who is) the most righteous of you.

Qur'an: 49: 13

Common Ground Between the Two Faiths

Both Islam and Christianity exhort men to virtuous deeds and a pious
life.[9] They condemn selfishness, falsehood, dishonesty, greed, hypocrisy, injustice, cruelty, malice, vindictiveness, pride, vanity, arrogance,
backbiting and violence. Both enjoin upon their followers faith and trust
in God, repentance, truth, purity, courage, justice, charity, mercy, self-
control and uprightness. To cite one concept common to the two faiths,
let us take the word "peace." In Christianity, peace is valued as a
behavior for the followers of the faith:

> Blessed are the peacemakers: For they shall be called the children of
> God.
>
> Matthew 5:9

Identical with this we find that the Holy Qur'an exhorts the Muslim
people to be peace-loving:

> And the servants of the Beneficent God are they who walk on the earth
> in humility, and when the ignorant address them, they say, "peace."
>
> Qur'an: XXV: 63

The Factors Affecting the Relationship

Considering the similarity between Islam and Christianity, one
would think that the relationship between the followers of the two faiths
would be characterized by respect and mutual understanding. However,
in reality, there are some factors which are divisive and disruptive of
the relationship. These factors include the role played by self-serving
politics and politicians; the mass media which is controlled by certain
groups of people; and some tel-evangelists who openly preach hate and
intolerance.

The Promising Future

The current dialogue between Muslims and Christians promises a
better relationship and mutual cooperation. These dialogues are taking
place on international, national, regional, and local levels. The seeking
of common ground in the two faiths and the analysis of the points of

disagreement can lead to understanding, respect and mutual tolerance. Bishop Griffin expressed the need for dialogue between Muslims and Christians when he wrote:

> Our society is so diverse and changes so quickly that the common and enduring values that religious people of all faiths stand for must compete with contrary practices and attitudes. If in the course of this dialogue, we Christians and Muslims can come to an understanding of our religious and ethical common grounds, we will be better able to stand together, giving a common witness to the larger community in central Ohio.

The Bishop also spoke of his hope that the dialogue would not just help us to understand one another's faiths and cultures, but would also "cement a bond of similarity based on the fact that we are all religious people."[10]

NOTES

1. Quotations from the Qur'an are from Abdullah Yusuf Ali, *The Translation of the Holy Qur'an* (Al-Madinah, Saudi Arabia: King Fahd Holy Qur'an Printing Complex).
2. W. Montgomery Watt, *The Faith and Practice of Al-Ghazali* (London, 1953), p. 20. See also W. Montgomery Watt, *Islam and Christianity Today* (London: Routledge and Kegan Paul, 1983).
3. Thomas Merton, *Conjecture of a Guilty Bystander* (New York, 1968), p. 44.
4. See Muhammed Ata-ur-Rahim, *Jesus: A Prophet of Islam* (London: MWHL London Publishers, 1979); and J.D. Shams, *Where Did Jesus Die?* (London: The Ascot Press, 1978).
5. Marilyn Robinson Waldman, ed., *Muslims and Christians, Muslims and Jews, A Common Past, A Hopeful Future* (The Islamic Foundation of Central Ohio, The Catholic Diocese of Columbus and Congregation Tifereth Israel, 1992), p. 35.
6. Jamal Badawi, *Muhammad in the Bible* (Halifax, N.S.: Islamic Information Foundation); Abdul-Ahad Dawud, *Muhammad in the Bible* (State of Qatar: Sharia Courts and Islamic Affairs).
7. See *The Gospel of Barnabas*, translated by Lonsdale and Ragg (Oxford: Clarendon Press, 1907) and M.A. Yusseff, *The Dead Sea Scrolls* (Indiana: American Trust Publications).
8. See Ulfat Aziz-us-Samad, *A Comparative Study of Christianity and Islam* (Lahore, Pakistan: Muhammad Ashraf).
9. See Joseph Stoutzenberger, *The Christian Call to Justice and Peace* (Winona, MN: St. Mary's Press, 1994).
10. See M.R. Waldman, *Muslims and Christians, op. cit.*, p. 109.

6

MUSLIM-CHRISTIAN RELATIONS IN AFRICA:

CHALLENGES AND PROSPECTS FOR DIALOGUE

Badru D. Kateregga

Introduction

ISLAM AND CHRISTIANITY are two monotheistic traditions which are almost as traditional to Africa as are the traditional religions of the continent. Both Islam and Christianity claim hundreds of millions of followers in Africa. No doubt Islam and Christianity are part and parcel of the African heritage on the strength of history, culture, numbers and influ-ence. Be that as it may, history bears testimony that in many parts of this vast continent, relations between adherents of these two great religions have been far from harmonious. More often than not, they have been characterized by disagreements, acrimony, misunderstanding and outright conflict. For the purposes of this paper, while generally discussing Muslim-Christian relations in Africa, an attempt will be made to highlight the problems and challenges of Muslim-Christian dialogue in Africa from a historical, theological and social perspective.

As the Muslim-Christian encounter in Africa is a historical

phenomenon, a brief survey of the spread of Islam and Christianity in Africa is inevitable. However, for specific analyses, our attention will focus mainly on East Africa.

Islam and Christianity in Pre-Colonial Africa

While Christianity has been well entrenched in North Africa, Egypt, Northern Sudan and Ethiopia since the third century after Christ, it was suddenly confronted by the arrival of Islam, which penetrated the same region four centuries later, almost wiping out the once vibrant African Christianity that had produced great scholars and theologians such as Tertullian, Origen, Clement of Alexandria and Augustine.[1]

The Portuguese Missionaries
and Their Encounter with Islam

In the fifteenth century, Africa experienced the first phase of European Christianity. The Roman Catholic Church dispatched priests from Portugal who attempted to carry on missionary work on the west and eastern coasts of Africa and along the Congo estuary, but their mission achieved no success at the coastal areas except in the Congo estuary. In east Africa, where Islam had arrived around the eighth century A.D., the Portuguese who arrived in 1492 found already a chain of Muslim towns stretching from the Barawa Coast in Somalia down to Mozambique in the south. The relationship the Christian Portuguese were ready to enter into with the local Muslim and African population was that of subjugation. At the time of their invasion, the area had prosperous trading relations with other Muslim states in the Arabian peninsula and the Indian sub-continent. The forceful occupation of Muslim towns and total destruction of many others struck a big blow to east African Muslim civilization. During the period of occupation, the Portuguese made an effort to introduce Christianity, but whatever little success they may have had did not survive their departure following their defeat by the Omani Arabs in the eighteenth century. As the Christian missionaries were meant to support the Portuguese invaders, they did very little to endear themselves to the Muslim coastal dwellers, and hence their lack of impact in the area. By their negative attitude and actions towards Islam and Muslims, they aided in poisoning Christian-Muslim relations in Africa.

For west Africa, the first noticeable expansion of Christianity took place at the end of the seventeenth century, when the liberated Christian slaves returned to settle in parts of western Africa along the coast stretching from Sierra Leone to present-day Nigeria. In their newly found homes/settlements, they led an exemplary Christian life which attracted their neighbors.

Similarly, Islam made a peaceful penetration into the deep interior of west Africa through the agency of Muslim merchants and the traveling scholars/clerics. The camel caravans that crossed the Sahara desert had brought northern Muslims into contact with western Africa as early as the tenth century A.D. Apart from gradually introducing Islam, the Muslim clerics had a civilizing impact on the area. They taught Africans how to read and write in Arabic and how to recite the Qur'an. Through their education, Arabic became the lingua franca of many parts of Black Africa. They established famous religious institutions of high learning which attracted students from across the continent. What is important to note at this stage in pre-colonial west Africa is that believers in both Christianity and Islam, though they did not engage in theological discussions/dialogues about their faith, were at least not fighting each other in the name of God. An exception to this was, however, witnessed deep in the east African interior in the central Ugandan kingdom of Buganda. Islam was introduced into the kingdom of Buganda by the Zanzibar-based Omani Arabs and their Swahili agents in the early 1840s.[2] The liberal king of Buganda (Kabaka), Suna II, listened with keen interest to the teachings of Islam as propagated by his guests. He tolerated Islam and showed interest to learn but did not convert.

Suna II's successor, Mutesa I (1860-1884), permitted more Arabs to visit Buganda and it was during his reign that the real process of Islamization began. The King himself adopted Islam in the period 1865-1875, and since he was an absolute monarch, he forbade his subjects to believe in anything else. He declared Islam the state religion, with strict punishment for violators of any aspects of the Islamic Shariah. Such imposition of religion from the top and the intolerance that accompanied it inevitably led to conflict.

No sooner had Islam enjoyed this privileged position of being the established religion in Buganda than it was faced with the arrival of Christian missionaries—the English Protestants arriving in 1877 and the White Father Roman Catholics in 1879. With their arrival, the competition between the imported religions became dirty. Catholics rivaled for "souls" with Protestants, and, when necessary, the two combined against Muslims. Mutesa, an intelligent King, did on some occasions engage the leaders of the Roman Catholics, the Protestants and the Muslims in a healthy dialogue. At one such meeting he asked them why Islam or Christianity should be the suitable religion for his Kingdom. After the usual heated arguments and exchange of insults, the Christian missionaries challenged the Muslims by bringing the contentious issue closer home. They put it to Kabaka Mutesa to ask his "pagan" butchers to slaughter a cow and give it to the Muslims and see if they could eat it. The Muslims quickly retorted by putting it to Mutesa to ask the Christian missionaries to take in marriage any one of his women subjects. The two questions also turned out to be of fundamental theological and social significance to King Mutesa, who had just murdered two hundred Muslim young men (pages) for, among other things, refusing to eat meat slaughtered by his (Mutesa's) uncircumcised "pagan" butchers. Equally important was the fact that Mutesa had just abandoned Islam to take on Christianity after the arrival of European Christian missionaries whom he had personally invited. Unfortunately, despite his pleas, both the evangelical Catholic and Protestant missionaries refused to baptize him into any of their sects because he had refused to divorce his three hundred wives to remain with only one![3]

After toying with Islam and Christianity for some time, Mutesa declared himself a Muslim again, but this time allowed his subjects to choose whatever religion they wanted. As a result, he lost control of religion in his kingdom. From thence, the competition between the three religious groups became intense and distasteful. Mutesa once complained to a Protestant missionary that foreign teachers (meaning missionaries) were always at each other's throats, calling one another liars. It was therefore difficult, he went on, for the Baganda to decide which book is true, the Bible as taught by the Protestants, the Bible as taught by the Catholics or the Qur'an. Mutesa's disappointment was justified. The attitudes and methods used by the foreign "soul seekers" were themselves a fertile source for dispute and conflict. The foreign teachers, Muslim or Christian alike, were ill equipped to conduct dialogue. They were all theologically bankrupt. They were not well groomed even in the study of their own religious traditions. They confronted each other with open hostility. They were not ready to discuss theological and social issues of common concern in a friendly manner. The doors for dialogue were still locked tight. The events of the next phase (the colonial period) only paint a more gloomy picture.

Muslim-Christian Relations in the Colonial Era—The Problem of Dialogue

Scholars of religious history in Africa all agree that Uganda has been one of the major hot beds for religious conflict. This cannot be doubted if we closely examine the relationship between Islam and Christianity in colonial Uganda.

Uganda became a British colony of the protectorate status in 1890, at a time when the religious conflicts were at their peak and the role of colonial agents in fueling such conflicts cannot be underrated. In these conflicts, the faithful died defending Islam or Christianity or even traditional religion. At one time (1888-1890) after a serious conflict, a whole group of Christian "readers" or converts were expelled from Buganda to Ankole and Tanganyika by the victorious Muslims. At a later time (1890-1893), after being defeated by a combined force of Christian exiles and Buganda traditionalists with the assistance and logistical support of Mr. Stokes (a former missionary turned gun runner) and the famous captain (later Lord) Lugard of the Imperial British East African Company, the entire Muslim community, which included my own grandfather, was expelled from Buganda. They took refuge in the neighboring Kingdom of Bunyoro, which welcomed them. Colonial agents such as Lugard physically participated in driving out Muslims from Buganda, their motherland. The Muslim refugees expelled from Buganda took on proselytization wherever they went, but they suffered because the British Christian colonizers were, as a matter of policy, not prepared to see Islam gain a foothold in Uganda. Thus as a policy, colonialism curbed Muslim influence in Uganda and sustained Christian dominance over Islam—from its inception right through to independence in 1962.

Education in the Colonial Setting

The British colonialists left the important task of educating the masses in the complete control of the evangelical missionaries. The missionaries set up schools where they educated their new converts. Christian education/Bible teaching was central to the curriculum of the day. These schools, which were given grants-in-aid by the colonial governments, also devised a system of education suited to the needs of the time and kept upgrading it to keep abreast of social requirements.[6] As a result, they were in a position to offer the colonial administrators qualified personnel whenever necessary. Consequently, the graduates of these schools came to occupy key positions in the colonial and post colonial governments. To date, this remains a thorny political issue in Muslim-Christian relations in Africa.

Muslims came off worse with this colonial arrangement. They were already a dispirited group, conquered and humiliated by the Christians who enjoyed government support. They had no means to start their own schools, and the Colonial government was not ready to sponsor state schools where Muslims could send their children without fear of conversion to Christianity. The Muslims were only too aware that the Christians were using their schools as ideological tools to combat Islam and oriental influence. The system had been tailored to produce educated Roman Catholics and Protestants.[7] Given that scenario, the Muslims, who had strongly resisted Christianization and undergone persecution, were not ready to send their children to the mission schools. They had, therefore, a double duty of protecting their children from the growing Christian influence, which had the full backing of the colonial administration, and at the same time bringing up their children in an Islamic manner and style. The few parents who stealthily sent their children to the missionary schools got the shock of their lives when some of their children converted to Christianity. The result was that Muslims took a rigid stance towards Western education as offered by the Christian mission schools. They stuck to their Qur'an schools/ Madarrasahs, with all the known limitations. Unfortunately, both the colonial rulers and the missionaries seem to have been happy with the status quo. The consequence was that Muslims were reduced to the status of second-class citizens in Uganda. Intellectual leadership bypassed them, as did political leadership. In such a situation, where members of one religious community believe they are superior, no one would be prepared to enter into dialogue about anything, as dialogue is a two-way street and a game of equal partners. In the colonial setting, one of the greatest social resources for dialogue—education—was unfortunately tangled up in conflict. This was a lost opportunity for both communities. A classroom can serve as a useful tool for dialogue.

Looking at another part of east Africa, colonial Tanzania, the Christian-Muslim situation appears a little different from Uganda mainly because the country witnessed two types of colonial masters—the Germans from 1894-1918, and thereafter the British under a U.N. mandate. The Germans ruled Tanzania (formerly Tanganyika) using Muslim chiefs and headmen, just as Umanis based in Zanzibar had done before. They also used Kiswahaili—written in Arabic script—as the major language of official communication. They used Akidas and Jumbes as cadres in the extension of their administration. Islam and Muslims were at this stage not ostracized by the German rulers. As *pax germanica* prevailed in the country, there was a steady influx of immigrants from the interior to the coastal towns, where subsequently people were exposed to Islam.

As already observed, initially Muslims were favored for colonial posts because they were literate. As more contemporary education became available, the situation changed. This happened during the British Mandate. While the Germans had set up at least five secular schools to train junior manpower for colonial duties, the British, under their mandate, as they did in Uganda, Kenya, Nigeria, Ghana and elsewhere, left education in the entire control of Christian missionaries. Although Muslims approached the administration seeking recognition of their schools, their requests were rejected.[8] Therefore, the entire system of traditional Islamic education was, by the stroke of a pen, forced by the colonialists to remain outside the mainstream of educational developments which were geared to modernization. Hence Tanzanian Muslims, like their counterparts elsewhere in East Africa (Uganda and Kenya) in particular and British colonized Africa in general, remained at a disadvantage as the country moved toward independence. Although at this point the Muslims constituted the majority population, they lacked Western education and a unifying body to coordinate, articulate and promote their interests within the nation. Since the destiny of the colonized peoples was not entirely in their hands, maybe it is not fair to apportion blame to any one religious community for the failure to enter into conversation/dialogue.

Theological and Social Issues at Stake

It can be deduced from this study that the nineteenth century witnessed a fundamental change in the religious geography of the African continent. It was at this time in history that Europe and the United States increased their interest in Africa. This is the period in which European colonialism with all its faces—ugly and beautiful—engulfed Africa. In most cases, Christian missionaries from Europe penetrated the interior of the "Dark Continent" either shortly before or simultaneously with the colonial invaders. Therefore, the image the Africans developed of Christianity is very much colored by colonial rule, with all its implications. The two were seen as hand in glove.

Another strange feature of Christianity as presented to the Africans by the European and American missionaries was that it was sectarian. Different church structures and traditions were imported from abroad and the Africans just absorbed them root and branch without even understanding their meaning or background. These denominations were more concerned with producing "perfect" Anglicans, Roman Catholics, Lutherans, Quakers, etc., than making their flock good followers of Jesus Christ. In their effort to capture more converts, denominations not only engaged in homiletical propaganda but also actively engaged themselves in physical fighting. The Catholic-Protestant war in 1892 in Uganda is a case in point. The result was that Africa was presented with not a single image of Christianity but several. In a situation of this nature, it was impossible to engage in a meaningful Christian-Muslim dialogue when the denominations themselves badly needed a theological dialogue. Ecumenism had no advocates at this point in time.

It should also be acknowledged that the Christian missionaries of this phase, together with their African assistants, though devout, zealous, sincere and dedicated, were not theologians by any definition. Some of them had very little education, and most of the African catechists (evangelists) were either illiterate or only had little formal education. They were all loyal to their mission—practical evangelism, education and medical care. They were not concerned in the least with any academic or theological issues that could arise from the presence of Islam and Christianity in Africa. Dialogue, though necessary, was never an issue to be contemplated or entertained. When Kabaka Mutesa of Buganda involved the leaders of the Christian factions and the Muslims in a theological debate about the Holy Book(s), their message and the truth, all religious leaders put up a poor show because none of them had been theologically prepared for dialogue of this nature. Polemics was the order of the day.

At the social level, what happened when the European colonizers (especially the British) left the control of the entire educational system in the hands of the European Christian missionaries, was, according to Muslim opinion, the greatest injustice meted out to Muslims in Africa, whose ramifications can still be felt to this day.

However, the picture I am describing so far was not so predominant in French African colonies because most of the French possessions were already dominantly Muslim when they conquered them; therefore, there was little they could do to change the religious demography of such countries. Equally true was the fact that although the French did not prohibit the establishment of missionary schools, they seriously advocated LAIC, i.e. non-confessional education. In the LAIC policy, the French colonial government provided state education to all citizens of the colony. This was necessary because their colonial philosophy was based on "assimilation" and their overseas territories were regarded and legally treated as extended/external constituencies with representation at Paris. This could perhaps, among other things, explain why we have had fewer cases of Muslim-Christian conflicts in the former French colonies of Africa than in the British ones, where "divide and rule" was the official colonial policy.

As a result of the British colonial policy, an existing and fairly well-developed system of Muslim education in Uganda, Tanzania, Kenya was suddenly thrown out and replaced by an alien "Western" system. Muslims who had been literate in Arabic and Kiswahili (like King Matesa), which they wrote using Arabic script, were officially declared illiterate! So within the short period of colonial rule, Muslims here fell from being the educated elite to a class of illiterate masses. Akidas and Jumbes, used as agents of German colonization in Tanganyika, were gradually replaced by their Christian-trained counterparts. Kiswahili had to undergo major surgery when the Arabic script was dropped as a form in which it was always written and replaced by the Roman script. Rev. Rowling of Namirembe, Uganda, argued successfully against the teaching of Kiswahili in Uganda, because according to him, it would increase Muslim influence in the country.[9] Perhaps the biggest recorded insult came from Bishop Cessian Spiss who argued thus: "Muslims have no morals and are deceitful. To educate them is useless, they are friends of Government out of greed alone."[10] Maybe similar insults could have come from Muslims as well but modern scholarship has no record of the same. The prejudice, intolerance and negativity towards anything un-Christian only helped to fuel the tension not only between Muslims and Christians but also among some Christian Africans. The growth, for instance, of the independent Churches, to date numbering six thousand and accounting for twenty percent of the Christian followers in Africa, is a case in point. Constantin Mwikamba is of the view that degradation and humiliation of Africans during the colonial times, imposition of Western culture, persecution of church members by the established churches/authorities, and the erosion of African values are some of the main causes for the growth, proliferation and continuation of the independent/separatist churches in Africa.[11] In a social situation where Muslims were unhappy with Christians, where Christian factions were not cooperating with each other, and where the Christian African independents were uncomfortable with their colleagues of the established denominations, dialogue was an absolute necessity. Unfortunately, it never took place.

The Post Independence Era—The Way Forward

In the first decade or so of post-colonial Africa, the Christian-Muslim situation did not change dramatically. The neo-agents of colonialism simply took over where their masters had left off. At least this was what obtained in Uganda. There was, however, one major difference. Freedom of worship was enshrined in the post-independence constitution, but, unfortunately, the religionists did not look at this constitutional development as a strong bridge to enable them to cross over and talk to each other, at least on matters of common destiny. However, a significant change in Uganda's political and religious history took place in 1974, when Uganda, a multi-religious nation with a secular constitution and Christian majority, applied and gained membership in the Jeddah-based Organisation of Islamic Conference (OIC). Although the admission was requested during the reign of the famous Idi Amin, all the subsequent governments, including the current NRM under Yoweri Kaguta Museveni, have duly honored Uganda's membership in the OIC. Through membership in this august Muslim body, Uganda, with its long history of religious conflict, has taken a positive practical step toward peaceful dialogue with the world of Islam, putting behind the history of the nasty encounters of the past.

In this effort, Uganda is not alone, for to date, twenty-three African countries are fully fledged members of the 52-member state OICI, with Mozambique, in December 1994, making the most recent addition. Many of these African OIC member states have a large population of Christians, with six of them led by Christian presidents. Of all the African member states of the OIC, only the Federal Republic of Nigeria has had its membership contested by some of its Christian citizens. According to Kunirum Osie, the Christians saw this act as a subtle way of making Nigeria an Islamic state, contrary to the tenets of the constitution.[12] In bold advice to the Muslims and Christians of Nigeria, which I also subscribe to in the context of Africa as a whole, Osia rightly observes that if Muslims and Christians in Nigeria sincerely search their Qur'anic and Biblical traditions and teachings, study and understand them, appreciate their contents and contexts, they will find that both religions have more points of convergence than divergence. Additionally, by engaging in sincere dialogue, both groups could reduce considerably the nagging religious conflict in their country.[13] This timely prescription holds true with all African countries already discussed where there is religious tension, misunderstanding and hostility. It holds true for Sudan, where decades of ethnic/racial conflicts between the south and north have now been given a religious garb—surprisingly, a re-orientation readily appreciated by both parties to the conflict. It is the best promise for good neighborliness. It is the ideal way for Muslims and Christians to move forward.

Conclusion

The history of Muslim-Christian relations in Africa is long, spanning thirteen centuries. It is also tainted with conflicts that have been propounded in the name of religion. While this study is by no means exhaustive, an attempt has been made to give a clear picture of the long, torturous journey Muslims and Christians in Africa have walked together to reach the current stage. This is the stage of practical dialogue where, for instance, six African Christian presidents are currently happy members of the OIC Summit. This is the stage where Iddul-Fitri/Iddul-Adhuha festivals have been gazetted as national public holidays in many African countries, including those with Christian majorities, such as Kenya. This is the situation where the unthinkable happened, when in Christian-dominated Malawi, a Muslim was popularly elected president recently. At this stage, we notice an interesting development where Christian and Muslim N.G.O.s in Kenya and Uganda can now sit together and discuss issues of mutual interest peacefully and a situation where, in 1989, the Geneva-based World Council of Churches sponsored the Second Christian-Muslim Colloquium in Africa on "Religion and Life" at Arusha, Tanzania. About thirty Muslim and Christian scholars and leaders from English-speaking Africa participated. The Rt. Rev. Michael Keili (Anglican Bishop of BO, Sierra Leone) and myself were honored to be the chairpersons of this historical colloquium. All of these developments in Africa, which were unheard of in colonial times, are clear signs of promise for an emerging Muslim-Christian dialogue in Africa.

The prospects for dialogue become greater as Africa faces new challenges and problems whose dimensions call for united, concerted action. This could be the holocaust in Rwanda, the ethnic wars in Somalia, Burundi and Sudan, famine in Ethiopia, refugees in Zaire, Tanzania or Uganda, extremist fundamentalism, etc. All these challenges demand that the people of faith in Africa rise above their checkered past and learn to understand and know each other, in order to develop areas of mutual cooperation and joint action where there has been none. Lessons of the past should not be used to build walls that separate but should instead help us to construct new bridges of amity, accord, and cooperation as we strive together for the betterment of Africa and humankind as a whole, as well as in service to God whom we all cherish.

NOTES

1. See J.S. Mbiti, *African Religions and Philosophy* (London: H.E.B., 1969), p. 229.
2. B.D. Kateregga, "Religion and Conflict in Uganda," in *Dialogue & Alliance*, Vol. 7, No. 1, Spring-Summer (New York: IRF, 1993), p. 34.
3. See T.W. Gee, "A Century of Muhammadan Influence in Buganda, 1852 - 1951," *Uganda Journal,* Vol. XXII, 1958, pp. 139-150.
4. A. Kasozi, *The Spread of Islam in Uganda* (Nairobi: Oxford University Press, 1986), p. 37.
5. B.D. Kateregga, *The Arab and Egyptian Factor in the History of Islam in Uganda 1850-1900*, M.A. Thesis, University of London, 1975, p. 46.
6. A. Kiyimba, "The Problem of Muslim Education in Uganda, Some Reflections," in *Journal of Muslim Minority Affairs*, Vol. 7, No. 1, Jan. 1986 (London), p. 248.
7. Ahmed Abdallah, "The Ambivalence of African Muslim Education," in *East African Journal*, NB 7, February 1965, p. 8.
8. S.V. 'Sicard, "Islam in Tanzania," *CSIC Papers*, No. 5, Birmingham, Sept. 1991, p. 4.
9. Kiyimba, *op. cit.*, p. 251.
10. C. Spiss, in *Tanganyika Notes and Records*, No. 62/63, 1964.
11. C. Mwikamba, "Ethnic Religion: Conflict and Social Changes in Kenya," in *Dialogue & Alliance*, Vol. 7, No. 1, Spring-Summer (New York: IRF, 1993), p. 54.
12. K. Osia, "Resolving Religious Conflict in Nigeria: A Search for Points of Convergence," in *Dialogue & Alliance*, Vol. 7, No. 1, Spring-Summer (New York: IRF, 1993), p. 42.
13. *Ibid.*, p. 43.

7

CHRISTIAN-MUSLIM DIALOGUE:

PROBLEMS AND CHALLENGES

Ataullah Siddiqui

Introduction

THIS ESSAY intends to highlight, briefly, the circumstances in which Christians entered into dialogue with the Muslims as well as with other religions. Our primary focus will be the World Council of Churches and the Vatican; the Evangelical Churches and others are not our priority here. We will highlight the factors that led to Muslims participation in dialogues organized and sponsored by Christians and, therefore, Muslim initiatives of dialogue will not be discussed here. We will further identify some of the Muslims' apprehensions about dialogue. We will also indicate the current developments within the churches on dialogue and will point out some key challenges for Christian-Muslim relations.

Dialogue—The Context

The dialogue agenda was set by the Christian churches against a background of modernity. Such organized effort began first following the two World Wars and their impact on Europe and consequently on the churches themselves.

Modernity brought "reason" to the center stage of human conduct and became the sole arbitrator of all human actions. It challenged centuries of theological beliefs which were now tested by the criteria of reason alone. This dominant modern thought even began to question "unquestionable" beliefs—such as God, Revelation, Hell, Heaven and Judgement. Gradually, anything beyond the reach of reason was declared irrelevant. A new epistemology widely and confidently took root in the Western world.

Christianity inevitably had to respond to the impact of modernity. The question was how to bring Christianity into conformity with the demands of modernity. Any "supernatural" beliefs, for example, would have to be explained "within reason." Hence, Adolf Harnack (1851-1930) attempted to declare such metaphysical aspects of Christian theology "as an alien intrusion from Greek sources (Hellenization)."[1] The reaction to such a development was equally assertive, and Christian fundamentalists laid emphasis on the Word of God and the Scriptures as the literal expressions of the Word and the Truth.

Against this background, Christian missionaries held their most important conference yet in Edinburgh in 1910. This conference discussed various issues, but it also aired the "missionary message in relation to non-Christian religions."[2] Although this sub-theme was to re-examine missionary methods in various parts of the world, the debate engendered during this conference subsequently opened up several issues about the nature and relevance of the Christian mission to other religions. Dialogue was one attractive option which emerged as a result of such discussions.[3] After several engaging meetings and consultations, dialogue, by 1970, had become a part of the World Council of Churches' programs. The Roman Catholic Church had already accepted dialogue as an option for enhancing new relations with non-Christians by 1964. The Evangelical churches initially resisted dialogue with other religions, but nonetheless later accepted it as a useful mission tool.

The Muslims experienced almost the same impact from modernity as Christianity, but with an added dimension. Most Muslim countries were under the direct, in some cases indirect, control of Western colonial powers.[4] They faced the challenges of epistemology and the reinterpretation of Islamic jurisprudence on the one hand, and the political and economic control of the Western powers, who had drastically changed the social fabric of the Muslim societies, on the other. The missionaries' vigorous missionizing activities, especially that of the Protestants, further compounded the Muslim predicament. For it was not only the land where they had lived for generations which was at stake, but also their souls. This was the very reason why Muslim leadership, mainly the *'Ulama'*, opposed the colonization of Muslim countries, just as they opposed the Christian mission.[5]

Dialogue, nevertheless, became an attractive option for the Muslims. A large number of Muslims who graduated from secular institutions gradually became influential in the creation of nation states. They wanted to mold their countries on the European model, and they became the flag bearers of nationalism and Westernization. But there were inevitably internal struggles between various factions once these countries became independent. Some preferred a Western style secular government and wanted to change, amongst other things, the legal and educational system, while others opted for a socialist style of government with a command economy. Religious groups and especially the *'Ulama'* saw these developments in contrast to religious beliefs. Western style governments would, they believed, bring all the "evils" of Western society and "moral decadence" with them, and socialist style governments would implement an atheistic "Godless society" in Muslim countries. In such circumstances, the call for dialogue with Christians, especially from the West, was a very attractive option. The Muslims saw the churches as an ally in their fight against materialism and socialism on one hand, and injustice of any kind on the other. Furthermore, the newly-created Muslim states were independent as well as being on an equal footing in the international political arena. They were, for example, members of the United Nations just like other nations. Therefore, in a sense, dialogue between Christians and the Muslims was a dialogue of "common cause" between "equal" partners. Against this background, the Muslims were invited to and participated enthusiastically in the "First Muslim-Christian Convocation" in Bhamdoun (Lebanon) in 1954.[6]

Problems in Dialogue

The dialogue which began in Bhamdoun as a "united front" against "atheism" and "social evils" in society gradually shifted its emphasis to social/political issues and theological questions affecting the two communities. However, Muslims never relinquished the hope for a "united front."[7] The dialogues organized by the World Council of Churches and the Vatican's Pontifical Council for Interreligious Dialogue are examples of such Christian efforts.[8]

However, the organized initiatives of the churches faced a number of problems. First, in the absence of a single representative body of Muslims, dialogue organizers approached the "Official *'Ulama'*" to represent the Muslims in various debates. Once such a body became "representative," however, Muslims questioned whom they were representing. The Muslim governments have no mandate from the Muslim community on the one hand, and the *'Ulama'*, who have been appointed by such governments with limited freedom to speak in the mosques, are further limited in any attempt to "represent" the Muslim community outside their own countries. They are cautious in dialogue rather than vocal representatives of the Muslim community. Therefore, they confine their presentation as much as possible to quotations from the Qur'an and the Ahadith. Muslims, especially the *'Ulama'*, have another difficulty, and that is language. Most of the dialogues initiated by Western Christians use English, French or other European languages as their basis, while the *'Ulama'* are well versed in Arabic or "Eastern languages," i.e. Turkish, Persian, Urdu. When such groups meet in dialogue, their language is loaded with the religious and cultural milieu of their own country. Therefore, dialogue at times becomes nearly impossible, an unbalanced exercise.

The second problem was that of trust.[9] The term "dialogue" itself raises a number of questions in the minds of Muslims. The question was, and to some extent still is: is dialogue a genuine effort for "reconciliation" and "bridge-building"—terms commonly used to describe the purpose of dialogue—or is it yet another method employed by missionary "strategists" to serve the purpose of "evangelization"? This question of trust also has another dimension. The term "dialogue" was initially used by the Christian churches in a particular context. Some view dialogue as a part of the secular heritage of the West. They argue that when Muslims deal with Christians in the West, they are in fact dealing with secularism as well. As one Muslim writer puts it:

> Christianity is, and ought to be, an antithesis to Secularism. Yet it became tied to a particular culture, a particular scholarly trend and the historic experience of a particular people. Instead of explaining the Bible and Jesus' ministry within changing circumstances, [its] cultural setting and different languages, [both] scripture and Jesus were made to serve the ends of European Secularism.[10]

As another Muslim writer puts it:

> We are not really facing for the most part the problem of dealing the Christianity, we are facing the problem of dealing with Secularism in a

particular guise—let us say with a good leverage of Christian faith; but nonetheless by our standards. . .essentially a secular outlook. . . .The modern Christian often seems to be more the child of that tradition than the child of Christianity.[11]

The third problem arises from history—from both the colonialist and orientalist traditions. In relation to dialogue, Muslims describe six elements of the "historical equation of colonialism and Christianity." They are "crusade, curiosity, commerce, conversion, conquest and colonization."[12] For example, the British entered into a trade treaty with the Mughal Emperor Jahangir in India, and subsequently obtained a considerable number of concessions under Shah Jahan which opened the floodgates for trade with India. The greatest beneficiary of this was the East India Company. The Company, which not only supplied arms and textiles but also carried missionaries, gradually shifted its emphasis from commerce and curiosity to the conversion and colonization of India. This is an example from one country; many other countries in the Far East and Africa faced similar problems.[13]

The tradition of "Orientalism" is understood as an effort to bring the knowledge of the Orient, by translation and fresh writings, to European languages. But the purpose went beyond this noble intention. Such "knowledge" fell into "the service of the empire" of the Western colonial nations, for commercial, diplomatic and missionary purposes. This process continued for centuries. The image of Islam and especially of the Qur'an and the portrayal of the Prophet in Orientalist writings deeply scarred the Muslims minds.[14]

Both colonialism and the Orientalist tradition gave the impression that the West was determined to "disintegrate" Islam, and that Muslim countries would never be allowed to exist independently of the West.[15]

All three of these broad but major factors played an important role in shaping the perception and misperception of Christian-Muslim relations and consequently had an impact on organized dialogues.

Gradual Shift in Dialogue

Let us look, very briefly, at the gradual shift which took place within the WCC regarding Christian-Muslim dialogues. The WCC began its organized dialogue program by establishing a Unit on Dialogue with People of Living Faiths and Ideologies (1971). The Unit began its activities by inviting Muslim scholars, mainly those who studied or lived in the West, to participate. These international dialogues initially began with explorations which emphasized understanding "the other" and a quest for the relevance of religion to the contemporary world. For example, the theme of the Broumana (Lebanon) dialogue (1972) was "The Quest for Human Understanding and Co-operation."[16] By 1986-87, the WCC had moved from dialogue at the international level to dialogue at a regional level and, therefore, organized colloquia at a regional level.[17] There, the representatives, both Christian and Muslim, were from the respective regions, and the issues were more or less geared to regional problems and priorities. By 1990, the WCC restructured itself and the Dialogue Unit was merged with the Secretariat. Now, it is known as the Office on Inter-Religious Relations. Today, the office focuses on complex issues, but increasingly, this is becoming the agenda for the Christian-Muslim dialogue of the next century.[18]

The Vatican's position since *Nostra Aetate* (1964) has also moved considerably. It is not out of place to identify two important documents. First, the *Nostra Aetate*—which speaks about Muslims (and not Islam)—was in fact prepared under the political climate of the time. Conciliar Fathers were considering Jewish-Christian relations and a statement on those relations, but the bishops from the Arab countries feared that to accept a document which speaks only of Jewish-Christian relations would be seen by Arab Muslims as the Second Vatican Council taking a pro-Jewish stance and, perhaps, by extension, a pro-Israeli view which would eventually damage the Church's image amongst Middle Eastern Muslims.[19] The original text underwent further revision and incorporated a statement on Muslims in the final session of the Council. The second point is equally important. While the Second Vatican Council was still in session, Dr. Hamidullah, after consultation with leading Muslims in France, wrote to the Pope to "officially disavow and declare annulled" the Church's "unjustifiable resolutions of former Councils, synods and other writings of anti-Islamic character."[20] The request seems reasonable and would have been a great step forward in Christian-Muslim relations.

The *Nostra Aetate* was promulgated, and the dialogue initiative was taken as a human concern or an "involvement in the world." But gradually, this concern was eclipsed and now it seems that dialogue is directly back in the fold of mission.[21] The WCC also faced a similar problem and, by 1991, openly acknowledged the difficulty of accepting dialogue as a human concern. Its Seventh Assembly report noted "our continuing problems in understanding religious plurality and God's relationship to people of other religious tradition."[22] The central difficulty remains the difficulty of "mission to" and "dialogue with." This lack of clarity in defining the relation between the two is summed up well by Dr. Samartha in one of his earlier writings:

> Dialogue emerged out of the womb of mission and it has never been easy for mission to cut the umbilical cord and to recognize the independence of the growing child without denying the relationship.[23]

One of the reasons why both the Vatican and the WCC could not take dialogue as a human concern away from the traditional understanding of mission seems to us to reflect the constant pressure mounted by the Evangelical churches at the grass roots level, a pressure which increased just as dialogue became an important program for the WCC and the Vatican. In 1970, the Frankfurt Declaration speaks about dialogue as "a fundamental crisis";[24] the Evangelical churches saw such a development as devaluing terms like "salvation." [25] Four years later, during the Mission Conference in Lausanne (1974), "dialogue" was understood as a tool for evangelism. Some of the papers very clearly stated that the "purpose is evangelism, the procedure is dialogue."[26] This is the tone set by the Evangelical churches ever since. 1990, as pointed out earlier, seems to have seen a turning point. The decade of the 90s was declared as the Decade of Evangelism, and dialogue seems to become, as Professor Talbi puts it, "a kind of scaffolding for mission agencies."[27]

Challenges

In Christian-Muslim relations, there are several challenges at various levels. First, there are theological challenges, where more debate and discussion is required. Then there are social challenges such as interreligious marriages, especially those between Roman Catholics and Muslims.[28] There is a whole range of challenges, but I have chosen three broad challenges, which may overlap. I believe that urgent attention to all these challenges is required if Muslims and Christians are really to play an important role into the next century. They are questions of justice, issues of the Shari'ah and of human rights.

Question of Justice: Justice covers a wide range of areas. It includes justice in our family, in social affairs, in areas of law and economy. While there is a growing realization that justice is widely available, in reality only few can afford it, especially in the judiciary and political domain. But here I would like to point out the area of just perception of the "other." The significant growth in Islamic revivalism, by which I mean Muslims' efforts to restructure their social, economical and political lives within the framework of the Qur'an and Sunnah in a peaceful environment and with constructive dialogue, has been lumped together within the derogatory connotation of "Islamic fundamentalism." Let me make myself clear that I have no sympathy with those who kill, maim or sabotage innocent people, their lives and property, in the name of religion or democracy. The fall of the USSR and its satellite regimes created a vacuum in the West and a new villain was discovered—that of "Islamic fundamentalism." While it is surprising that western powers and western mass media will "discover" such "villains" in the Middle East and in North Africa, what is even more intriguing is that some of the Churches discover it among the Muslims of former Yugoslavia who were far more secular and integrated in western culture than any Muslims anywhere else. Muslims became an issue of "Islamic Fundamentalism" even before the crisis began.

During 23-25 April 1990, a special meeting for European Church leaders was called at Geneva. The agenda was "the present situation in Europe." Prior to the meeting, the organizers sent out a questionnaire. Question No. 3 asked its members: "What are the ecumenical changes and challenges your Church is facing at present?" In response, concerns were mainly raised by the representatives of Yugoslavia, France, England and the USSR. It is worth quoting the answers summarized in paragraph thirty-nine by the organizer. It says:

A special challenge confronting this Christian "fellowship" is Islam in Europe. The important thing here is not to fall short of the human rights proclaimed in Europe, but rather to give consistent support to religious freedom and tolerance. On the other hand, a clear distinction must be made here in respect of fundamentalist currents of all kinds whose aim is the destruction of tolerance and the abolition of human rights.

Then Islam is picked out for special mention as if it fits the bill all of the time. It says:

The Serbian Orthodox Church for Yugoslavia warns European Christians against pan-Islamic fundamentalist currents which it sees at work in the Kosovo area. It asks for the support of European Christians in opposition to these currents which are preparing a "holy war" against Europe.[29]

Islam is presented and implied as a destructive force, one which is against "tolerance" and for the abolition of "human rights." Muslims are preparing for a "holy war" against "Christian fellowship" and "against Europe." Here, in the last decade of the twentieth century, once again we hear the churches of Europe using the language of the Crusades. It is no wonder that one of the Muslim sociologists wrote an article on Bosnia under the title "Bosnia, the Latest Crusade."[30]

This does not mean that all Church leaders and ordinary Church members see Islam in this light. But it does suggest—in the case of Bosnia and its contemporary crisis or similar other situations—that despite our dialogue efforts of a quarter of a century, all such efforts can be swept away by emotions, and we are quite capable of creating an unjust "image" of others. "Fear" becomes our guiding principle, not "justice" as our scriptures command. The Bible says, "Hate what is evil, love what is right, and see that justice prevails" (Amos 5:15), and the Qur'an urges "O ye who believe! Stand out firmly for justice, as witnesses to God, even as against yourselves, or your parents, or your kin, and whether it be (against) rich or poor" (Al-Nisaa 4:135). Achieveing justice is one of the important challenges both Christians and Muslims have to face together.

The Issue of Shari'ah: Although this issue overlaps in some way with the issue of justice, it needs to be stated separately.

The Seventh Assembly of the World Council of Churches takes the question of Shari'ah seriously and states:

> Many Christians, especially in Africa and Asia, feel threatened by Islamization and the introduction of the Shari'ah law. The WCC must take this very seriously in its dialogue with people of other faiths.[31]

Let me begin by saying that it is easy to demonstrate the "implementation of Shari'ah" but difficult to implement its spirit. The WCC's sense of "threat" is the result of that "demonstrative" aspect of "Shari'ah" which some military regimes adopted in the past. I, as a Muslim, am threatened by that too.

The spirit of Shari'ah goes much deeper and wider than just punishment laws. For Muslims, Shari'ah incorporates aspects of daily life, including prayers, *Zakat*, fasting and *Hajj*. Muslims living Islam is what Shari'ah is. Thus, to equate Shari'ah simply with "law" as perceived in a secular society is a mistake.

Today, a large body of Muslim thinkers and jurists are trying to formulate a new model of jurisprudence relevant for our times. If Islam is for "all times and places," then this includes quite literally places where non-Muslims are partners in nation building. Benefits to a nation —financial or otherwise—are shared by all and so are the losses. Therefore, in such circumstances, simply transplanting an historical model of *fiqh* into new circumstances would be unwise. The objectives (*maqasid*) of Shari'ah, as Ibn al-Qayyim states, are

> . . .wisdom and welfare of the people in this world as well as the Hereafter. This welfare lies in complete justice, mercy, well-being and wisdom. Anything that departs from justice to oppression, from mercy to harsh-ness, from welfare to misery and from wisdom to folly, has nothing to do with Shari'ah.[32]

If we keep these objectives in mind and search for a new meaning of pluralism, then obviously non-Muslims and Muslims have to work together. Then, especially, the Christian-Muslim dialogue is not only desirable but imperative.

I believe a dialogue of co-existence between the two communities will help to reduce the existing tension or "threat" and will generate the trust which is so important for living in peace and with dignity.

Use of Human Rights: The assertion of human rights evolved during the last 100-150 years and became a part of the UN Declaration. This gave an individual some basic rights, such as speech, association, etc. It made citizens more involved in decision making; authorities and states became much more accountable to the people. These are worthwhile developments and humanity needs to be vigilant against any erosion of them.

Human rights are not something which are static; rather, they are a growing concept evolving and incorporating new aspects and needs. Religions can also play an important role in expanding human rights. The growing consumerism and the growing concentration of wealth has created an "underclass" both in rich Western cities as well as in poorer countries. They are the victims of economic inequalities. Their right to live and live with dignity is denied. Because the dimension of ethical values is missing from the human rights discourse, a new vision for human dignity is called for. Here is the opportunity and challenge for both Christians and Muslims alike to provide that missing dimension.

There is also another challenge. Today, the "Human Rights talk is power-talk."[33] Human Rights have been used in the service of "New World Order." It is used for the extension of Americanization/Westernization both culturally and politically. Its "will" has been used, unfortunately, through international forums, such as the UN Security Council. Millions of people have starved in order to conform to this "will." Double standards have been used in international politics in the name of human rights and democracy.

The Muslims' and Christians' search for human dignity has already begun. The World Council of Churches moved to recognize human rights at a conference held at St. Polten in 1974 where it incorporated several clauses on human rights into its constitution. One of them is "the right to human dignity." Muslims, at the turn of the Hijrah century, adopted the "Universal Islamic Declaration of Human Rights" in September 1981. In December 1994, in Kuala Lumpur, a Conference of Muslims and non-Muslims was called under the theme "International Conference on Rethinking Human Rights." Participants urged the conference towards a multi-faith dialogue on the question of human dignity. Perhaps this is the area where Muslims and Christians together could move the debate on human rights issues to issues of human dignity and incorporate wider aspects of human concerns.

Conclusion

I began my essay by pointing out the context in which Muslims and Christians felt the need for religious dialogue. The challenges posed by modernity to both Muslims and Christians and subsequent developments show that both communities have not moved as far as they wished during the last twenty-five years. Generally, the problems of perception and misperception have been used for the benefit of various constituencies of both communities. I believe one of the reasons that we cannot achieve what we want is perhaps because we focus our efforts on dialogue very narrowly. Dialogue is understood to be between the two religions, but it would be more beneficial if we emphasized the dialogue between the two civilizations. Perhaps it would not be out of place to say that dialogue between the two epistemologies is also needed. In essence, I believe the scope of our dialogue needs to be widened.

NOTES

1. See also, prior to Adolf Harnack, German theologians such as Heinrich E.G. Pankus (1761-1851) and David F. Strauss (1808-1874) who explained the supernatural events of the Gospel narrative "scientifically" and "objectively" in an attempt to "desupernaturalize" them.

2. See N. Lossky, *et al.* (eds.), *Dictionary of the Ecumenical Movement* (Geneva: WCC, 1991), p. 325.

3. I have left out a large part of the debate, beginning with the Edinburgh Conference in 1910 up to the formation of the "Secretariat for Non-Christian Religions" (known since March 1989 as the Pontifical Council for Interreligious Dialogue [PCID]) by the Vatican and Dialogue with the People of Living Faiths and the Ideologies Unit under the World Council of Churches which merged into the General Secretariat of the WCC in 1990. For development and debates during this period, see H. Kraemer, *The Christian Message in a Non-Christian World* (London: The Edinburgh House Press, 1938), and C.F. Hallencruntz, *Kraemer Towards Tambaran* (Cleering, 1966) and also N. Lossky, *et al.* (eds.), *op. cit.*

4. See Y.H. Haddad, "Muslims and Contemporary Colonialism—Some Facts and Figures," *MCC Newsletter* (August 1974), pp. 7-11.

5. For the impact of modernity and the Christian mission on Muslims, see A.A. Powell, *Muslims and Missionaries in Pre-Mutiny India* (London: Curzon Press, 1993); Khurshid Ahmad, "Dini Adab" (in Urdu), in *Tarikh Adbiyat Musalmanan-e-Pakistan wa Hind* (Lahore: Punjab University, Vol. 10, 1971), pp. 262-376 [English translation is in progress]; Deliar Noer, *The Modernist Muslim Movement in Indonesia 1900-1942* (Kuala Lumpur: Oxford University Press, 1973); Zaki Badawi, *The Reformers of Egypt* (London: Croom Helm, 1978); Zahia R. Dajani, *Egypt and the Crisis of Islam* (New York: Peter Lang, 1990); W.C. Smith, *Modern Islam in India* (Lahore: Sh. Muhammad Ashraf, 1963); E.I.S. Rosenthal, *Islam in the Modern National State* (1965).

6. See "Continuing Committee on Muslim-Christian Co-operation: The Proceedings of the First Muslim-Christian Convocation," Bhamdoun (Lebanon), 22-27 April 1954.

7. For example, Dr. Hassan Abd-Allah Turabi's paper "Inter-Religious Dialogue: Challenges and Horizons" presented at the Inter-Religious Dialogue Conference held in Khartoum, 8-10 October 1994. He called for the "establishment of a world religious front to combat the challenges of secularism."

8. See Stuart E. Brown (ed.), *Meeting in Faith: Twenty Years of Christian-Muslim Conversations Sponsored by the World Council of Churches* (Geneva: WCC Publication, 1989); Michael Fitzgerald, "25 Years of Christian-Muslim Dialogues: A Personal Journey," *Proche-Orient Chretien*, Vol. XL (1990), pp. 258-271 and "Twenty-five Years of Dialogue," *Islamochristiana*, Vol. 5, No. 15 (1989), pp. 109-120. See thematic classification "The Organized Dialogues," pp. 41-78 and "Christian-Muslim Dialogue—A Chronological Listing," pp. 187-196 in my Ph.D. thesis, "Muslims' Concern in Dialogue: A Study of Christian-Muslim Relations since 1970," University of Birmingham (UK), 1994.

9. In a one-day bilateral dialogue between Muslims and Christians on 5 May 1982, in Marawi, a report sums up the Muslim suspicions in four questions asked by the Muslim participants of the Christians:

    1. Why do Christians want dialogue with Muslims?

    2. Why is it that people (whether Christians or Muslims) feel so unsafe in Mindanao? Do Christians feel safe with so many soldiers around?

3. What do Christians expect Muslims to do to reduce anti-Muslim prejudice?

4. What do Christians mean by integration? What are the changes you expect Muslims to make in order to be "integrated"? See the full report in *Dansalan Quarterly*, Vol. III, No. 4 (July 1982), pp. 222-32.

Although this is dominated by the country's political tensions, I believe that the first question is one often asked by the Muslims who participate in local level bilateral dialogue.

10. My interview with Gai Eaton, Editor of *Islamic Quarterly*, London, on 18 April 1991.

11. Ziauddin Sardar, "The Ethical Connection: Christian-Muslim in Postmodern Age," *Islam and Christian-Muslim Relations*, Vol. 2, No.1 (June 1991), pp. 59-60.

12. See M.A. Anees, "Historical Light on the Present Situation of Christian-Muslim Relations," *Newsletter of the Office of Christian-Muslim Relations*, Hartford Seminary, No. 38 (July 1988), pp. 1-7.

13. See the citations in Reference No. 5.

14. See Edward Said, *Orientalism* (London: Routledge and Kegan Paul, 1978). Also A.L. Tibawi, "English-speaking Orientalists: A Critique of Their Approach to Islam and Arab Nationalism," *Muslim World*, Vol. 53, Nos. 3 and 4 (1963), pp. 185-204; also in *The Islamic Quarterly*, Vol. 8, Nos. 3 and 4 (1964), pp. 23-45 and 73-88. Also his "Second Critique of English-speaking Orientalists and Their Approach to Islam and the Arabs," *Islamic Quarterly*, Vol. 23, No. 1 (1979), pp. 3-54. Norman Daniel's book, *Islam and the West: The Making of an Image*, first published in 1966. The revised edition is published by Edinburgh University Press, in 1993 (reprint). His *Islam, Europe and Empire* (Edinburgh, 1966) is equally important.

15. Referring to the Gulf War, Professor Mahmoud Ayoub said: "I believe that the devastations that were done in Iraq would not have been done to another country if the country was a Christian or predominantly a Buddhist or a Hindu or whatever." It happened because there "is that anti-Islamic sentiment and often it translates itself to anti-Arab sentiment." Interview with Ataullah Siddiqui on 20 April 1991 in London.

16. This was the theme of the dialogue in Broumana. See S.J. Samartha and J.B. Taylor (eds.), *Christian-Muslim Dialogue. Papers presented at the Broumana Consultation, July 1972* (Geneva: WCC, 1973).

17. See the Regional Colloquia reports from 1983-1989 in Stuart E. Brown, *op. cit.*, pp. 133-181.

18. Here some of the important issues were raised by the WCC in a booklet, *Issues in Christian-Muslim Relations: Ecumenical Considerations* (Geneva: WCC, 1992).

19. A.J. Hastings, *Concise Guide to the Documents of the Second Vatican Council, Vol. 1* (London: Darton, Longman and Todd, 1968), p. 197.

20. Reply to my questionnaire which I sent to more than 130 Muslims who I believed had participated in Christian-Muslim Dialogues at some level. The reply is dated 5 March 1991.

21. First the document, *The Attitude of the Church towards the Followers of Other Religions*, published in 1984. Then Pope John Paul II's Encyclical, *Redemptoris Missio* (1991) states clearly in Chapter V that "inter-religious dialogue is part of the Church's evangelizing mission." In order to clarify the confusion between "mission" and "dialogue," the Pontifical Council for Inter-Religious Dialogue and the Congregation for the Evangelization of Peoples jointly published another document in 1991, *Dialogue and Proclamation: Reflections and Orientations on Interreligious Dialogue and the Proclamation of the Gospel of Jesus Christ*.

22. M. Kinnamon (ed.), *Signs of the Spirit. Official Report, Seventh Assembly* (Geneva: WCC, 1991), p. 104.

23. S.J. Samartha, "Guidelines for Dialogue," *The Ecumenical Review*, Vol. 31 (1979), p. 130.

24. The text of the Frankfurt Declaration appeared in *Christianity Today*, 19 June 1970, see p. 1, and also in D. McGavran (ed.), *The Conciliar-Evangelical Debate: The Crucial Documents 1964-1976* (California: William Carey Library, 1977), pp. 283-293.

25. R. Winter (ed.), *The Evangelical Response to Bangkok* (South Pasadena: William Carey Library, 1973), p. 31.

26. G.W. Peters, "Contemporary Practices of Evangelism," in J.D. Douglas (ed.), *Let the Earth Hear His Voice*, International Congress on World Evangelization, Vol. 1 (Minneapolis: Worldwide Publications, 1975), p. 186.

27. M. Talbi, "Unavoidable Dialogue in an Unavoidable Pluralist World: A Personal Account," *Encounters: Journal of Intercultural Perspectives*, Vol. 1, No. 1 (March 1995), p. 66.

28. "A new document by Italian bishops advising Catholic women not to marry Muslims reflects the Vatican's fear of the advance of Islam in Europe." The report suggests that the British, Swiss, Belgian and French bishops had produced similar papers in the past. *Catholic Herald*, 5 March 1993.

29. See the document, "Special Meeting for European Church Leaders on the present situation in Europe," meeting held in Geneva, 23-25 April 1990.

30. Akbar Ahmed, "Bosnia, The Latest Crusade," in *The Arab Review*, Vol. 1, No. 4 (Spring 1993), pp. 7-11.

31. M. Kinnamon (ed.), *Signs of the Spirit, op. cit.*, pp. 92-93.

32. Ibn Qayyim al-Jawziyyah (691-750 CE), *A'lam al-Muwaqqi'in*, Vol. 3, p. 14 (1955) quoted in M.U. Chapra, *Islam and the Economic Challenge* (Leicester: The Islamic Foundation and The International Institute of Islamic Thought, 1992), p. 1.

33. S. Parvez Manzoor, "Human Rights: Secular Transcendence or Cultural Imperialism?" (Review Article), *Muslim World Book Review*, Vol. 15, No. 1, p. 9. See the special issue of *Islamochristiana* on Human Rights, Vol. 9 (1983). Jacques Waardenburg, "Human Rights, Human Dignity and Islam," in *Temenos Studies in Comparative Religion*, No. 27 (1991), pp. 151-182. Chandra Muzaaffar, "From Human Rights to Human Dignity," paper presented in International Conference on Rethinking Human Rights, Kuala Lumpur, December 1994. See the 5th Muslim-Christian Consultation on "Peace and Justice," 12-15 December 1988, published by Geneva: Center Orthodoxe Du Patriarcat Occumenique Chambesy, especially Vol. 2, Chapter 2.

8

THE LANGUAGE OF DIALOGUE:

CHALLENGE AND PROMISE IN MUSLIM-CHRISTIAN DIALOGUE

Saba Risaluddin

Introduction

ISLAM AND CHRISTIANITY, like Judaism before them, are founded on the word—the revealed Word of God, preserved for us in our scriptures. We have internalized a sense of the power of words, yet too often we use words as means, and to ends, that are far removed from the ethos of justice and compassion articulated in our holy texts. We may even appeal to our texts to justify the indefensible, while those whose discourse makes no reference to scriptures—be they secularists, or people for whom religion is so personal a matter as to have no relevance to the world of politics—may unthinkingly or cynically use words in a way that obscures our understanding. In a post-modern society, which has lost its innocence about words, we no longer understand them—if indeed we ever did—as fixed, immutable and neutral in their impact. Vocabulary affects, often at a subliminal level and very profoundly, our understanding: political correctness (PC), though it may have gone too far and laid itself open to ridicule, is grounded in this belief and in the assertion that changing the words we use can change our understanding and our behavior. At the other pole from the well-meaning proponents of "PC" lie demagogues who use language as a means of control for their own ends. Developing sensitivity and scrupulousness towards the words we use is a crucial element in the process of any dialogue from which we hope to gain insights rather than merely assert our own creedal positions.

The Challenge of Our Historical, Social and Theological Heritage

The history of encounters between Muslims and Christians has been marked by many conflicts, sometimes of arms, frequently of words. Polemic and rhetoric have united to distort our understanding of our own and of the other's heritage. Let me give, at this stage, just one example of words that have become so charged as to be almost unusable by scrupulous commentators without exegesis. The words in question are, in a sense, a matched pair: "crusade" and "jihad." The word crusade reveals, in its dual origin from the French *croisée* and the Spanish *crusado*, that it is intimately linked to Christian symbolism and belief, exemplified in the Cross. The Crusades, in the most neutral, dictionary definition, were military expeditions to recover the Holy Land from the Muslims—a holy war, if you will. The Spanish etymology of the word is symbolic; Christendom felt itself to be profoundly wounded by the triumphant expansion of Islam into Europe, and most successfully in Spain; the Crusades, even more perhaps than the *reconquista* of Spain itself, were an expression of a Christendom seeking to regain its self-respect. Another, more tendentious way of describing them is as ventures devised, or at least exploited, to address the problem of younger sons in a Europe under the pressure of social and economic change as greater prosperity and security provided fewer outlets for martial energies—ventures which had little to do with religion, though religious zeal, at this time of an undoubted general upsurge in religious fervor, was whipped up to encourage support. Their ostensible purpose was betrayed by the slaughter of Jews on European soil by the first Crusaders, the rabble followers of Peter the Hermit, even before they reached the Holy Land, and then by the mass killing of Arabs, both Muslim and the Crusaders' co-religionists, in Jerusalem; the blood is said to have flowed so deep as to reach the horses' knees.

If I dwell on the ignoble aspects of motivation and the bloodier elements of the Crusades, it is not to arouse the ire of the Christians among us, but to underscore the irony of present-day usage of the word crusade as wholly positive, a striving for desirable ends: a crusading journalist is one who exposes public evil or wrong-doing, for example.

Jihad is also commonly translated as holy war, with connotations for the Western mind of fanaticism and aggression, of crazed fighters with the Qur'an in one hand and the sword, or latterly the Kalashnikov, in the other. This undoubtedly has deep roots in this same Christian fear of Muslim might in the early days of Islamic expansionism, as well as more recent resonance in the rhetoric of Saddam Hussein and others who misuse the word in an effort to justify their actions. For, as all Muslims know, the word derives from the Arabic root meaning "to strive." It may include taking up arms in self-defense; the Qur'an explicitly permits this,[1] and equally clearly bans aggression, warning that even self-defense may, if carried too far, become an evil; fighting must stop as soon as the threat is repelled. But as a tradition of the Prophet makes clear, armed struggle is the lesser jihad; the greater jihad, which is continuous, is the internal struggle of all of us to discover and submit to the will of God.[2] Understood in this sense, Yassir Arafat's call for a jihad for Jerusalem, which struck such fear and loathing in many Jewish and even some Christian hearts, takes on a very different color, though it is hard to deny that it was politically inept to use a word which has become so loaded that its pristine meaning is unavailable to the majority of his non-Muslim hearers, who have been indoctrinated in the belief that Palestinianism equals terrorism and who are probably unaware that the Palestinian National Charter calls for equal citizenship for Muslim, Christian and Jew in Palestine.

As these examples suggest, our assumptions about each other are colored, and indeed often distorted, by our historical, theological and social heritage; almost fourteen hundred years of shared history, at times painful, at times fruitful, have left deep and often unexpressed, or even unrecognized, traces in our individual and collective psyches. The ways in which we perceive past events, past encounters, often differ radically. It is not my purpose to examine our entire shared history, but to consider briefly our differing perceptions of certain phases of encounter.

The debt which the West owes to Muslims is still hardly acknowledged, hardly recognized outside the realms of academia. There is a vague awareness that Greek philosophy was preserved and transmitted by Muslim philosophers such as Ibn Sina (Avicenna) and Ibn Rushd (Averroes), but this awareness seldom goes as far as a consciousness that the Renaissance, the very foundation of modern European thought, culture and political structures, could not have happened if Muslims had not preserved, developed and transmitted much more than just Greek philosophy. Still less, perhaps, are Muslims aware that as early Islamic thinkers began to reflect on their holy texts, they drew upon many strands of thought, including that of Christian theologians, while both Muslims and Christians turned to the Neo Platonists for philosophical insights. We have a shared hellenistic heritage as well as common Abrahamic roots. There were, from the first, creative interchanges between as well as polemical tracts by the two communities. Yet it is the polemic that lingers in the psyche, while the creativity is claimed by each civilization as its original contribution to succeeding generations.

Europe's debt to Islam is traceable above all to the period of Muslim rule in Spain, or as the Muslims call it, al Andalus. During the period of *la convivencia*, the living together in harmony, that lasted broadly from soon after the conquest in the eighth century to around 1250, al Andalus was a center of learning for the Christians of the rest of Europe as well as for the Muslims, Christians and Jews who lived there. Almost any northern European scholar worthy of the name would, sooner or later, find his way to al Andalus to study with the theologians and philosophers of that extraordinarily rich culture. This was a very different encounter from that of the Crusades: for the Christians here found themselves relating to Muslims, not as the infidel to be banished from the holy sites by the sword, but as sophisticated and subtle thinkers to be admired and emulated, even if only in the sense of learning from them how to sustain and develop a different theology. But at the same time, the Christians of the region nurtured the understandable resentment of the conquered, and sought to regain what they saw as their lands from the Muslims, resulting in a long-drawn-out struggle known as *la reconquista*, marked by successes and defeats, by shifting alliances which sometimes brought together Christian and Muslim, and finally by the fall of the last Muslim stronghold, Granada, in 1492.

Both before 1492 and after, Muslims and Jews suffered grievously at the hands of the Inquisition, an institution which has seared the collective memory. More than the memory, two monuments express for me, a Muslim, the contrast between the Muslim and the Christian civilizations in Spain: the Great Mosque of Cordoba and the Alhambra. The first, a vast, tranquil space marked by the rhythm of countless columns, is violated by the triumphalist insertion of a cathedral into its very heart. It is said that the Christian rulers of Cordoba (which fell as early as 1236) sought the permission of the Emperor Charles V, who had yet to visit Spain, to build the cathedral, which he granted. When he finally visited Cordoba, he exclaimed, "You have built that which could have been built anywhere, and in so doing have destroyed that which was unique in the world." The Alhambra, high on its hills above Granada, is the work of the Nasrids, last of the Muslim rulers of Al Andalus. It is a more complex, more delicate, more ornate creation than the awe-inspiring simplicity of Cordoba's mosque; the craftsmanship of the carvings and calligraphy, the play of light and shadow through intricate screens, the magic of the secluded courtyards with their sparkling fountains, are no less moving. And next to this place of ethereal beauty is the massive, crude palace of Charles V, a monument to imperial might if not to aesthetic values.

If the memory of al Andalus evokes for Muslims a nostalgia for lost greatness—cultural and intellectual more perhaps than political— colonialism remains a far more immediate and painful experience, contrasting with the days of political power in successive Muslim dynasties and empires. The great empires of the West themselves may have fallen, but the borders of many of today's nation-states were imposed by the colonial powers, imperialism is thriving in US foreign policy, and the colonization of the mind by the dominant Western cultural paradigm continues apace. Muslims have yet to come to terms with the legacy of colonialism, and we are all too apt to lay all our ills at its door rather than to acknowledge that it is part of our history and that we had better start to develop some creative strategies for asserting our role in the world of today rather than merely bemoaning our post-colonial condition. In the following section, where I consider current issues, I shall touch on some of the ways in which our inherited world order militates against social justice, an area where Muslims and Christians could find common cause on behalf of the dispossessed, disempowered and oppressed peoples of the world. Here, too, I shall discuss some of the ways in which language impedes understanding.

Current Issues

First of the issues which were proposed for discussion under the heading "current issues" in the paper originally sent to us was "fundamentalism." It seems very appropriate to tackle this at the outset, for more even than "crusade" or "jihad," this is a word which lies like an obscuring cloud over our understanding of each other. Originally coined to describe a Protestant Christian movement in North America that asserted the inerrancy of the scriptures, it has become irrevocably associated with Islam, and lurking behind it the suggestion of terrorism or fanaticism. It is worth mentioning in passing that the French word *intégrisme*, which has come to have many of the same connotations though often used with greater care, is also loaded, deriving as it does from a Catholic doctrinal tendency to deny the possibility of interpreting the apostolate in the context of modern society.

In the discourse of Western politicians and commentators, "fundamentalism" is used to describe such disparate manifestations as the vocal opposition of the professional middle class to rulers seen as corrupt or as puppets of the West, the anger of the disenfranchised in Algeria or of those opposed to the Middle East peace process, and even the power-holders themselves in, among other countries, Saudi Arabia and Iran—than which it would be hard to discover two more divergent interpretations of Islam. Used in a scrupulous sense to describe those who believe Muslims should draw inspiration solely from the Qur'an and Sunna, "fundamentalism" legitimately describes state doctrine in Saudi Arabia, while Iran exemplifies the corresponding phenomenon expressed through Shi'ite theology: thus the one word, even carefully used, conceals polar opposites in philosophical and ideological terms. Used in the careless sense, it also—and far more insidiously—obscures not merely the distinction between powerholders and those who challenge them, but also differences in mindset between true "fundamentalists" as just defined, and those who can be called, in a manner more likely to illuminate our understanding, Islamists.

Islamism is a term that is increasingly used to describe other so-called fundamentalists. It is defined (by Yahya M. Sadowski, senior fellow in the Brookings Foreign Policy Studies program[3]) as a post-modern doctrine, "an attempt to reconstruct a new communitarian ideology by men (and an occasional woman) who have been exposed to, and grown disenchanted with, modernity." Sadowski considers as Islamists the Muslim Brotherhood in Egypt, the Sudanese regime, groups challenging the military-backed rulers in Algeria and groups such as Hamas that are challenging the leadership in the Palestinian entity. A third type of Muslim mindset sometimes characterized as fundamentalist would more properly be called traditionalist; here, religion and its accretions of tradition tend to be conflated. To quote Sadowski again, "'traditionalism,' in which rural elites swath their interests in the banner of the Prophet, is a third distinctive variety of political Islam."

The word "fundamentalism" to describe a narrow or extremist mindset is sometimes associated with other religions than Islam, of course; the destruction of the Ayodhya mosque and some at least of India's communal violence is attributed to "Hindu fundamentalism," for example. It could also apply just as appropriately to the secularists or liberals who so freely attribute it to Muslims; for example, to those who supported Salman Rushdie's right to say and write whatever he would, however insulting and painful, about Islam, while denying Muslims the right of reply. Freedom of speech, it seemed, was an absolute right for liberals only.[4] The undoubted inappropriateness of much Muslim response to Rushdie's book *The Satanic Verses* is irrelevant to the argument about freedom of speech, however much it may have exacerbated the tensions between supporters and opponents of the writer. That Muslim voices were unwelcome except as a contribution to the image of Muslims as "fundamentalists" is amply demonstrated by the fact that, after Khomeini issued his *fatwa* against Rushdie in February 1989, the counter-*fatwas* of, among others, Dr. Zaki Badawi in London and Ayatollah Mehdi Rouhani in Paris went unreported, and remain little known even among Muslims themselves. Christian voices raised in our support, however, were given some small prominence, and did not go unnoticed or unappreciated by us.

It should be clear, then, that the assertion of Willi Claes, Secretary-General of NATO, in February 1995,[5] that "Islamic fundamentalism" is as great a threat to the West as communism ever was, demonstrates how urgent is the need to understand what we mean by the word, for to discuss as an "issue" or a single "-ism" a word which is called upon to bear so many different and mutually irreconcilable meanings, to say nothing of the weight of irrelevant associations which accompany it, is to invite misunderstanding and incomprehension. Just as communism, during the Cold War years when it was called on to fulfil the function of the "enemy," the significant other, was understood as monolithic, so the successor to communism in the demonology of foreign policy, "Islamic fundamentalism," is similarly misrepresented as a monolith, as the world's one remaining superpower, the United States, repeats the fateful error of preparing for a global confrontation between two largely fictitious blocs, "the West" and "Islam." The risks of this becoming a self-fulfilling prophecy are too great for us to allow such discourse to go unchallenged.

The position and role of women in our faiths is another area rich with misunderstandings and mutually incompatible perceptions. From being perceived, in medieval times, as a religion of self-indulgence and sexual licence, Islam has come to be seen in the West as repressive towards women (an attitude which is woven into perceptions of "fundamentalism"). Lately, the issue has become focused on the *hijab*, around which an entire mythology has developed. It is described variously as a symbol of male oppression, or as a religious obligation, or as a means of liberating Muslim women from the unwelcome attentions of men, or as a political statement of identity in a society perceived as hostile or indifferent, or as a cultural expression, or even as profoundly sexy, exemplifying for some men the desirability of the unattainable.[6] Some Muslim women—whether they wear the *hijab* or not—assert that the real issue is not what women should or should not wear on their heads but the behavior of men, and believe that Western feminism has served women ill by seeming to demand for them no more than sexual freedom and the right to paid work outside the home, or even the right to behave as badly as men, instead of seeking to redefine society so that women no longer need resort to a particular style of dress to repel unwanted advances (or, indeed, the antithesis of this, feeling they will attract male attention only with plunging necklines or thigh-high skirts). What is undeniable is that feminism, be it "Western" or other, has so impressed itself upon political, social and intellectual discourse that it has become impossible to ignore its claims to our attention. The debate has stimulated much interesting work by Muslim women theologians and thinkers, who are engaging with text and tradition—with words and their interpretation—in new and challenging ways; it is an exciting time to be a Muslim woman, despite all the tensions and difficulties of a world in which Muslims are often seen as unwelcome or problematic. And Christian feminist theology can surely inspire and encourage Muslim women struggling to come to terms with their male-interpreted heritage.

To the extent that the debate within Christianity addresses the question of women as priests, it might seem inaccessible or irrelevant to Muslims—for we have, of course, no priesthood, and, except in Shi'ism, no religious hierarchy similar to that of Christianity. But those of us who believe Muslim women should be allowed to lead the prayers of a mixed congregation can identify, perhaps, with Christian women who yearn to be priests. I recall here a debate in the university town of Oxford, in which I and a Roman Catholic nun participated with an

Anglican priest and a rabbi. The question of women's ordination arose (this was in Britain, before the Synod voted to permit women to be ordained) and the Anglican priest, who was of course a man, expressed sympathy with women who believe they have a vocation to the priesthood. The nun snorted in derision at the very idea of Anglicans being priests at all, whatever their gender—in her view, only Roman Catholics could truly be priests, and only male Roman Catholics at that.

The priesthood is, of course, not the only issue exercising Christian women. Of far more immediate concern to many, especially Catholics, is family planning. At the UN Conference on Population Control and Development in Cairo last year, controversy over the terms of the draft Declaration was fueled, even before the conference began, by Muslim countries and the Vatican. Appeals to religious values and political responses became entangled with each other, helped along by an uncomprehending Western media which, from its largely secular perspective, saw the bogey of "religious fundamentalism" lurking behind every phrase, but failed to see the "secular fundamentalism" of extremist groups seeking to manipulate the Declaration to endorse sexual promiscuity. In the event, the informal alliance of Muslims and Catholics, hindered by attempts to misfocus the debate on abortion rather than on the real issues, but helped by constructive lobbying from Muslim countries such as Pakistan and Iran, led to changes in the wording of the closing statement so that a consensus could be reached. There is, of course, a fundamental difference between the Muslim and the Catholic —or at least the Vatican—position on birth control; the Vatican opposes it utterly, whereas in the main the Muslim concerns were not about the moral rights and wrongs of birth control itself, but about the means, and perhaps the motives, of population control.

The media coverage of Vatican-Muslim resistance to an agenda which was perceived as promoting sexual liberties succeeded in masking the diversity of experience among Catholic and Muslim countries alike, where there are both models of good practice in population control and examples of societies in which rights—above all, women's rights—are abused either through repressive or coercive population control programs or because of pressure to bear large numbers of children. In societies where most women are illiterate and where tribal or patriarchal traditions dominate, the debate has been seen primarily in terms of the ethics of sexuality, and above all of the control of women's sexuality as the locus of male honor, often framed in highly selective religious language that ignores the egalitarian ethos and the values of compassion and responsibility towards the more vulnerable members of society that underpin the world's great faiths.

Human rights in the broader sense is another issue that could unite us, not merely as Muslims and Christians, but as people of faith, all faiths, with humanists and people of good will the world over. Alas, it is not always so; squabbles over definitions all too often take precedence over expressing shared outrage at violence and oppression. In a secular world, "rights" is generally assumed to mean human rights or civil rights, with positive connotations. But, as the UN conference on human rights in Vienna in 1993 revealed, there are many interpretations of the word. Even after the agreement that human rights are universal, there remains debate about the balance between individual, collective and group rights, and between individual freedoms and the restrictions that are deemed necessary to maintain a society in which it is possible to be fully human. For many people of faith, the anthro-pocentric nature of the secular concept of rights is rebarbative; respon-sibilities come first, and rights flow from the responsibilities of each human being towards every other, as well as towards the rest of creation, responsibilities that form part of our necessary submission to a greater force —call it God, or Nature, or what you will.

Demagogues—I use the word here in its modern, pejorative sense— do not disdain to use the language of rights to assert their exclusivist claims. It is my belief that far more dangerous than fundamentalism, even if we could agree on what that word means, is the resurgence of extremist nationalism, of fascism. We need to be on our guard against a politics of identity which fragments society, often violently, into narrower and ever narrower groups of "us" defined against a hostile "them." Only a framework within which expression and dissent are freely articulated will allow for a sense of identity with space for wider loyalties. Diversity and difference lie within each of us as well as in the societies we inhabit. And an acknowledgment, even a celebration of diversity, is integral to our faiths, either explicitly, as in the following Qur'anic verse, or implicitly in the assertion that the message of our scriptures is for all humankind:

O humankind, behold, We have created you all out of a male and a female, and have made you into nations and tribes, so that you might come to know one another. Verily, the noblest of you in the sight of God is the one who is most deeply conscious of Him. Behold, God is all knowing, all aware.

Qur'an Surah 49, al Hujurat, v 13

It is imperative that this kind of speculation about words, which may seem very remote from the lives of people who are struggling against poverty, hunger, disease, or who are the victims of violent conflict, become grounded in reality. Poverty, hunger, disease and warfare are not horrors that descend upon people out of a void—they are the result of the policies of self-interest elaborated by the richer nations, or more precisely by the rich people of the rich nations and their allies among the elites of the poor nations, who are adept at using words to justify their actions or mask their motives, and have, in the mass media and in instantaneous global electronic communications systems, greater power to do so than ever before. Almost the only weapon we have in the face of this power is the hermeneutics of suspicion.

Few of us are now taken in, if we ever were, by the notion of a New World Order that might actually look different from the old, unless we take more of the same—more poverty, more hunger, more conflict, afflicting more people in more regions of the world—to be something new. The world is now a much more dangerous place than when communism was some kind of counterbalance to the West. The Soviet Union and the United States, before the collapse of communism, were each prepared to cry foul when the other transgressed too blatantly the norms of decency. Now even that frail underpinning of morality has been abandoned. In every other respect, the old certainties are still in place, the same five powers hold permanent seats on the UN Security Council and the accompanying power of veto, enabling them to ignore the fine words of the UN Charter and sundry Declarations when they wish, and to invoke these same words when it suits them. These same five control 90% of the world's arms trade—half of it is in the hands of the United States and Britain, which have all but destroyed their non-armaments manufacturing capacity in the name of the free market, but support with massive government intervention their armaments industries, and must, therefore, create markets by creating conflicts, the threat of conflicts or the fear of an enemy—for which purpose Islam (or "Islamic fundamentalism") is a ready substitute for communism.

I would like to dwell briefly on the way language has been used in discussion of the conflict in Bosnia, and its effect in muting or silencing even the voices of those from whom one would hope for clarity and courage, including all too many religious leaders; for Bosnia is a tragic paradigm for the end of the twentieth century, and its tragedy lies in part in the realization that we have learned nothing from the terrible wounds inflicted on Europe fifty years ago, but are, rather, repeating many of the same mistakes and allowing many of the same evils to go unchecked and unchallenged. The genocide in Bosnia has been characterized, at least in the West, by public apathy only rarely illumined by moral outrage and political or humanitarian action. It is my view that this apathy is due very largely to the language used by politicians and commentators to describe the conflict—language designed to obfuscate and confuse, leaving the public with the impression that the Balkans is a region of vicious inter-ethnic or tribal rivalry regularly, throughout history, spilling over into armed conflict, against which we can do nothing except, perhaps, provide a little food, a few blankets for the elderly, or a hospital bed for the occasional child we airlift out of the war zone, amid great fanfare.

Vile atrocities are being committed against women, children, the elderly, against families, against the whole fabric of society in Bosnia, and yet there is hardly a hint of this in the urbane discourse of "neutrality" of the United Nations, and the resultant paralysis of political will among those capable of influencing events towards a peaceful resolution in the Balkans. It is all of a piece with the disturbing silence of the churches; with all too few honorable exceptions, church leaders have not condemned the fascist policies that have led to so much suffering, which has been experienced above all by the Muslims of Bosnia. Indeed, I have often found myself, a Muslim, wondering if I am encountering yet another manifestation of the darker side of the collective Euro-Christian psyche, with its long history of polemic against Islam and its complicity with the excesses of imperialism and the conquest of "lesser breeds." The Orthodox church, in particular, is deeply implicated in fomenting the attitude of mind—Serbs as hapless victims, never as perpetrators of atrocities—that has fed the conflict.

The following passages are from an open letter sent by Patriarch Pavle of Serbia in June 1993 to fellow Christians of all denominations.

The present day war in Bosnia. . . develops *horribile dictu* into a war of religions, because our Muslims here do not distinguish their religion from their nationality. The Croats fight to extend by force Roman Catholicism. The Serbians in Bosnia resist the united Muslim and Catholic armies in order to protect themselves and their Orthodox Church and nation from subjugation. . . .In the media war the Croats have the support of the powerful Vatican network and our Muslims have the aid of the international Muslim League—we Serbians, however, have no longer the Orthodox Tzar of Russia to protect us. Therefore we expect from you, good Christians, to defend us against the sordid calumnies such as detention camps and raping of Muslim women. As educated churchmen, you are qualified to know the history of Christian Serbia suffering from Turkish yoke and from concentration camp (Jasenovac) instigated by the Roman Catholics in Croatia.

At a United Nations Association prayer meeting for former Yugoslavia at St. Martin in the Fields in London's Trafalgar Square, at which I was privileged to be a speaker, the Serbian Orthodox priest who took part quite shamelessly used the occasion to promote the same propaganda line. Its paranoid tones, and specifically its Islamophobia, are all too clear. Contrast that with the reality—Russian troops joining the UN blue helmets in Bosnia despite their overt camaraderie with Karadzic's men, while Turkish troops (at the time of writing) are still not permitted to form part of UNPROFOR because they are seen as sympathetic to the Muslims.[7]

Other Christian denominations have not been so overtly hostile to the victims, but all too often the response seems to have been framed by the Christian principle of "turning the other cheek." This may be an admirably stoic and forbearing response by a victim, but as a response to the suffering of others it is grotesquely lacking in another Christian virtue, that of compassion. Much Christian discourse seems to be dominated by the rhetoric of the peace movement with its roots in the (very different) relationships of the cold war and the calls for nuclear disarmament, rather than turning to an older Christian tradition of looking to the interests of others, not your own.

The clever and cynical use of words has tricked the public into believing that the conflict is insoluble, and that international bodies and individual governments are thereby somehow absolved from taking decisive action. True, most of us now recognize that "ethnic cleansing" really means genocide. But we swallow uncritically phrases such as "ancient ethnic hatreds" when the reality is that the hatreds are the result, not the cause, of the atrocities being perpetrated; or the phrase "warring factions," as though aggressors from both outside and within an internationally recognized UN member state were somehow equivalent to the legitimate, democratically-elected government of that state, and as though aggression were much the same as the desperate attempts by a largely unarmed defense force to save its civilian population from destruction. This dubious equivalence goes as far as giving the self-appointed leaders of the aggressor factions an honored place at the negotiating table beside the legitimate representatives of the Bosnian government. Indeed, it goes much further, favoring the aggressors by maintaining an arms embargo which affects only the defenders, and making numerous concessions to those who have gained territory by force and terror while pressuring the victims to admit that they have lost the war.

"Civil war" is another misnomer. Yes, the conflict has taken on many aspects of civil war, but it was started by external aggression, and those who would destroy the hapless state of Bosnia-Herzegovina are still supported by both men and supplies from Serbia and Croatia. Worse, extensive evidence of such external support, and even of actual cross-border attacks, is repeatedly withheld or its truth denied by the UN and others.

Small wonder that many Muslims the world over are coming to believe that behind this real-politik which favors the aggressors and turns a blind eye to atrocities and genocide is Western fear and hatred of Islam. This belief is fostered and encouraged by another duplicitous use of words, the continual characterization of the Bosnian government as "the Bosnian Muslims," or at best as "the Muslim-led Bosnian government." It is true that the major victims of the conflict are the Bosnian Muslims; but the Bosnian government as established by Aliya Izetbegovic's SDA, whatever its failings, was explicitly multi-national and multi-cultural, composed of all three major national groups that form the population of Bosnia, as is the highly disciplined and motivated but still desperately ill-equipped Bosnian defense force; and Prime Minister Haris Silajdzic has led a successful campaign to keep the SDA committed to a multi-ethnic vision. Furthermore, about thirty percent of marriages in Bosnia are "mixed," which means that probably at least half the population is a partner in, the product of, or closely related to, "mixed" relationships.

The mirror image of the use of the word "Muslims" to equal both "victims" and "Bosnian" is the demonization of all Serbs by equating "Serb" with "aggressor." The very inconsistency of this in the face of policies that favor the aggressor demonstrates how words have been corrupted by misuse. This particular abuse is sinister: it has utterly marginalized and silenced the Serbian voices of opposition to Milosevic in Serbia and to Karadzic in Bosnia.[8] And by silencing them, it has ensured that they are powerless to maintain the struggle against ultra-nationalist and fascist policies in the Balkans. Further, constructive alternative policies for a resolution of the conflict in former Yugoslavia proposed by such opposition groups have been ignored or contemptuously dismissed by UN and EU negotiators and members of the

Contact Group. Contrast this to the considerable, and often quite un-critical, support of the opposition to Tito at a time when communism, not Islam, was the West's "enemy" of preference.

Perhaps, in a Europe where mainstream political discourse has moved sharply to the right in recent years, we should not be surprised to find fascism regarded as less of a threat than communism; yet many of us believe that fascism is the common threat faced by all; that it is a threat that should unite the Western, post-Christian world and the world of Islam, at a time when instead we find Western politicians talking up the threat of Islam as the successor enemy to communism. Bosnians, rather fewer than half of whom are at least nominally Muslim, have been tragically caught up in this Manichean discourse.

Perhaps the most alarming abuse of words, however, is the phrase "peace plan." We are to believe that the destruction of a UN member state, its division into "ethnic regions" (as though that were possible in so mixed a population), and the forcible expulsion or killing of any citizen who does not "belong" in the regions won by aggression are a sound basis for peace. On the contrary, such fundamental injustice will leave behind only bitterness, will foster the hatreds which have been created by appalling suffering, and will leave about two million people homeless and even stateless.

All this is bad enough; but Bosnia is more than just the sum of its people's suffering. The response of the international community repre-sents a complete betrayal of all the high principles on which the United Nations is founded: human rights, the equality of all people, the right of member states (enshrined in Article 51 of the UN Charter) to defend themselves against aggression or, if unable to do so, to be defended by other member states. Bosnia represents the first real challenge to European collective foreign policy, and Europe has failed utterly. What has happened to the Europe I and others of my generation thought we were signing up to, when we voted "yes" to the referendum on whether Britain should join the EC? I thought we were taking a major step towards the creation of a Europe, and beyond that a world, in which all who lived—regardless of skin color, culture, religion, ethnicity—would be full citizens: no longer just a white, Christian Europe but a multi-cultural, multi-religious, and thereby greatly en-riched Europe.

Bosnia shows us that far from this perception of Europe in the minds of our governments, the world is still ruled by those who have a Manichean view of the world—them and us. This permeates all their policies, from their desperate need to find a successor enemy to communism (ready-made, they believe, in the shape of Islam) to their attitude towards refugees and asylum seekers as "others" to be kept out, not suffering fellow human beings to be given shelter and succor. Europe is in danger of becoming a nation-state writ large, with fortress walls to keep out all those who do not conform to the image of "Europeans" that the power-holders have decided upon. And the world's only remaining superpower, the United States, seems trapped in a politics of indecisiveness towards Bosnia, though it has not hesitated to intervene in regions where its vital interests (i.e. its determination to control the world's major oil deposits) were supposedly at risk and where there seemed small chance of American casualties.

In speaking of this, I am reminded of the Gulf War, described as a war with remarkably few casualties, as though a quarter of a million dead Iraqis, conscripts and civilians alike, counted for nothing—not to speak of the soaring infant mortality and the agony of the Iraqi people since the fighting ended and the monstrous Saddam Hussein was left in control of his suffering country as a local strong-man who had tasted the might of Western arms and could be relied upon, perhaps, to behave tamely thereafter. Sanctions in Iraq, still applied with maximum rigor as I write, are causing extreme suffering to the Iraqi people while leaving Saddam and his coterie untouched, and indeed serving to undermine such endeavors to unseat him as the people may have strength for. Beyond that, they are likely to result in the collapse of civil society into ungovernability by any successor to Saddam, whatever manner of person he may be. This same Saddam, of course, was propped up and armed by the West during the Iran-Iraq war in the name of regional balance, for which one may read, in an attempt to undermine the Islamic revolution in Iran. That revolution was, predictably, also pre-sented as a threat; there was much rhetoric about the risk of its spreading to the rest of the Muslim world, despite the very distinct nature of Iranian Islam; and indeed no similar regime has yet emerged elsewhere.

Our faiths may have originated, like Judaism before them, in the Middle East, but the Christianity which dominates the Western world developed, above all, in Europe, and I do not think I am being unjustifiably Eurocentric in suggesting that Europe still plays an important role in world politics—it has, after all, been the starting point for two world wars this century and it is, today, the single largest economic bloc in the world. We are seeing today the third European genocide of the twentieth century: first the Armenians in 1915/16, then the Jews at the hands of Hitler, and now the Bosnian Muslims. The century began in

1914, in Sarajevo. It is going out in bloodshed, in the 1990s, in Sarajevo. Bosnia is crucially important for all of us, and above all for Muslims and Christians, for it lies on a double fault-line. In Bosnia, Western, Catholic Christianity meets Eastern, Orthodox Christianity, and Christendom meets Islam. None of us, wherever we live, can turn away from Bosnia. And in Chechenya the airpower of another Orthodox Christian state, Russia, has been used to devastating effect against another mainly Muslim people, the Chechens, accompanied by near-silence from politicians and church leaders. Small wonder that Muslims are asking themselves the same question about Chechenya as they ask about Bosnia—is it because the victims are Muslims that the world is silent?

Not all our endeavors lie in the global arena or confront evils of such magnitude as genocide. Racism of a less vicious kind is a daily reality for many people, and here is another form of prejudice where language plays a considerable part in forming our understanding. Much well-meaning discourse about the ills of discrimination focus on color-racism in simplistic, literally "black" and "white" terms, leaving groups from visible minorities who do not think of themselves as black—Chinese, for example, or, probably, a majority of South Asians—feeling excluded or marginalized. A broader anti-discrimination language speaks of racism and anti-Semitism, which includes Jews but excludes Muslims, exacerbating Muslim anger in the face of policies seen as grotesquely favoring Israel against the Palestinians in the Middle East, not to mention the fact that in some countries—Britain and France come to mind—it is above all Muslims, not Jews, who are the victims of discrimination, harassment and even violence. In France, for example, *l'affaire des foulards*[9] has reached alarming proportions, and whereas in the early stages of the secularist campaign against the *hijab*, Jewish boys were prepared to wear the *kipah* in solidarity with the Muslim girls who wished to wear the scarf, now that Charles Pasqua's Islamophobia has so deeply tainted French politics, the Jews are keeping a low profile. Their fear, in the light of twentieth century history, is understandable; perhaps if Christians were to demonstrate their solidarity with the Muslims of France, the Jews might again find the courage to do so. Meanwhile, events in France demonstrate that secularism as state policy is no guarantee of religious freedom; the legacy of the French understanding of imperialism, which is essentially assimilationist (as against the British emphasis on discipline and racial superiority), is fueling discord and violence beyond the borders of France itself, most tragically in Algeria.

We as Muslims and Christians need to stand side by side in solidarity with each other and with other believers to assert this freedom for all. Having been rather hard on the Vatican in regard to its stance on birth-control, I must now pay tribute to the work of the Pontifical Council for Inter-Religious Dialogue and, in particular, to the work of its Office for Islam, whose head displays a keen awareness of the destructive nature of Islamophobia. There are, too, many other organizations, often Christian in origin, that are working to overcome mutual misunderstandings and fear and the hostility that all too often accompanies the fear of the unknown.

In my concluding passages, I shall consider briefly how a shared commitment of this kind may both deepen our understanding of each other and lead to real change for the better in the lives of women and men.

Guidelines for Dialogue Today and Signs of Promise

Among the issues that we address as Muslims and Christians in dialogue, there are shared concerns and there are those that are deeply divisive. Of course, this is over-simplistic; some issues may be divisive within our faiths and serve to unite like-minded groups between the faiths. I propose the distinction to alert us to the possibility of developing a deeper understanding of each other, of learning to value each other, by beginning where dialogue is easy. And, by and large, it is easy when we focus on shared concerns. Later, as trust and friendships develop, we may discover the divisive issues to be less threatening than we thought.

To this I would add what I believe to be essential if our discussions and debates are to lead to understanding and trust: be prepared to be self-critical, both of ourselves as individuals and of our community, our leaders and would-be leaders. Defensive or polemical responses to justified criticism lead nowhere, except perhaps towards entrenched mistrust. There is, of course, a fine line between self-criticism and disloyalty to one's group or community; but silence in the face of rhetoric or actions that are morally indefensible is also a kind of disloyalty. If justice has any meaning, we must affirm it everywhere, not selectively, turning a blind eye to abuses when perpetrated by our own.

That a shared commitment to justice can unite people of diverse origins and beliefs, and can triumph over exclusion, repression and violence, we have seen in South Africa. Though the anti-apartheid struggle was against brutal minority white domination, it was never an anti-white struggle, but a fight for justice in the ethical sense, a struggle with a powerful moral dimension against the legalized lawlessness of the apartheid regime; and it joined people of faith with secularists and atheists, women and men—for it was also a struggle deeply informed by concepts of gender equality—united in a common purpose. There remains much to be done to redress the terrible effects of so many years of injustice, but so long as the commitment to justice remains undiminished, and provided that the dominant political and economic elites and interest groups of the world do not seek to impose their will on the nascent democracy, the people of South Africa may yet create a society in which all can participate as equal partners.

The South African struggle for justice was sustained not only by the extraordinary courage of the people themselves, but also by the knowledge that ordinary people the world over, many of them remote from any experience of discrimination let alone repression and violence, supported the anti-apartheid movement. In Britain alone, the movement had, at its height, over 25,000 members, not to mention the tens of thousands more who supported its aims without formally joining it as members. Contrast this with the apathy towards genocide in Bosnia, which I have already discussed. The explanation for such apathy that is sometimes proposed is "compassion fatigue." What is our compassion worth, if it becomes fatigued the more it is needed? The very phrase sounds as though it was invented by the same spin-doctor as "collateral damage" (killing or maiming innocent civilians), "pre-emptive strikes" (aggressive acts of war, often against civilians on the grounds that they are harboring "terrorists"), or "new world order" (more of the same old order, only with greater, and growing, economic and political inequalities). A far more likely explanation, it seems to me, is the profound sense of disempowerment that this vaunted new world order creates in us.

One of the most damaging effects of the break-up of the Soviet Union is that we now live in a world in which any sense of an alternative to the Western cultural paradigm and to capitalism has almost disappeared, and, with it, much of the hope that the world might one day be a place in which it is safe to be human, rather than, as now, desperately skewed against the majority of its people. How is it that people of faith have, so far, failed to present the values expressed in our religions as just such an alternative? Perhaps documents such as the Global Ethic represent a tentative step in this direction; without wishing

in the least to discount the contribution of other faiths, I would argue
that the responsibility lies above all in the hands of people of the two
faiths here represented, for ours are the faiths of almost one half of the
world's population, and above all, ours are the faiths in which the
Western cultural paradigm, which dominates the world today has its
roots (I have already drawn attention to the shared Abrahamic and
Hellenistic elements in our heritages).

We who are gathered here, though we may not belong to the power-
holding elites, do at least have the inestimable privilege of being able
to voice our concerns. This privilege carries with it responsibilities. Not
least, we owe it to the silenced majority to speak on their behalf. We
face risks, of course, in speaking out. In seeking to mobilize public
support, to encourage popular organizations and movements, to articulate our demands in the political arena, we risk mobilizing something
very different: the wrath of political and economic elites whose power
or wealth our demands would threaten. Being willing to accept those
risks, which can be considerable, even including the risk of torture or
death, calls for a rare level of courage and dedication. Bleak though the
world may seem, we learn from history and from the world of today
that such courage and commitment can lead to profound changes. And
if our meeting as Muslims and Christians does not go beyond the
necessary dialogue in which we learn to know and value each other to
a shared commitment to do whatever is within our power to reassert the
moral and ethical values of our faiths for the benefit of all mankind,
then we are failing ourselves, we are failing humanity, and above all we
are failing in our duty to God. Our care in using words with respect for
their power can be one measure of our submission to the will of God
expressed in the Divine Word.

NOTES

1. Qur'an Sura 22, *al Hajj* [Pilgrimage], vv. 39-40: "To those against whom war
   is made, permission is given to fight, because they are wronged; and verily God
   is most powerful for their aid; they are those who have been expelled from their
   homes in defiance of right, for no cause except that they say 'Our Lord is
   Allah.'" Sura 2, *al-Baqara* [The Heifer], v. 190: "Fight in the cause of God
   those who fight you, but do not commit aggression, for God does not love
   aggressors." Sura 8, *al-Anfal* [Spoils of War], vv. 60-61: "Against them make
   ready your strength to the utmost of your power, including steeds of war, to
   strike terror into the enemies of God and your enemies. . . But if the enemy
   incline towards peace, do thou also incline towards peace, and trust in God."

Sura 42, *al-Shura* [Consultation], vv. 36-42: "Whatever you are given is but for the enjoyment of life in this world—whereas that which is with God is far better and more enduring. It shall be given to all who attain to faith and in their Sustainer place their trust; and who shun the worst sins and shameful deeds; and who, when they are angry, readily forgive; and who respond to their Sustainer and are constant in prayer; and whose rule is consultation among themselves; and who spend on others out of what We provide for them as sustenance; and who, whenever tyranny afflicts them, defend themselves. But requiting evil may also become an evil; hence, whoever pardons his enemy and makes peace, his reward rests with God—for verily He does not love evildoers. Yet indeed, as for those who defend themselves after having been wronged, no blame attaches to them; blame attaches only to those who oppress others and behave outrageously on earth, offending against all that is right: for them there is grievous suffering in store. But if one is patient in adversity and forgives—this is indeed something to set one's heart upon."

2. The word *jihad* derives from the Arabic triliteral root j-h-d, to endeavor or to struggle, so that the essential meaning of jihad is to strive in the way of God. The oft-quoted saying of the Prophet recounts that on returning to Medina from battle he said to his companions, "We are returning from the lesser jihad to the greater jihad." The words used for war are *al-Harb* and *al-Qital*. Today, certain extremist Muslim groups regard armed *jihad* as the only legitimate form, dismissing the notion of a moral jihad; some Western scholars, for example, Bernard Lewis, seem to support this notion on historical grounds, asserting that jihad has always meant the Caliphate's military effort to establish political supremacy (though it did not imply coercive conversion to Islam). In reality, both ideas—the militant and the moral—have existed alongside each other since the earliest days of Islam.

3. Yahya M. Sadowski, "Bosnia's Muslims: A Fundamentalist Threat?," *Brookings Review*, Vol. 13, No. 1, p. 10. The term is also used by the newly-launched Washington-based journal *TransState Islam* (Khalid Duran, ed.), which sees the key notion distinguishing Islamism from Islam as "the central role of politics and the concept of an ideological state."

4. For a fuller discussion of the "Rushdie Affair," see M.M. Ahsan and A.R. Kidwai (eds.), *Sacrilege versus Civility: Muslim Perspectives on* The Satanic Verses *Affair* (Leicester: The Islamic Foundation, 2nd ed. 1993).

5. Inter Press Service, 18 February 1995, quotes Claes as saying to German TV: "Fundamentalism is at least as dangerous as Communism once was. Please do not underestimate this risk." Claes also "told British and Belgian media" that "Muslim fundamentalism at the conclusion of this age is a serious threat, because it represents terrorism, religious fanaticism and exploitation of social and economic justice." IPS report that "a French diplomat described Claes' statement as an 'invitation for terrorism on NATO territory,'" and southern European countries were "quick to downplay Claes' talk of a 'new enemy'" because they are "nervous of finding themselves on the front line against potential Islamic fundamentalist threats." Concern at Claes' comments therefore focuses not around the Islamophobia tenor of his views but on the perceived increased risk from "Islamic fundamentalists" presumably angered by his remarks.

6. See, for example, Yasmin Alibhai-Brown, "Sex, Veils and Stereotypes," *The Independent*, London, 22 December 1994.

7. For a critique of the role of the UN in Bosnia, see B. Cohen and G. Stamkoski (eds.), *With No Peace to Keep. . . UN Peacekeeping and the War in the Former Yugoslavia* (London: Media East West, 1995).

8. A rare exception is to be noted in late 1995: one of the four recipients of the 1995 Right Livelihood Awards (often referred to as "the alternative Nobel prize") was the Serb Civic Council of Bosnia-Herzegovina. The press release states that "The Serb Civic Council (SCC) has resolutely refused to succumb to the ethnic hatred that has so disfigured Europe in the war in Bosnia-Herzegovina. The Award's Jury honors in the SCC 'the forgotten voice of all those Bosnian Serbs who have under extremely difficult circumstances maintained their support for a humane, multi-ethnic, democratic Bosnia-Herzegovina and rejected the war of genocidal apartheid waged by the regime in Pale.' The SCC works by political means for a peace in Bosnia which protects human rights and pluralistic parliamentary democracy."

9. See, for example, *Times*, London, 27 November 1989; *Guardian*, London, 11 December 1989. The then Education Minister of France, Lionel Jospin, asked the Conseil d'Etat to rule on the matter. Its ruling was that in the name of freedom of expression, the wearing of signs of religious affiliation by pupils could not be forbidden, but that in the name of the secular state and tolerance for the opinions of others, such pupils could be disciplined if deemed to have put pressure on others, or indulged in provocation, propaganda or proselytism. By 1994, French attitudes (both governmental and popular) appeared to have hardened. Muslim girls arriving at the Lycée Romain-Rolland near Paris were banned from class for wearing the *hijab*. The Education Minister, François Bayrou, issued a circular banning "ostentatious" religious symbols. These moves need to be seen within the context of the hardline policies of France's Interior Minister, Charles Pasqua, towards immigrants and "fundamentalists," fueled by fears of the growing tension and violence in Algeria. See also *Guardian*, 15 September, *Le Monde*, September 1994, *Guardian*, 6 October 1994. A similar case occurred in Britain (Altrincham girls' grammar school): see *Guardian*, 23 January, 26 January, 1990. The Board of Deputies of British Jews criticized the French government's 1994 decision as "an infringement of religious liberties"; the Jewish community in France has also protested at the ban.

9

PERSONAL THOUGHTS ON MUSLIM-CHRISTIAN DIALOGUE

ᶜAbdullāh Noorudeen Durkee

PRAISE BE TO ALLĀH, Lord of all the worlds who, through His Eternal Word, does not cease to be praised: The Universally Compassionate, The Singularly Mercy Full, Who by His Mercy has stirred up within us gratitude for His goodness wherewith He has enriched us and inspired us to praise and glorify Him.

The limits of favour and the bounds of praise were extended when He promised to those grateful for His bounty still more blessings; and He spread wide the carpet of His Assembly to those who remember Him. He has brought into subjection all things according to His Wisdom and Equity, as He has willed, by His Power, so that by His Authority the mover remains still and the still moves. The Controller of expansion (*baṣṭ*) and contraction (*qabḍ*), "The Knower of the Unseen (*al-ghayb*); not even the weight of an atom, or less than that or greater than that, either in the heavens or on the earth escapes Him." (Q34:3[1]) "He is the First and the Last, The Outer and the Inner (*al-ᵓawālu wa-l-ᵓākhiru wa dhāhiru wa-l-bātin*)." (Q57:3)

We praise Him with the praise of those who know Him with true knowledge of Him. We give thanks with the expressions of gratitude of those who acknowledge the perfection of His goodness and favour. We bear witness that there is no deity other than Allāh alone, having neither companion nor partner, with an affirmation to which no doubt is attached and before which no door closes from accepting.

We testify that in speaking of human perfection, we speak first of our liege-lord Muḥammad, the Perfect Worshipper (ʿabdu-l-llāh), His Slave and Prophet and Messenger chosen from the treasure house of pure nobility, selected from a family of honour. Allāh bless and save him, with a blessing that will bring us to him and gather us around him on the Day of Assembly and Reckoning. May Allāh be pleased with his family, his helpers, his descendants, the people of his household, his illustrious companions, the best of friends, as long as a star will shine, the moon shall rise and a cloud shall float above the face of the earth.

By praising the Prophet, so at the same time we must praise all the Prophets and Messengers, blessings of Allāh and peace be upon them, for, as I bear witness that Muḥammad is the Prophet and the Messenger of Allāh, so do I bear witness that there are upwards of some 124,000 Prophets that Allāh has sent to the people of the world, and from these I bear witness to the Prophethood (nubuwa) of Adam, Idris, Nūḥ, Hud, Saliḥ, Lūṭ, ʾIbrāhīm, Ismaʿil, Isḥāq, Yaʿqūb, Yūsuf, Shuʿayb, Mūsā, Hārūn, Dawūd, Sulaymān, Ayyub, Dhu-l-Kifl, Yunus, Ilyās, al-Yasaʾ, Zakarriyah, Yaḥya, and ʿIsā who are all related, peace and blessings be upon them, and we do not discriminate between any one of them, known or unknown, they are all brothers without exception.

And of these I bear witness, knowing that Allāh has sent more than 104 Divinely Revealed Books, that Allāh sent the Tawrah to ʾIbrāhīm and Mūsā, the Zabūr to Dawūd, the ʾInjil to ʾIsā and the Qurʾān to Muḥammad, peace and blessings be upon them all.

These Books were sent specifically for the purpose of promulgating the Divine Law (sharīʿah) that regulates the transactional basis (dīn) of life between the self (nafs) and Allāh and the self and all the other selves (an-nās, al-jāān, al-malāʾikah) that exist in the world, with great attention to the relationships that exist between members of families, communities, tribes, nations and people of other religious communities, and specifically among the monotheistic People of the Book, pre-eminently the Jews, the Sabians and the Christians.

I bear witness that, as the Prophet Muḥammad is the Seal of all the Prophets (khātama-n-nabiyyīn) (Q33:40), just so is the Qurʾān is the Final Testament in accord with the last ʾāyat in the Revelation (nuzūl) which says (in English translation),

"This day I have completed for you (akmāltu lakum) your religion and completed my favour on you and have chosen for you the way of surrender (al-ʾIslām) as your religion." (Q5:3).

As a Muslim, ʾinshāʾllāh, I take note that Allāh has devoted more than 1,300² verses (*āyāt*) in al-Qurʾān to speaking of previous Prophets and Messengers, peace be upon them all, as well as earlier revelations and other religions. My understanding conforms itself to what Allāh has said regarding these, and all other, subjects. What may or may not be true in any other earlier Revelation is not a matter upon which I speculate. To the degree that Allāh confirms "that which was revealed before you," (Q2:4) I accept the content of earlier Revelation. When there appears to be a discrepancy between what I find in Qurʾān and any earlier Revelation, I accept what Allāh has said by way of verification, mindful that there have been those who "listened to the Word of Allāh and then used to change it, after they had knowingly understood it." (Q2:75) I am deeply aware of the saying of Allāh, "Woe to those who write the Book with their own hands and say, 'this is from Allāh.'" (Q2:79)

I am, you might say, a "Unitarian" (*muwaḥḥid*), as indeed all Muslims are, and as such I reject at every level, and in every dimension, any possibility of duality or trinity (*thalīth*) and any possibility of any form of incarnation (*ḥulūl*) or hypostasis (*uqnūm*) with Allāh who is One before and without number.

As this is an essay which was specifically written for a conference dealing with the "problems and challenges of Muslim-Christian dialogue," I wish to make my own position clear from the beginning and so spare the reader any possible doctrinal or sentimental misunder-standing. In terms of the "problems" of Muslim-Christian dialogue, I do not believe there is anything much to be gained by discussion of the issue of what is sometimes called Christology, as it does not seem possible that Christians and Muslims can ever come to any common understanding on this issue without compromising the very basis of our differing belief (*ʿaqīdah*). Equally, I have little hope that any discussion that centres around the assumed Passion of Christ, and specifically the question of crucifixion and vicarious salvation, will yield any new understanding. Surely by now we have learned this over the past fourteen hundred years of our, often bloody, dialogue.

I would also say that, after many years of deeply considering the issue, I have come to believe that the Prophet and Messenger that we, as Muslims, know as ʿIsā, peace be upon him, bears only a passing resemblance (*shubbiha*) to the Jesus of Christian doctrine. I accept this as so without any attempt to reconcile the Jesus of Christianity to ʿIsā, peace be upon him, for if they were to be truly reconciled there would no longer be the need for anything called "Christianity" as such. This is in accord with the Words of Allāh:

﴿ قُلْ يَـٰأَهْلَ ٱلْكِتَـٰبِ تَعَالَوْاْ إِلَىٰ كَلِمَةٍ سَوَاءٍ بَيْنَنَا وَ بَيْنَكُمْ
أَلَّا نَعْبُدَ إِلَّا ٱللَّهَ وَ لَا نُشْرِكَ بِهِ شَيْئًا
وَ لَا يَتَّخِذَ بَعْضُنَا بَعْضًا أَرْبَابًا مِّن دُونِ ٱللَّهِ ﴾

QUL YĀĀ ʾAHLA-L-KITĀBI
TAᶜĀLŪ ʾILĀ KALIMATIN SAWĀʾI BAYNANĀ WA BAYNAKUM:
ʾALLĀ NAᶜBUDA ʾILLĀ-LLĀHA WA LĀ NUSḫRIKA BIHI SḫAYʾAÑ
WA LĀ YATAKḫIDḫA BAᶜADUNĀ BAᶜḌAN
ʾARBĀBAM-MIN DŪNI-LLĀH

Oh People of the Book
[Let us] come to an agreement between us and you
that we shall worship none but Allāh and ascribe no partner to Him
and none of us shall take as lords other than Allāh.
(Al ᶜImrān 3:64)

I should also say, that in as much as I see an unbridgeable gap between the Christian notion of Jesus and the Prophet ᶜIsā, peace be upon him, I also see an even more daunting gap between what is variously meant or has been understood over the past millennium by the term God (Θεος) and Allāh.

The word "God", which can also be spelled "god", yields such derivatives as goddess, goddesses and gods, is simply not the same at all as the word *Allāh*, which has neither root nor derivative.

Even in the Era of Ignorance (*jahiliyyah*), when the dwellers in the Arabian Peninsula in general, and Makkah in particular, had forgotten the teachings of the great Muslim *hanīf*, the Prophet ʾIbrāhīm, peace be upon him, and had fallen into idolatry, superstition, fortune telling and magic, the Name —Allāh— never changed its meaning nor was anything ever associated with that Name, which always remained inviolable unto itself. Throughout the time of the desert Semites, the word 'Allāh' has always meant the One that is God without either other or partner.

It is thirty years since the Second Vatican Conference (Vatican II) declared that,

God's saving will also embraces those who acknowledge the Creator, and among them especially the Muslims, who profess the faith of Abraham and together with us adore the one God, the Merciful One, who will judge men on the Last Day. (Article 16)

Yet despite calls of various, mainly Christian, Orientalists for greater understanding or even, in the case of Dr. Massignon's call many years in the past, for a "spiritual Copernican revolution," there remain fundamental differences between Muslims and Christians that cannot be truly bridged, no matter how many people talk for however long about "paradigm shifts", without either Christianity losing its doctrinal relevance or 'Islām yielding what can never be yielded if 'Islām is to continue in accord with its origins in Divine Revelation (al-Qurʾān).

The questions is if Christians are prepared to accept that salvic grace also exists outside of the church, are they also prepared, insofar as they accept the Hebrew Prophets, peace upon them all, to accept the Arabic Prophet, peace be upon him? After all there cannot be two sources of Revelation if God is truly One any more than there can, in Truth, be any source of Grace or Salvation other than God which is to say Allāh.

Having then accepted that Muslims *"together with us adore the one God"*, and they do so because they received a message from a prophet then, consequentially, what else can the Qurʾān be but the Word of God? The only question left is whether it is *ipsissima verba* or the human word of a prophet. On the issue of the Divine Revelation of the Qurʾān, there is no possiblity of any other understanding, for that is a basis of our belief, as the Incarnation, at whatever level, is a basis for Chrisitan belief.

If only from the perspective of consequentiality, Muslims can never believe in other than a Divine Origin for the Qurʾān, for if we were to accept, say through a process akin to historical criticism, that the Qurʾān was not the True Word of Allāh but rather it was a "message" filtered either through the Prophet, blessings of Allāh and peace be upon him, or through the early community as some Orientalists[3] have sought to prove, then we would have lost the bedrock basis of our belief and we would be lost in the same relativism in which modern Christianity seems to find itself — apparently unsure of exactly what or whom to believe in.

There is of course a lot to be said for swimming in the sea of not-knowing. I have been assured that not-knowing increases one's faith no end and that one need not think, say, about how exactly the Trinity actually works but instead concentrate on God and — simply worship that which is obvious to us all. But rather than rush time seeking a solution that cannot exist I would prefer to accept the present as it is and merely point to the gap.

For Muslims, the Qurʾān, is the Word of Allāh revealed orally to the Prophet Muḥammad, blessings of Allāh and peace be upon him. Cognately, for Christians, Jesus, peace be upon him, is the Word of God, as attested to both in the Qurʾān (Q4:171) and the Gospels (John 1:14).

The Revelation descended over the course of twenty three years and was recorded in writing by pious scribes (Q80:11-16). After the death of the Prophet, blessings of Allāh and peace be upon him, these writings were gathered into a single book according to the order that was established during the last Ramaḍān before the death of the Prophet, blessings of Allāh and peace be upon him. Both the contents and the order were well known and, in addition to being written down, had been memorised by hundreds of his companions, Allāh have mercy on them.

Within thirteen years after his death a number of complete copies were made by the most trusted of the Companions, Allāh have mercy on them, working under orders of the Khalīfah ʿUthmān. These copies were sent out in the four directions and a master copy remained in Madinah, to assure the accuracy of all future editions of the Holy Book.

There is no difference between those copies and any modern edition save in the addition of certain orthographical marks which aid the reader to fulfill the original command to "Read" or "Recite." (ʾIqrāʾ) (Q96:1)

The accuracy of these copies allows us to recreate, in the present, the original sonorous revelation which is, by way of metaphor, *the* Holy Sacrament of the Muslim, for when one reads the Word of Allāh, it is breathed into life and thus for us is the Word, so to speak, made flesh.

It is very important for non-Muslims to realise that Revelation *is*, not was, and as such is always new. For the faithful reader, the Qurʾān is Remembrance (*dhikr*), it is Guidance (*hudā*), it is Healing (*shifā*), it is Mercy (*rahmah*), it is Blessed (*mubārak*) and it is always Most Generous (*karīm*). It is also our ultimate means of discriminating (*furqān*) between what is right and what is wrong, what is false and what is true.

In truth, I could not really be a Muslim and have any other view, just as if you, the reader, are a Christian, then Jesus the Christ can be, for you, no less than the Word of God and your personal Savior. Given this and considering the reality of the times in which we find ourselves to be, it would appear to me that our best possible course is to leave discussion of all of that behind and agree to disagree if you like. For Muslims, this is possible in accord with the saying of Allāh,

LAKUM DĪNUKUM WALIĀ DĪN:

To you your religion and to me my religion.
(al-Kafirūn 109:6)

and in accord with:

> ✳ لَا إِكْرَاهَ فِى آلدِّينِ ۚ قَد تَّبَيَّنَ آلرُّشْدُ مِنَ آلْغَىِّ ✳
>
> LAĀĀ ʾIKRĀHA FI-D-DĪN:
> QAT-TABAYYANA-R-RUSḥDU MINA-L-GḥAYY
>
> There is no coercion in religion, the truth stands clear from the false.
> (al-Baqarah 2:256)

Having left our disagreements behind, we are free to find many areas of concord, such as the belief in Allāh, or if you like, "God," given that each of us in reality (*haqīqah*) have quite different understandings of what *that* might or might not Be; the belief in angels; the belief in scriptures; the belief in prophets and, of great possible significance in the present world, the belief that each of us is ultimately accountable to Allāh or God on the Day of Judgment.

> ✳ أَلَيْسَ آللّٰهُ بِأَحْكَمِ آلْحَٰكِمِيْنَ ✳
>
> ʾALAYSA-LLĀHU BIʾAḤKAMI-L-ḤĀKIMĪN
>
> Is not Allāh the most Just of Judges?
> (at-Tīn 95:8)

Let us leave Allāh to judge between us and cease judging each other.

> ✳ بَلَىٰ ۚ مَنْ أَسْلَمَ وَجْهَهُۥ لِلّٰهِ وَ هُوَ مُحْسِنٌ
>
> فَلَهُۥ أَجْرُهُۥ عِنْدَ رَبِّهِ
>
> وَ لَا خَوْفٌ عَلَيْهِمْ وَ لَا هُمْ يَحْزَنُونَ ✳
>
> BALĀ : MAN ʾASLAMA WAJHAHŪ LI-LLAHI WA HUWA MUḤSINŪN
> FALAHŪ ʾAJRUHŪ ʿINDA RABBIHI
> WA LĀ KḥAWFUN ʿALAYHIM WA LĀ HUM YAḤZANŪN
>
> Surely whoever surrenders his whole self to Allāh and is sincere,
> his reward is with his Lord and no fear shall be upon him nor shall he grieve.
> (al-Baqarah 2:112)

Allāh further relates to us (by way of its meaning in English) that, "They are not all alike. Of the People of the Book there is a staunch community who recite the Signs of Allāh in the night and prostrate themselves. They believe in God and the Last Day and they enjoin the doing of what is

right and forbid the doing of what is wrong and they vie with one another
in performing good deeds; and these are among the righteous. Whatever
good they do they shall never be denied the reward of having done so for
Allāh has full knowledge of those who consciously guard themselves
[against all impurity] for [the sake of] Allāh." (Q3:114)

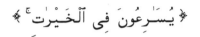

YUSĀRIʿŪNA FI-L-KhAYRĀT

Vie together in good works
(ʾAl ʿImrān 3:114)

This verse points, in this writer's humble opinion, to the best possible,
and most productive, way in which we can relate to and with one another
as members of different faith groups. Surely if Muslims, Christians and
Jews worked out their various differences by way of competing with one
another in the carrying out of good works, everyone would benefit.
Surely there can be no doubt that such a way of relating to one another
would go a long way to alleviating, if only in a small way, so much of
the oppression and suffering evident everywhere around us.

Just as both the Old Testament and the New Testament contain
ample directions for Jews and Christians from the same One God to live
righteous and wholesome lives, so Muslims find in both the Qurʾān and
the Wisdom Sayings (aḥadīth) of the Prophet, blessings of Allāh and
peace be upon him, a complete program of good works (khayrāt) that is
built from the ground up on such basic wisdom as, "He whose neighbour
is not secure against his mischief shall not enter the Garden of Paradise,"
to the broader directions and prescriptions from Allāh as in,

WA BAShShIRI-L-LADhĪNA ʾĀMANŪ WA ʿAMILŪ-Ṣ-ṢĀLIḤĀT

And give good news to those who believe and perform righteous deeds.
(al-Baqarah 2:25)

From a Muslim perspective, there is no belief (ʾimān) without action
(ʿamal). Belief without action is, at the very least, casuistry and, perhaps,
at a deeper more cynical level — utter hypocrisy. Belief without action
can only be seen as a failure to honour our pre-eternal covenant to live as
the faithful worshipful slaves (ʿabīd) and representatives (khulafāʾ) of
Allāh upon the earth. (Q7:172)

Equally, action without belief is, for the Muslim, ultimately worthless. Any reward for such action is merely temporal for, "they have purchased the present life at the price of the world to come."(Q2:86) This conjunction — this marriage — of belief and action, *'āmanū wa 'amilū*, is an oft recurrent pairing which can be found in numerous *'āyāt* in the Qur'ān from beginning to end (Q2:25 to Q103:3).

We trust that our Christian interlocutors have long since put behind them any idea that because we, as Muslims, understand at the deepest level that everything and every event is being determined by Allāh, that perforce we Muslims believe that humans are but "helpless tools of an arbitrary God" or that ours is a fatalistic faith.

As Josef van Ess in an article[4] *Islamic Perspectives* succinctly put it from the Christian perspective,

I believe...Judeo-Christian and Islamic theology (could agree) on two major points:

- The world is governed not by blind chance or obscure destiny but by the gracious and merciful God. Creation and conservation, presence and judgment, are expressions of his freely granted compassion.

- God's absolute freedom does not threaten man's relative freedom, but makes it possible and powerful. In this sense, the Infinite represents not the far limit of the finite, but its enablement and fulfillment.

In a sense it is this very understanding that lies behind the idea of jihād which simply means concerted and conscious struggle.

Jihād, as struggle or combat, exists both internally, in the sense of the struggle each of us must wage with our own self which is called the greatest jihād (*jihādu-l-'akbar*), and externally as the lesser jihād (*jihādu-l-'asghar*), which is the necessary (*darruri*) struggle with all those forces of oppression (*dhulm*) which act to restrict one's individual or communal capacity to worship and live in accord with both the Mercy and the Rigour of the Divine Law.

Externally or internally (*dhāhiri 'aw bātini*), this combat is among the greatest of the good works and deeds of true righteousness, for it touches on the very most basic issue of the struggle between inspired consciousness (*taqwā*) and ignorance (*jahl*) — ignorance which is synonymous with oppression (*dhulm*) — an oppression which inevitably begins with the self.

RABBI 'INNĪ DhALAMTU NAFSĪ

Our Lord, truly I have oppressed my self.
(an-Naml 27:44)

In our vying with one another in performing righteous deeds, can there be a more accessible place to begin than within our "own" selves? Is it not in our own selves that the struggle (*jihād*) between inspired awareness of Allāh and ignorance is so clearly visible?

There is a phrase from a pop song momentarily in vogue at some point during the past thirty years that goes, "It starts out with your family and later it comes round to your soul." With apologies to the song-writer I would suggest that it might be more correctly phrased, "It starts out with your soul (*nafs*) and later comes round to your family."

If one accepts the full implications within the conjunction — the marriage — of belief and action, ʾāmanū wa ʿamilu, fully aware that:

• the world is governed not by blind chance or obscure destiny but by the gracious and merciful God. Creation and conservation, presence and judgment, are expressions of His freely granted compassion.

• God's absolute freedom does not threaten man's relative freedom, but makes it possible and powerful. In this sense, the Infinite represents not the far limit of the finite, but its enablement and fulfillment, then surely it follows that part of that enablement and fulfillment in one's own being is an ecstatic freedom that results from the alignment of one's self to the dynamics of Being.

If one can align one's self, and especially do so in partnership with one's mate, who is also motivated by the same inspired awareness, then the very next step is to work to align one's whole family to that Being.

Let me just digress to clarify my use above of the word *Being*. God, or Allāh, to again give That which we speak of its proper Name, is not some *body* any more than Allāh or God is any *thing*. I would rather not get caught up in a long ontological discussion, so perhaps it will suffice to say that, from a certain perspective, as much as we can say Allāh is a Being so we must realize that Allāh *is* Being. At every level outwardly and inwardly, in time and eternally, there is, and can be, no other god but God (*lāā ʾilahā illa-llāh*), which is to say no other Being other than Allāh as both The Named and Event, Noun and Verb.

What we constantly experience, to whatever limited degree we can, is the wave momentarily manifest as particle. When, through worship, one becomes quite still, it is possible to sense at the center of the wave a universal mercy (*rahmah*) and specific compassion (*rahīm*), the ground of all being, which alone animates (*rūh*) or spiritualises (*rūh*) all that which is, or at least that which we can experience, always bearing in mind that it is we who are limited and contingent whilst That which is Allāh is unlimited and everywhere self-established. Allāh remains both beyond all form and simultaneously that which inspires (*bi-rawah*) all form.

One either lives one's life unconscious of this Being and remains ignorant (*jahl*), or through action (*'amal*) or grace (*barakah*), by wayfaring (*sulūk*) or through attraction (*jadhb*), ignorance is overcome, momentarily or constantly, eternal in the moment, and one is blessed by the vision of the ultimate interconnected unicity of all that Is or can Be — the only Wave that ever Is.

Perhaps there is the responsibility of some kind of abstract belief in Being but it is very difficult to be motivated by abstraction. Experience or tasting (*dhawq*), on the other hand, is a strong motivator which is, perhaps, part of the meaning of the command to "Seek ye first the kingdom of heaven and all else shall be added unto you." (Luke 12:31) Rather than digress further along what is, for this writer, a very seductive and compelling avenue of thought, let me return to my central idea of our vying with one another in good works.

If one proceeds from within to without along the lines I am suggesting, then, inevitably, one must begin by working goodness with one's self and one's mate and then in one's family and, if one is very successful — in the ever wide-spread community.

If you can accept that personal experience (*dhawq*) or certainty (*yaqīn*) is required if one is truly to be inspired and motivated in the great struggle against all forms of oppression — the combat on behalf of the Angel on the part of the Faithful Lovers — as some refer to jihād, then it follows that the holy warrior (*mujahid*) must be one who has seen the true nature of Being, and having seen it, must be accounted as a witness (*shahīd*). The witness can, in the light of what he or she has seen, never be content with ignorance and oppression, darkness and delusion. Not incidentally (*shahid*, witness) is the same word for "martyr" in Arabic.

For it so often follows that once one has seen behind the curtain, so to speak, it is quite impossible to any longer accept the posturing of those who strut through the world leaving wreckage and destruction in their wake, unaware that they are actually walking in the Holy Valley of Tuwa (Q20:11-15). It behooves us all to remove our shoes and realize that the world is not at all a stage but a prayer carpet and that surely we will all stand naked before the same Merciful and Just God to be judged in accord with our belief and actions whilst in this world.

One must also struggle to bring an end to ignorance and oppression in one's own community, for it is not only the "other" who covers up (*kufr*) the Truth. We must all seek to redress in our own faith communities the balance between intelligibility and sensibility; between transconscious and transmutated spirituality and the historico-collective revelation. This lest the world of belief be subverted from within and be burned, as it is so often, by the fires of fanaticism and hatred.

Ultimately, perhaps, for the believer (*muʾmin*) our vying in good works must be a struggle on behalf of "all sentient beings," as Gautama, a buddha, phrased it, though here we must be very careful of entertaining hubris and its mate, pride (*kibr*).

The Prophet, blessings of Allāh and peace be upon him, said, "No man can be called a believer until he loves for his brother what he loves for himself," which is not far off the command of Jesus to "love your neighbor as your self." (Matthew 19:19)

I am drawn to observe that the words *neighbor* and *brother* (and *sister* as well) suggest that, in all cases, these are not some abstract "others" but those closest to us in accord with the ḥadīth: "the believers are all brothers to one another." One's neighbor is someone known, as is one's brother or sister. I mention hubris and pride in terms of larger missions, for it seems, at least such has been my experience, that the wider the web or net is stretched, the more prone we are to leaving the human particular (brother, sister, neighbor) in favour of the inhuman abstraction, which can lead to a kind of spiritual fascism which, I believe, is at the root of most fundamentalist movements in the world today.

Neighbors and brothers, as well as sisters, are spirit, intelligence, feeling, flesh and blood and so less susceptible to abstraction. One's brothers and sisters live in one's house. One's neighbor lives next door — a human not unlike one's own self.

Allāh, on the tongue of the Prophet, blessings and peace be upon him, advised us, in what is known as Ḥadīth Qudsī, "Know that no one with even an atom (*dharrah*) of pride shall enter the Garden of Paradise."

This saying frightens me deeply. Pride is so subtle. Thus, in imagining possible spheres, I prefer to take care of pride and hubris by working in a milieu where I find it is just barely possible that one might succeed in one's efforts to work goodness. For my own self, as I have tried to make clear, this means working goodness toward my own self, toward my family and toward my neighbours.

Beyond that is both the immediate and wider community in which I live and work. This includes, because I am also a teacher, a wider faith community in which I also include those people of good will with whom open dialogue is possible. Beyond that, I don't know. At night I walk in the fields and look at the stars. Now, at the time of the new moon, the sky is dark. The stars blaze forth fiercely against deep velvet. The world is filled with people. Like the stars, who can count them but Allāh?

Lao-Tzu put it this way: "No need to leave your door to know the whole world. No need to peer through your windows to know the Way of Heaven. Therefore the wise one knows without going, names without seeing and completes without doing." (Tao 47)

﴿ يَـٰٓأَيَّتُهَا ٱلنَّفْسُ ٱلْمُطْمَئِنَّةُ ۚ
ٱرْجِعِىٓ إِلَىٰ رَبِّكِ رَاضِيَةً مَّرْضِيَّةً ۚ
فَٱدْخُلِى فِى عِبَـٰدِى ۚ وَ ٱدْخُلِى جَنَّتِى ﴾

YAĀĀ'AYATUHĀ-N-NAFSU-L-MUṬMA'INNAH •
'IRJPIĪĪ 'ILĀ RABBIKI RĀDIYATAM-MARDIYYAH •
FA-DKhULĪ FI 'IBĀDI • WA-DKhULĪ JANNATĪ

Oh you whose self is become at peace
return to your Lord pleased and well pleasing.
So enter with my worshippers — enter My Garden.
(al-Fajr 89:28-30)

There are some who find it a bit "other worldly" when we say that Allāh has told us that we were created solely for the purpose of worship, and there are others who understand it just as it is, for true worship has no limit and no bounds.

﴿ وَ مَا خَلَقْتُ ٱلْجِنَّ وَ ٱلْإِنسَ إِلَّا لِيَعْبُدُونِ ﴾

WA MĀ KhALAQåTU-L-JINNA WA-L-'INSA 'ILLA LI-YA'BUDŪN •

I have not created the Jinn or People except that they worship Me
(adh-Dhāriyāt 51:56)

So far as to "how" we are to continue our "dialogue," I would suggest we get out of our talking shops and spend our time vying with one another in good works and leave it to Allāh to judge on the basis of "whoever surrenders his whole self to Allāh and is sincere, his reward is with his Lord, no fear shall be upon him nor shall he be grieved."(Q2:112) Surely this is not far off the order, "Thou shalt love the Lord your God with all your heart and with all your soul and with all your mind. This is the great and first commandment. And a second is like it, You shall love your neighbour as your self. On these two commandments depend all the law and the prophets." Matthew 23:34

The Prophet, blessings of Allāh and peace be upon him, said, "No one can be called a believer who eats his fill while his neighbour remains hungry by his side" and reminded us, "When you make soup add some more water remembering your neighbours." It really isn't all that complicated. And in that bowl of soup I find my end.

By way of closing I would like to share the following ʾāyat as I have found it to be of great meaning in my own attempt to understand how to proceed in life. Perhaps you, dear reader, will also find it useful:

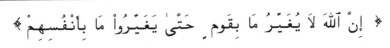

> ʾINNA-LLĀHA LĀ YUGhAYYIRU MĀ BI-QŌWMI
> ḤATTA YUGhAYYIRŬ MĀ BI-ʾANFUSIHIM •
>
> Allāh does not change what is in a people
> until they change what is in them selves.
> (ar-Raʿad 13:11)

I thank Allāh for allowing me an opportunity to speak to you, the reader, through these words. I hope my words have helped and not hurt. Any mistakes you may find are my own and I apologise for them.

و الله أعلم

and Allāh Knows best

NOTES

[1] The letter 'Q' refers to the Qurʾān. The chapter number precedes the verse number as, for example, in (Q1:7). Where the Arabic is present I use the name of Sūrah (Chapter) before the number of the chapter and the verse. as in (ar-Raʿad 13:11).

[2] Over thirteeen hundred verses out of 6,247 verses or in nearly one fifth of the Qurʾān refer to previous Prophets and Messengers, peace be upon them all. The Prophet Muḥammad, peace and blessings be upon him, is referred to by name in only four verses.

[3] Beginning in 1800's with Geiger and Hirschfield and continuing into the late 1900's with Wansborough and/or even Neuwirth.

[4] *Christianity and the World Religions,* Hans Küng et. al., Doubleday Day & Co., Garden City, NY 1986, see Chapter Four, Islam and the Other Religions: Jesus in the Qurʾan, Josef van Ess: Islamic Perspecitives.

PART III

ISSUES

10

ISLAM AND THE CHALLENGES OF CONTEMPORARY LIFE

Habibur Rahman Khan

WE LIVE IN TIMES whose potentials, achievements, perceptions, and violations are at complete odds with each other. There is a vast amount of hunger and equally vast resources and potential to feed the hungry. Never in history has humanity enjoyed such opportunities to educate everyone for individual fulfillment and salvation and yet millions and millions go uneducated and have no opportunity to use any part of the human collective resources. There are innumerable struggles and killings whose rationale fails to a reasonable mind. There are many opportunities and means for the modern world to right these wrongs, yet people seem to look on them as if it is no one's business. We have enough knowledge to reject discrimination based on color, creed, sex and religion and yet vast numbers of Muslims around the world are targets of aggression, coercion and genocide, all because Islam is perceived as the new enemy in place of communism and socialism. But it is not merely the problems of the Islamic World alone which bring us together.

People of faith around the world, particularly of the house of Abraham, have much in common, but short-sighted greed for worldly gain has prevented their faiths from playing their true role in bringing about peace, human cohesion and the opportunity for individual fulfilment and salvation. The modern secularized world has realized that neither modern tools and gadgetry nor manuals of competent administration can remove the world's misery in the midst of plenty.

Humanity needs a new relationship with the Creator and the creation, and a moral dimension for performance which transcends the differences built on greed, color, and differentiated creeds. I am convinced that this gathering must define its role in that large perspective that the modern world, already changed into a global village, presents. The first step is that we must be true and straightforward between ourselves. Contemporary religious leadership has often played politics and has not attempted to remove the cobwebs of willful ignorance about the real teachings of each other's faith. Such efforts could remove or at least reduce the barriers of mutual misunderstanding which stand in the way of peace, amity and mutual respect. A vast amount of media material has, for example, portrayed the teachings of Islam as the real reason for what is identified as the poor lot of women in the Muslim world. Any fair reading of the Bible and the Qur'an would not support such a proposition. Then why does this perception persist in the West?

But I am not here to pick quarrels about what has been done in the past. I am here to jointly thank Allah or God (by whatever name we call Him) for what has already been achieved the world over. We must, however, share guilt for what has not been achieved when we have the means for doing more. Several factors can be identified. One significant reason is the modern western world's commitment to power and its advantages. Those who wield power feel convinced that their power is living proof of their wisdom and superiority. Their political slogans reflect their superior wisdom. The church, I must regretfully add, has not played the role it could have played. It has acted as a handmaid of western imperialism. The single indisputable objective in the social field of all religions is that truth, morality and law should prevail over power. This should be so under all conditions.

Christianity and Islam are the two largest religions of the world. Amity between them should save us many Bosnias, Chechniyas, Palestines and Kashmirs. It is not my purpose to recount and extol the excellence of the teachings of Islam. Rather, I must confess that notwithstanding Islam's teachings giving an honored status to the progeny of Adam and guaranteeing freedom, opportunity, fulfilment and salvation to every Muslim, male or female, much can be found in the traditional religious literature of the Muslim world which states the contrary. The same is true for other world faiths. The tragic aspect of modern times is that most women in the West have come to believe that most of the gains of their sex in property rights, voting rights, right of divorce, of work, of participation in all spheres of life is the direct result of secularization, their having freed themselves from the stranglehold of the church. Even the current debate over living together outside marriage, of the legitimacy of children born out of wedlock, and the right of abortion seem to have pitched women and people who support them against the church. The same approach is being recommended to the Third World. This is totally unnecessary because property rights, the right to work and earn, and retain property belong to women from the inception of Islam. The right to choose a spouse and to divorce if the marriage does not prosper are also there. The right to education and participation in economic, social and political affairs have been guaranteed to Muslim women by Shariat law from its inception.

But rights identified in the Christian West as achievements obtained in protest against established religion have created massive problems in the West. The search for freedom and equality has doubtless given women a new social face but has added countless problems to their lives. On the new terms of equality, women are expected to play a role similar to that of men. The first demand is that she complement the family income economically. The result is that she now must do a full day's work to become entitled to an equal wage and yet undertake all the household chores as before. Gone are the privileges of womanhood and some of the major protections. Running a family has become a big burden. The desire to escape carrying the burdens of others has deprived every family unit of the help, company and solace of loved ones. Bringing up children and facing the work of running a household singlehandedly is a problem that those who live in the West know well. The psychological devastation that children suffer under this system and the stressful life that a man and woman endure without help is a special problem of modern times. Because under the new law of inheritance accepted by the West, the man and wife must share equally the common property on divorce, men who can afford marriage often avoid it. The new rules of the game are such that a woman has to sleep with many men before she can land a husband. A genuine opportunity for marriage is just not there for many. Sex without responsibility and outside marriage has left women vulnerable and devastated, and it is women who have to carry most of the burden of single-parent families, a situation which further aggravates the existing problem. The problems for Muslim women, however, have arisen for different reasons and require different handling.

It is a matter of fundamental importance that sex without moral responsibility receive severe social disapproval. It is also essential that the family as the basic unit wherein the woman is the center of the whole micro-organization must be restored. People must be reminded that the order of nature is such that a human being must first receive life, nurture, education, training, tools and capital to become productive and free. Then we must likewise play our roles by providing these elements free to others, primarily to our own progeny but also to others. Parents must nurture by their children as they were nurtured by their parents two or three decades earlier. People must be made to realize that the stage of the world is not merely a bazaar for exchange, but a place wherein important relationships which provide meaning to human life must be nurtured in a frame of correct relationship with the Creator and the world around us. The woman in a family in the role of the mother or of wife is crucial to the establishment and continuance of all relationships based on love. These must be restored. Humanity is suffering because love is wrongly identified only with sexual pleasure and all the important relationships which make for the happiness of mankind are emptied of this component. The Qur'an says that God has placed love and compassion between a man and his mate (Q 21/30) and made each like clothes to the other. Clothes are, as we know, a source of warmth, protection and beauty to the body. Such should be the lives of spouses. The Qur'an says that men have rights over the women and women have right over the men, but the obligations of the men are greater (Q 34/4). A hadith says that Paradise is under the feet of the mother. Another hadith of the Prophet (P.B.U.H.) further says that the best among you are those who are kind to women folk. The Qur'an speaks of two women—the wife of Pharaoh who nurtured Moses, and Mary the mother of the Christ—as examples of virtue for all those who believe in God.

The rat race in which modern humanity is involved does not yet recognize the limits of loveless sex and lust. Young people indulge in it as a numbers game without noticing the scars that the human personality and especially the female personality suffers on this account. Such an approach of the sexes to each other has to be unlearned. It has been firmly rejected by Islam and Christianity. The affection which leads a person to hold the hand of the other can and must build a chain of friendship, affection, equal honor, fulfilment and salvation around the world, and the key role is to be performed by women.

Notwithstanding the vast technology and knowledge of material things, humanity has unfortunately overlooked some very significant dimensions of human life. Harmony must be cultivated by realizing its radical significance in the achievement of human development and salvation. We are trustees of vast powers, but on the other hand, the realization of the responsibilities to harmonize our efforts with the universal requirement of harmony is largely absent. What environmentalists speak about is part of this development, and this harmony can be achieved only if the family unit is given due importance as the cradle for the development of personalities who know how to give and share with grace and compassion, who recognize each other's rights even when resources are scarce. The meaning of good government in this context would be a government searching for human bonding and harmony. Governments have attempted to play God and have failed. Socialism claimed that it could do so and, as a result, humanity suffered this barren experiment for seventy years. Capitalism survived because it was intellectually humbler about the role of governments. Unfortunately, in the new world order, capitalism, in cooperation with political and military power, is pressing for an arrangement of affairs which would assure the absolute domination of power and wealth. This will not do. This could not be done in the past and it cannot be done in the future. The State and the capitalist monopolies just do not have the stuff in them with which mutual respect, human bonding and sense of belonging are built. The world has run terribly short of the humility and humanity which enables us to respect others.

If the family and blood relationships are to be re-integrated in the reconstruction of human society, then some radical thinking is required of the religious leadership of the Muslim-Christian world.

Apart from the different roots of problems for Christian womanhood and Muslim womanhood, there are some totally new factors:

1. The new technological revolutions have rendered male strength and strength-related stamina obsolete. Similarly, the task of defense of family and larger social groups has been taken over by the society.
2. The changing pattern of instruction and education has put these tasks progressively in female hands. A change is taking place in the intellectual leadership of mankind. In the fields of health, medicine and teaching, labor is dominated by women.
3. In the new technology of media communication, electronics, and

entertainment, female employment is greater than ever before.

4. The new pattern of employment, coupled with other factors mentioned above, is going to radically affect the social structure, power structure and particularly the family. How this issue is to be resolved is a question which requires a concerned re-consideration.

Male aggressiveness and recklessness must be tamed. The significance of the male in the emerging world of a global village has undergone a change already. If he is no longer the sole bread-winner, the defender and the educator, his role has already changed. Attempts to revive the *status quo* will not do.

Development of a culture capable of accepting variety and diversity, of sharing of knowledge, of producing good things of life, and above all, of upholding peace as a prime value is not only the task of Christian and Muslim communities but of all communities that share a theistic perception of the universe, a conviction that morality and law stand above power, and that life and the earth are Divine gifts to all humankind.

11

ORIENTALISM AND THE STUDY OF EACH OTHER:

THE STORY OF GEOFFREY PARRINDER

Martin Forward

IN RECENT YEARS, many western scholars of Islam have been accused of being orientalists. The English comparative religionist Geoffrey Parrinder (b. 1910) has written extensively enough on Islam for the question to be asked whether he can meaningfully be deemed to be among their number. As well as sections in his thematic works, and occasional references in several more publications, he has written a major book on *Jesus in the Qur'an* (1965, reprinted 1976 and 1995). He wrote about Islam as one of *Africa's Three Religions* (1976; a reprint of his *Religions in Africa* [1969]). He has written a number of articles about Islam in West Africa and general reviews of Islam or aspects of that religion in other books.[1]

This essay defines an orientalist and investigates whether Parrinder is to be accounted among them.

The Nature of an Orientalist

The *Oxford English Dictionary* records that the first use of the word "orientalist" was about 1780. It meant a student of the orient. "Orientalism," the study of the East, dates back to 1812.

In more recent decades, particularly during the last twenty years, "orientalism" and its other grammatical forms have been used in an unfavorable sense, mainly of western scholars of Islam. They stand condemned of writing condescendingly about the orient, and of being involved as agents of imperialism to bring about its denigration and the destruction of many of its religions and cultures. So, for example, Abdallah Laroui defined "orientalist" as "a foreigner—this case a westerner—who takes Islam as the subject of his research," and continued:

> We find in the Orientalists' work an ideological (in the crudest sense of the word) critique of Islamic culture. The result of great intellectual effort is for the most part valueless. . . .The caste of Orientalists constitutes part of the bureaucracy and, for this reason, suffers from limitations that badly inhibit the free creation of new approaches or even the application of those that already exist.[2]

The most scathing critique of orientalism in recent years has been that of Edward Said, by birth a Palestinian Christian, now an American citizen and a secularist. In his influential book *Orientalism*, he described and condemned the phenomenon in three long chapters: "The Scope of Orientalism"; "Orientalist Structures and Restructures"; and, "Orientalism Now."[3] Said's basic point, passionately made, is that "modern orientalism," from the eighteenth century onwards, has created a stereotype of the gullible, untruthful, illogical, misogynistic, sexually insatiable, cruel and untrustworthy "oriental" male, and of the passive female. According to Said:

> The principal dogmas of Orientalism exist in their purest form today in studies of the Arabs and Islam. Let us recapitulate them here: one is the absolute and systematic difference between the West, which is rational, developed, humane, superior, and the Orient, which is aberrant, undeveloped, inferior. Another dogma is that abstractions about the Orient, particularly those based on texts representing a "classical" Oriental civilization, are always preferable to direct evidence drawn from modern Oriental realities. A third dogma is that the Orient is eternal, uniform, and incapable of defining itself; therefore it is assumed that a highly

generalized and systematic vocabulary for describing the Orient from a Western standpoint is inevitable and even scientifically "objective." A fourth dogma is that the Orient is at bottom something either to be feared (the Yellow peril, the Mongol hordes, the brown dominions) or to be controlled (by pacification, research and development, outright occupation wherever possible).[4]

In a series of later works, Said has extended and illustrated these basic points. His book *Covering Islam*, with its sub-title "How the Media and the Experts Determine How We See the Rest of the World," emphasizes that his chief concern is with the West's attitude to Islam.[5]

Yet Said has an inadequate historical perspective on the relations between Islam and the West. William Montgomery Watt, "one of the last living and best-known traditional orientalists,"[6] has shrewdly observed that Said realizes some of the important differences between nineteenth-century stereotypes and earlier ones, but:

there is one central question which he omits. How can it be that previous European perceptions of the Muslim as a warrior spreading his faith by violence and the sword was transformed into a perception of the Oriental as a pusillanimous, weak and ineffectual person. It would surely be better to see the nineteenth century perception of the Oriental as something new which became possible after the western European powers had ceased to regard the Ottoman Empire as a military threat.[7]

If Said, a literary scholar, is no historian, neither is he a religionist. He is ignorant of much that is central to Islam. One example is that Said condemns Sir Hamilton Gibb, whom he calls "the greatest name in modern Anglo-American Islamic studies" for "his assertion that the Islamic master science is law, which early on replaced theology." In Said's view, this was an assertion "made about Islam, not on the basis of evidence internal to Islam, but rather on the basis of a logic deliberately outside Islam."[8] Yet Gibb was right. He was intent upon correcting impressions of European students who conformed Islam's central concerns to Christianity's.[9] Moreover, Said is also uninformed about the religion of his birth, especially the reasons for its troubled relations with Islam. For example, he condemns Dante (1265-1321) for putting, in his *The Divine Comedy*, Muslims, Avicenna, Averroës and Saladin into the Inferno along with pre-Christian virtuous heathens: "Even though the Koran specifies Jesus as a prophet, Dante chooses to consider the great Muslim philosophers and king as having been fundamentally ignorant of Christianity."[10] Whatever Dante's motives, Said does not appear to understand that qur'anic definitions of prophecy hardly align with Christian ones. Muslims who rely upon the Qur'an for their information about Jesus remain fundamentally ignorant of Christianity; and an implication of Said's thesis is that interpreting others from one's own perspective is destructive and dehumanising. Moreover, Saladin (properly Salāh al-Dīn, 1138-1193) was not a philosopher, and to call him king is (ironically, given Said's thesis) rather a western designation to describe his authority as a Muslim political ruler.

In one of his most recent books, *Culture and Imperialism* (1993), Said's polemical skills are turned upon literary and musical figures. He protests too much. For example, in his dissection of Verdi's opera *Aida* as a "hybrid, radically impure work that belongs equally to the history of culture and the historical experience of overseas domination,"[11] it is easy to lose sight of Verdi the humanist and freedom-fighter, as well as the paid entertainer. To be sure, *Aida* has an exotic location in ancient Egypt, but it explores issues of love, patriotism and parental manipulation that are universally relevant. To seek to establish it as an orientalist work is to miss the point. Ironically, Said misinterprets because he is obsessed by his own agenda, just as he believes orientalists to be.

The former Pakistani diplomat, now Cambridge don, Akbar Ahmed, points out that:

> However powerfully Said argues his case, the work of the older orientalists was marked by many positive features. These included a lifetime's scholarship, a majestic command of languages, a wide vision and breadth of learning and an association with the established universities.

Akbar Ahmed is right to point out that "Said's Arab passion may have ultimately damaged his own cause. The *rite de passage*, the ritual slaying of the elders. . ., has been too noisy and too bloody."[12] Nevertheless, Said's polemics have served to remind his readers of the intricate and compromised relationships between the western world and Islam. Unfortunately, they have also encouraged Muslims to dismiss as "Orientalism" the critiques of aspects of Islam by westerners. Orientalists write as outsiders and from particular perspectives, but that does not mean that their views are necessarily unconstructive and that they write nothing that Muslims could profit by reading.

Parrinder has written in ignorance of the debate about "orientalism" or, at least, has disregarded it. His two chapters on Islam in his anecdotal book *Encountering World Religions* do not mention it at all, although it had become an important issue between Muslims and Christians when he wrote his book. Yet its major concerns interrogate his works on Islam. Does he describe only a western and Christian perspective on Islam? Does he despise what he describes? We shall look particularly at *Jesus in the Qur'an* and ask whether he could fruitfully have examined another range of issues between Muslims and Christians.

Parrinder's first encounter with Islam was in French West Africa, Dahomey and then Ivory Coast. It therefore makes little grammatical sense to call Parrinder an "orientalist." Because most western academics have engaged with Muslims either in the Middle East or South Asia, the term "orientalist" has made a certain sense. But Parrinder's geographical setting as a missionary and then teacher in West Africa (most of 1933 through 1957) illustrates the term's parochialism, given that Islam and Christianity are worldwide religions.

Jesus in the Qur'an

In Ibadan, Parrinder had some contact with the Ahmadiyya, a heterodox Islamic group founded in north India by Mīrzā Ghulām Ahmad (c.1836-1908). Ahmad had declared that Jesus had not died on the cross but was rescued by his disciples and went to Kashmir. He died and was buried there. Ahmad proclaimed that he himself was the spirit and power of Jesus. The Ahmadiyya accept him as messiah and mahdī ("the one who is rightly guided"), contrary to the orthodox Islamic view that Jesus is the messiah and Muhammad the last and greatest of the prophets. Writing in 1959 about their presence in Nigeria as a whole, Parrinder observed that the Ahmadiyya

> have become exceedingly active in literature, education and propaganda, claiming converts among Christians as well as among animists. . . .In Lagos they print literature and journals, and a weekly column every Friday in the chief English newspaper (the "Daily Times," with a daily circulation of over 80,000), is written by the chief Imam of the Ahmadiyya, and often contains anti-Christian propaganda, intended for literates.[13]

Parrinder was aware that the Ahmadiyya was not a large group. In 1953 in *Religion in an African City*, he wrote that they had only a small mosque which could not hold more than 100 people. Many years later in 1971, he estimated that there were only about 30,000 in West Africa as a whole. Nevertheless, it is reasonable to suppose that his interest in Jesus as the Qur'an presents him dates from his awareness of Ahmadiyya propaganda. Their agenda, that Jesus did not die, is one that he deals with and attempts to refute on the basis of qur'anic teaching.

Here we meet Parrinder the Christian missiologist and theologian, in this instance intent upon righting false information as well as mistaken perceptions about the founder of Christianity. He wrote that his interest in *Jesus in the Qur'an* "is chiefly theological." Thus, his major readership was western Christians, but he recognised that by the time he wrote (the book was first published in 1965), authors could hope for "a world audience." For this reason, he adopted Watt's device of avoiding the question of the authorship of the Qur'an by writing "the Qur'an says" rather than "God says" or "Muhammad says."[14]

Parrinder seems to have had two aims in writing the book. The first was irenical, making positive comparisons and links between Islam and Christianity. He wrote that:

There are differences between the Muslim and Christian apprehensions of God, but it would be fatal to any chance of understanding to doubt that one and the same God is the reality in both.

His second aim in writing, as the above quotation makes clear, was to aid understanding. He chose a particularly difficult topic, the long-standing, complex and destructive problem between Christians and Muslims of the person and works of Jesus Christ. Parrinder wrote that "it is to encourage study, self-examination, dialogue and searching the scriptures that this book has been written."[15]

The book is a thorough account of the qur'anic material about Jesus. Every reference there to him, his titles, and people associated with him are described. The book has 17 chapters. The introduction is followed by three chapters on the names of Jesus: "Jesus" and "Son of Mary" have a chapter each; and a third looks at other titles ascribed to him in the Qur'an. There are two chapters on "Zachariah and John" and "Mary." There is one on "The Annunciation" and another on "The Birth of Jesus." A chapter follows on "Works of Jesus" and another on "Words of Jesus." Then there is one on "The Death of Jesus" and another on "Jesus and the Future." The title "Son of God" has a chapter, then there is another on "Trinity." There is one on "Gospel" and another on "Christians." Then there is a "Conclusion" followed by a "General Index," "Quranic Index" and "Biblical Index."

Jesus in the Qur'an has proved an invaluable resource, so much so that it is to be reprinted by a third publisher in May 1995.[16] In order to both illustrate the measure of his achievement and also prepare the ground for some criticisms of the assumptions which lie behind his work, we shall examine his account of the death of Jesus.[17] This has been a particularly important area of dispute between orthodox Muslims, the Ahmadiyya and Christians.

Many Muslims believe that Jesus did not die, but was taken up by God and will return as a sign of the last day. However, Parrinder argued that the weight of the Qur'an, as opposed to many interpretations of it, is in favor of a real death. For example, the Meccan sūra 19:34/33: "Peace is upon me [Jesus], the day of my birth and the day of my death," indicates that Jesus died and that his raising up is at the general resurrection of all people when the world ends. Jesus's return to God is mentioned to in sūras 3:48/55 and 5:117, which most naturally refer to his death. Parrinder pointed out that the Arabic word *mutawaffīka*, used in these passages of Jesus, is used of people dying in sūra 2:241/240, and, in sūra 6:60, of believers being called to God in the night, raised up to complete an appointed term and returning to him.

The most contentious passage between Muslims and Christians about Jesus is sūra 4:156/157, which most Muslims see as a denial of the crucifixion. This in turn has led them to interpret 3:48/55 against its natural sense, to mean that Jesus did not die. Sūra 4:156/157 comes in a section (4:154-157/155-159) which he quotes in full:

> So for their [the Jews'] violating their compact, and for their unbelief in the signs of God, their killing the prophets without justification, and for their unbelief, and their speaking against Mary a mighty slander; and for their saying: "We killed the Messiah, Jesus the Son of Mary, the messenger of God," though they did not kill him, and did not crucify him, but he was counterfeited for them; verily those who have gone in different ways in regard to him are in doubt about him; they have no (revealed) knowledge of him and only follow opinion; though they did not certainly kill him. Nay, God raised him to himself. God is sublime, wise. And there is no People of the Book but will surely believe in him before his death, and on the day of resurrection, he will be regarding them a witness.[18]

Parrinder pointed out that the most widely held view among Muslims about this passage is that the Jews tried to kill Jesus but were unable to do so. This led him to examine two questions: did Jesus really die on the cross?; was there a substitute who suffered in his place? The canonical gospels affirm the first and have no suggestion of the second. Many Muslims, however, deny the first and affirm the second; they have slender support, so Parrinder contended, in the teaching of the second century CE Egyptian gnostic and Christian Basilides, whose views survive only in rather diverse interpretations by his opponents. The idea of a substitute, perhaps Judas Iscariot or Simon Cyrene, has been accepted by some notable Muslim commentators of the Qur'an. For example, Tabarī (d. 923) believed a Jewish chief called Joshua, whom God gave the form and appearance of Jesus, died in his place.[19] However, the passage hardly demands this interpretation, which does not seem its obvious import. The Arabic *shubbiha la-hum* (which is even more difficult to translate than Parrinder suggested) is rendered by Bell into English as "he [Jesus] was counterfeited for them." Louis Massignon offered "it [the crucifixion] appeared to them as such," a translation which Parrinder preferred. It is certainly possible that the Arabic words mentioned should be attached to the crucifixion and not Jesus. Then the meaning of a very difficult passage could be that the Jews did not kill Jesus rather than that he did not die.

It remains, however, a controversial and widely-interpreted passage. The Indian modernist Sir Saiyid Ahmad Khan (1817-98) believed that after three or four hours Jesus was taken down from the cross by the disciples and kept in a secret place, for fear of the Jews. Parrinder noted that this led to the Ahmadiyya view that Jesus eventually went to Kashmir and died there. Another view has been expressed by the Egyptian surgeon and educationalist, Kamel Hussein. In his book *Qaryah Zālimah*, translated by Kenneth Cragg as *City of Wrong*, he focussed on the events leading to Good Friday. This is a sensitive and moving account of the influence of Jesus upon a number of the participants involved in his arrest and condemnation, whether they be (to use the titles of three sections of the book) "In Jewry," "With the Disciples," or "Among the Romans." Yet in the final section, "Golgotha and After," the author (naturally, since he was a Muslim) reaffirmed the traditional Islamic belief that Jesus was not crucified. One of his characters, the Wise Man, observes:

There is one thing about the events of this day of which I am aware which you do not know. It is that God has raised the Lord Christ to Himself. He was the light of God upon the earth. The people of Jerusalem would have nothing to do with him except to extinguish the light. Whereupon God has darkened the world around them. This darkness is a sign from God to show that God has forbidden them the light of faith and the guidance of conscience.[20]

The author informed his translator that:

No cultured Muslim believes. . . nowadays [that someone substituted for Jesus on the cross]. The text is taken to mean that the Jews thought they killed Christ but God raised him unto Him in a way we can leave unexplained among the several mysteries which we have taken for granted on faith alone.[21]

Parrinder observed that "the significance of the cross Dr. Hussein sees to be in that men did crucify Jesus in intention, all their actions were bent towards it, and they utterly rejected the Christ of God." Parrinder had had

long discussions with Dr. Kamel Hussein. . . who took time off from a busy medical life to talk about problems of deep religious importance. The assurance that this book could be useful, and was not offensive to modern Muslims, encouraged the writer in final revisions and publication of a matter that had long been on his mind.[22]

It may not be offensive, but, for all its usefulness as a reference work, it perpetuates the mistaken apprehension that Christian relations with Muslims can be built upon the shared figure of Jesus.

In *Jesus in the Qur'an*, Parrinder noted some important facts about the qur'anic views of Jesus which show his importance to Muslims:

The Qur'an gives a greater number of honourable titles to Jesus than to any other figure of the past. . . .Three chapters or sūras of the Qur'an are named after references to Jesus (3, 5 and 19); he is mentioned in fifteen sūras and ninety-three verses.[23]

However, this evidence could be looked at from a different perspective. For example, over 6,000 verses of the Qur'an do not mention Jesus. A comparatively unimportant figure, Aiyūb or Job, is mentioned in over 200 verses. Certainly, Jesus is greatly honored, but Ibrāhīm (Abraham) and Mūsā (Moses) are more important qur'anic figures.

Indeed, if all references to Jesus were deleted from the Qur'an, the religion of Islam would not be significantly different, save in some of its mystical forms.

In fact, Jesus fits into qur'anic categories of what constitutes a prophet, as Islam interprets that concept. In the two religions, Jesus is a common figure, differently understood. Parrinder's comparative methodology has led him to accept too easily the notion that to examine the qur'anic material about Jesus from a Christian perspective might not only be inoffensive to Muslims, but even lead to more positive relations between them and Christians:

> To Christians and to Muslims, to historians and to general readers, this book offers a new study of what the Qur'an says concerning Jesus, together with similar sayings from the Gospel. It is hoped that this account of a matter of great common concern, by going back to the fundamental scriptures, will help to remove some misunderstandings and lead towards deeper appreciation of Muslim and Christian faith.[24]

A particular implication of Parrinder's work is that an informed exegesis of the Qur'an will reform Muslim belief. This aspiration is shared by some Muslim modernists, but has not so far been actualized. If it were, it would require the corpus of traditions about the prophet (the *ahadīth*) to be radically reappraised, because much of the information about, for example, Jesus' death being an appearance rather than an actuality is found in them. Since these traditions are granted by Muslims a revelatory status second only to the Qur'an, such a reappraisal would have to be large scale, and probably at least as convulsive for Muslims as modern biblical criticism has been for Christians.[25] It is arguably improper for an outsider to be a catalyst for such change, even one with the noblest of intentions. If Parrinder's suggested alternatives to traditional Muslim views not only about the death of Jesus but in other areas of qur'anic christology are convincing, then the meaning of the Qur'an has been astonishingly opaque to Muslim people of faith who have studied it with the seriousness of those who believe it to be the exact word of God.

Elsewhere, Parrinder condemned that belief. He wrote that "Christianity is not just tied to a book as 'word' of God, with all the dangers of fundamentalism which that entails, and which Islam must face sooner or later."[26] Why must it? Assuming that recent western intellectual pilgrimages must inevitably be charted by others may be a demonstration of the orientalist mindset. Certainly, Islam shows no signs of conforming to what Parrinder believes appropriate for a modern or perhaps postmodern religion.

In short, Muslims and Christians disagree so widely about Jesus that it is difficult to believe that greater appreciation can come by a textual analysis of the Qur'an. Muslims are committed to a belief that God is the author of the Qur'an.[27] This means that they take for granted the fact that the information in it about Jesus is true. Most Christians believe, on historical, dogmatic or other grounds, that it is largely inaccurate as a statement not just about what they believe, but also about whatever information can be uncovered on the historical Jesus.

Thus, on qur'anic as well as other grounds, Jesus is the focal point of division between the two religions. Christian and Muslim perceptions about him are so different, as are the means of creating those perceptions, that it is difficult to believe that he could ever be other than a divisive figure. This is perhaps harder for Christians to accept than Muslims, because Jesus is central to their faith, and is seen in their scriptures as a decisive and unifying figure for all creation (e.g. Ephesians 1, Hebrews 1), whereas, dogmatically and legally, he is of no importance to the center of Muslim faith. It might be particularly difficult for an ex-missionary like Parrinder to accept the irrelevance of Jesus, the more so when he is committed to the comparative method as leading to appreciation even where there is disagreement. Yet in the case of Jesus, comparing Muslim and Christian beliefs usually creates heat, not light.

That Jesus remains a divisive figure between Christians and Muslims can be illustrated from a relatively recent book review of Neal Robinson's *Christ in Islam and Christianity*. One of its reviewers, Ataullah Siddiqui, is clearly angered by it:

> Although it is useful to have a glimpse into the classical Islamic literature on the subject. . . he does not take the qur'anic Jesus, and for that matter the Qur'an itself, as the authentic expression of Jesus in its own right. He finds many influences, from many quarters, on the Qur'an and therefore on the qur'anic Jesus,. . . . seeing the Qur'an as borrowed material which prevents the qur'anic expression of Jesus being expressed freely.[28]

Robinson, not being a Muslim, is not bound to the historically inaccurate hypothesis that the Qur'an offers "the authentic expression of Jesus in its own right." Siddiqui misses this point. He is also oblivious of the offence Muslims can cause Christians by their appropriation and reappraisal of Jesus on grounds that, to them, seem wholly unconvincing.

Parrinder could perhaps have chosen a better bridgehead for establishing good relations between members of the two religions by exploring Jesus within the mystical traditions of both. He mentioned that "Jesus was taken as the pattern of poverty and the ascetic life" for many Sūfīs, but Sūfīsm is mentioned on only four pages of *Jesus in the Qur'an*.[29] Parrinder is ambivalent about Sūfīs, arguing elsewhere that "many wandered in the deserts of monism," a terrible fate in his estimation.[30]

Instead of exploring Sūfīsm, he could have offered a more innovative and imaginative look at the qur'anic material than he attempts. For example, the crucial passage on the crucifixion berates the Jews for disbelieving in the signs (*āyāt*) of God. The concept of signs is important in the Qur'an: it describes itself as "a book whose *āyāt* have been made distinct" (41:3/2). It would be possible for Muslims and Christians together to explore the focus and meaning of these signs and eventually for Christians to explain that Jesus is for them God's clearest sign of his presence in the world. This would not dissolve the disagreements between Muslims and Christians but it might set the debate within a more fruitful and creative setting than has hitherto been attempted by many scholars.

Otherwise, Parrinder could have proceeded theologically by reflecting on specific implications of the *logos* Christology for Christian-Muslim relationships, not least because this estimation of Jesus's importance has meant so much to him;[31] but of course he was not writing a theological book. Indeed he wrote that

> Although the interest of this book is religious and theological, it makes no claim to be either speculative or dogmatic theology. It has been said that the present time is for ploughing, not reaping, for making soundings, not plotting maps. Yet if the time is not ripe for major works of theological construction or reconstruction, the tools for the work need to be provided.[32]

The book he wrote is a remarkable achievement. As so often when reading Parrinder, one marvels at the breadth of reading, interpreted clearly and helpfully for the non-specialist. Moreover, he certainly achieves his aim of providing non-Muslims and even Muslims uncertain of the details of their faith with the necessary tools for locating the Qur'an's material about Jesus.

Yet, in relation to Islam, the feeling remains that Parrinder's wide reading not only for *Jesus in the Qur'an* but also displayed in his other works on Islam, has not been matched by a depth of personal acquaintance with Muslims themselves; in Africa, he preferred to study various forms of Christianity and primal faiths, and meet their adherents. Nor has his scholarship been met with a corresponding insight into the heart, still less the subtleties of the religion: he often displays sympathy, never empathy.

Parrinder: Orientalist?

In post-colonial or even (bearing in mind Edward Said's Palestinian origins) neo-colonial contexts, the term "orientalist" has served as a depreciatory word to channel the frustration and anger of many "orientals," particularly Muslims, with western condescension and misinterpretation. But it has been imprecisely, provocatively and polemically used, and has undeservedly stained the reputations of many scholars whose writings and criticisms have been imperfectly assessed and who have not been judged against their historical setting. It has also played down the fact that, whatever their failings, the desire of many of these Christian scholars to learn about other faiths has not often been matched by that of members of other faiths to understand what Christians actually believe rather than what is imputed to them.

However, more positively, "orientalism" could be said to define a tendency among certain western scholars to view other cultures and religions, especially Islam, through European and Christian categories. The answer to the question, does Parrinder describe only a western and Christian perspective on Islam (or, indeed, Judaism) is, by and large, yes. He comes at the material from a viewpoint shaped by questions and issues from his Christian convictions. He does not reveal much interest in the issues which Muslims and Jews pose for themselves. However, he does not despise what he describes. He discerns God at work in Islam and Judaism, and is candid and sympathetic about Christian history's terrible record in its dealings with both faiths. This sympathy, but also, perhaps, his lack of linguistic skills and sustained personal contacts with Muslims means that it would be untrue to call Parrinder an "orientalist." If his works on Islam do not demonstrate the remarkable academic achievements of the greatest of them, neither does he display their worst defects. Yet I would end this essay wistfully in the hope that Muslim and Christian scholars will, in future, transcend their communities' common history of mutual fear, ignorance masquerading as knowledge, and misrepresentation. To be sure, there are irreconcilable differences between us, about which God knows best; he will reveal these truths on the Day of Judgement. Meanwhile, can we hope to study each other's traditions with reverence and in the hope that we might achieve not only sympathy but empathy? Surely, present world circumstances not only commend this but command it.

NOTES

1. Geoffrey Parrinder's writings include: E.G. Parrinder, *Religion in an African City* (Oxford: Oxford University Press, 1953); E.G. Parrinder, "Islam and West African Indigenous Religion," *Numen* 6/2 (December 1959), pp. 130-141; E.G. Parrinder, *Avatār and Incarnation* (London: Faber and Faber, 1970); E.G. Parrinder, *Jesus in the Qur'an* (London: Sheldon, 1976); E.G. Parrinder, "Sufism," in G.S. Wakefield (ed.), *A Dictionary of Christian Spirituality* (London: SCM, 1983); E.G. Parrinder, *Encountering World Religions* (Edinburgh: T and T Clark, 1987).
2. See W.M. Watt, *Muslim-Christian Encounters* (London: Routledge, 1991), p. 107, where Abdallah Laroui is cited.
3. Edward Said, *Orientalism* (London: Peregrine, 1985), first published in 1978. See also Edward Said, *Covering Islam* (London: Routledge and Kegan Paul, 1981) and Edward Said, *Culture and Imperialism* (London: Chatto and Windus, 1993).
4. Edward Said, *Orientalism*, *op. cit.*, pp. 300f.
5. Edward Said, *Covering Islam*, *op. cit.*, where the term "experts" is used ironically.
6. A. Ahmed, *Postmodernism and Islam* (London: Routledge, 1992), p. 181.
7. W.M. Watt, *Muslim-Christian Encounters, op. cit.*, p. 109.
8. Edward Said, *Orientalism*, *op. cit.*, pp. 53 and 780.
9. W.M. Watt, *Muslim-Christian Encounters, op. cit.*, p. 110; H.A.R. Gibb, *Mohammedanism* (Oxford: Oxford University Press, 1969 rev. ed.), p. 7.
10. Edward Said, *Orientalism*, *op. cit.*, p. 69.
11. *Ibid.*, p. 147.
12. Akbar Ahmed's book *Postmodernism and Islam* assumes that, in the wake of modernism's passing, it is possible for Islam and the west to engage fruitfully with each other. However, he fails to grapple with the issue of whether Islam, since it has never accepted modernism, can meaningfully be related to postmodernism. His solution, that Islam breathes "the spirit of postmodernism," bypasses too adroitly issues of history and philosophy. The citations are from p. 180.
13. Geoffrey Parrinder, "Islam and West African Indigenous Religion," *op. cit.*, p. 137.

14. Geoffrey Parrinder, *Jesus in the Qur'an, op. cit.*, p. 10. See also W.M. Watt, *Muhammad at Mecca* (Oxford: Clarendon, 1953), p. x.

15. Geoffrey Parrinder, *Jesus in the Qur'an, op. cit.*, p. 173.

16. Geoffrey Parrinder, *Jesus in the Qur'an* was published by Faber and Faber in 1965, then Sheldon Press in 1976. Oneworld published it in May 1995. It has never been revised since it was first written. Parrinder refers to two schemes for versifying the Qur'an. The first is that of Gustav Fluegel (1834), and the second the Cairo edition of 1923. The former is not acceptable to Muslims, but the latter is used widely among them.

17 Geoffrey Parrinder, *Jesus in the Qur'an, op. cit.*, pp. 105-121.

18. Parrinder usually used Richard Bell's two volume translation of the Qur'an. It was first published by T and T Clark, Edinburgh in 1937.

19. Perhaps Tabarī was unaware that Joshua and Jesus are variant forms of the same name in Hebrew.

20. M.K. Hussein, *City of Wrong*, tr. K. Cragg (London: Gordon Bles, 1959), p. 183.

21. *Ibid.*, p. 222.

22. Geoffrey Parrinder, *Jesus in the Qur'an, op. cit.*, p. 14.

23. *Ibid.*, p. 16.

24. *Ibid.*, p. 15.

25. From early in Islamic history, there has been a science of *hadith* criticism, though its methodology (which stresses the integrity of persons who form the chain of transmission, rather than the context and content of the saying) seems unreliable to western and even to some Muslim scholars. In the nineteenth century, the Indian modernist Saiyid Ahmad Khan (1817-1898) applied western critical methods to the traditions of the Prophet Muhammad and deduced that very few were authentic (C.W. Troll, *Sayyid Ahmad Khan* [New Delhi: Vikas, 1978], pp. 138-144). In contemporary times, the Moroccan sociologist Fatima Mernissi (b. 1940) has particularly criticized as unauthentic most of the misogynistic *hadith* (F. Mernissi, *Women and Islam* [Oxford: Blackwell, 1991], pp. 25-81).

26. Geoffrey Parrinder, *Avatār and Incarnation, op. cit.*, p. 65.

27. As far as I am aware, only one Muslim writer, Syed Ameer Ali, has written that Muhammad is the author of the Qur'an. He believed it to be quintessentially Muhammad's moral teaching, but was a poor scholar of both Islam and Arabic (S.A. Ali, *The Spirit of Islam* [London: Chatto and Windus, 1922 rev. ed.], pp. 159-187).

28. A. Siddiqui, Review of *Christ in Islam and Christianity,* by Neal Robinson, in *Islam and Christian Muslim-Relations* 3, June 1992, p. 171.

29. Geoffrey Parrinder, *Jesus in the Qur'an, op. cit.*, p. 165; for his views of Sūfīsm, see pp. 88, 164-169. In a later article on Sūfīsm in *A Dictionary of Christian Spirituality*, Parrinder wrote that "Jesus was often taken as a pattern of mystical life and his poverty was emphasized, with his purity giving him the title 'seal of the saints,'" p. 365.

30. Geoffrey Parrinder, *Avatār and Incarnation, op. cit.*, p. 278.

31. Parrinder does indeed refer to the *logos* in *Jesus in the Qur'an, op. cit.*, pp. 47f. (the section of Jesus as the Word or *kalima*), where he briefly describes the

history of its origins in Hebrew thought, and comments that: "A revival of the use of the Logos-doctrine has been suggested today, as a means of approach to people in other lands to whom the Word of God has clearly been spoken." Yet there he leaves matters, at the point where the reader wants him to elaborate.

32. Geoffrey Parrinder, *Jesus in the Qur'an, op. cit.*, p. 14.

12

THE ROLE OF THE PROPHET MUHAMMAD IN MUSLIM PIETY

Reza Shah-Kazemi

MUSLIMS ARE RARELY referred to any longer as "Muhammadans."
It is now generally known that the religion of Islam is rigorously based
on the worship of God, conceived as the Transcendent Absolute,
supremely exalted above all creation; Muhammad was but a creature,
a "slave"—despite being God's Messenger; being but a man, he cannot
be regarded in the spiritual universe of Islam as an object of worship.
Implicit in the first testimony of Islam—"There is no god but God"—is
that there can be no legitimate object of worship except God. The
position of Muhammad in Islam, then, is in no wise to be equated with
that of Christ in Christianity.

If this altogether fundamental point is appreciated, the non-Muslim
may then be somewhat baffled by the intensity and depth of love
evinced by Muslims for the Prophet: what can explain the extraordinary devotion to his personage, a devotion sustained from generation to
generation down through the ages, expressed outwardly in the most
sublime litanies, hymns and poems from one end of the Muslim world
to the other?[1] How is it that a careful compiler of a handbook of
Muslim devotions, Constance Padwick, could say that the invocation

of blessings on the Prophet "has become an essential, sometimes it would seem the essential of the life of salvation and devotion"?[2]

The appearance of paradox is sharpened for the outside observer when he hears it stressed by Muslims that Islam, in contrast to Christianity, has no priesthood; the Muslim stands in a one-to-one relationship with God; he is, as it were, his own priest and has no need of any human intermediary. It is true that the Qur'an enjoins upon all Muslims the duty of emulating the Prophet and of rendering obedience to him; and it is true that his *Sunnah*, his manners, customs, actions and behavior, constitutes a basic source of Islamic law, subordinate only to the Qur'an itself. But this only partly explains the devotion to the Prophet; for it is one thing to submit to an external rule regarding action, and quite another positively to love the human embodiment of that rule. The Law orders the will, but the Prophet engages the very heart and soul of the Muslim.

One comes closer to a resolution of the paradox by moving from the outward dimension of action to the inner dimension constituted by the character of the Prophet; for his magnanimity is dazzlingly self-evident, and cannot fail to elicit respect, if not veneration, from any impartial observer of his life. It is a magnanimity that in certain respects contrasts with the sublimity of Christ; for it is not the super-human but the integrally human, that is presented by the Prophet; and this, in a manner that combines earthly realism with the very highest moral and spiritual ideals. There is here a beauty of soul, a degree of nobility and an all-encompassing totality that captivates the sentiment, imagination and intelligence of the Muslim, who cannot utter the name of the Prophet without invoking blessings upon him. This invocation derives from a celestial archetype, for according to the Qur'an:

Verily God and His angels overwhelm the Prophet in blessings. . . (XXXIII,56)

The Prophet manifested to perfection the full range of human virtues. Since his actions were carefully observed and later codified, and his sayings were memorized and subsequently recorded, we know more about his life than about that of any other founder of a religion; he therefore stands forth as a timeless ideal concretely actualized in human terms, an ideal to be emulated by all Muslims; for the Qur'an states:

Verily ye have in the Messenger of God a noble exemplar for whoever hopes for God and the Last Day, and remembereth God much. . . (XXXIII,21)

The extraordinary breadth encompassed by the Prophet's life on earth provides the believer with a range of precedents, norms and values that cover practically all conceivable dimensions of life; for he was at once contemplative and combative, an ascetic and a ruler of men, profoundly steeped in the next world while astonishingly success-ful in this. He experienced the loneliness and poverty of an orphan, was first a shepherd and then a merchant; he tasted the bitterness of ostracism, and also the joys and trials of married life—both monog-amous and polygamous; he was simultaneously military commander, religious judge and political statesman, organizing and administering the first Muslim state, seed of a world empire—all of this while never ceasing, as the Qur'an testifies, to devote long hours of each night in prayer:

Thy Lord knoweth that thou keepest vigil sometimes nearly two-thirds of the night, or half or a third. . . (LXXIII,20)

The Prophet is thus a "noble exemplar" not just in respect of what goes by the name of "religion"—narrowly conceived as it is in the West, but also in all aspects of existence. Life, for the Muslim, cannot be rigidly divided into religious and secular spheres, for the whole of one's existence, outward and inward, is rendered susceptible of sancti-fication, in the very measure that it be assimilated to the prophetic ideal.

While it may not be everyone's calling to be a judge or a ruler, it is certainly every Muslim's duty, in all circumstances, to live virtuous-ly in the context of the Shari'ah—the quintessence of which is worship of God; and if these two universal elements—prayer and virtue—are to be realized perfectly, it is to the Prophet's example that one must turn. Both the canonically binding and the supererogatory prayers are derived from his devotional practices, so that in the very act of prayer, the presence of the Prophet is keenly sensed. Similarly, in the practice of the essential virtues—humility, justice, generosity, sincerity, com-passion—the Muslim feels altogether close to the Prophet, the personi-fication *par excellence* of human virtue; as he said of himself: "I was sent to perfect the beautiful character traits."[3]

To imitate piously the Prophet's example, then, is tantamount to following the path to salvation. It should be noted that, in a very important respect, this imitation of Muhammad is quite different from the *imitatio Christi* of the Christian tradition; for the latter essentially involves purification and redemption through empathy with Christ's suffering and passion, while imitation of Muhammad implies participation in the stable equilibrium that is both condition and consequence of total conformity to the divine will: earthly equilibrium for the sake of heavenly ascent, virtuous action with a view to interiorizing contemplation.

But this imitation still cannot exhaustively account for the depth of the devotion to the Prophet; for there is in the soul of the Muslim something in the nature of an ontological affinity with the Prophet: love of the Prophet seems to be part of the very being of the pious Muslim's soul; it is a love that cannot be reduced to the level of sentiment alone. The Prophet is told in the Qur'an: "Verily thou art of a tremendous nature." (LXVIII,4)

Now, in order to appreciate the spiritual dynamics of the Muslim's relationship with the Prophet, it is necessary to make an attempt at understanding something of this "tremendous nature."

The best place to begin is the Qur'an itself; for when 'A'ishah, the Prophet's favorite wife, was asked what kind of character the Prophet possessed, she answered: "Have you not read the Qur'an? . . .Truly the character of the Prophet was the Qur'an."[4]

This points to an important aspect of the relationship between the divine message and the human messenger, between the transcendent content of revelation and its providential container; one who is deemed worthy of receiving and transmitting the message of God must possess a soul that is in total harmony with that message: there must be, not just receptivity to the divine Word, but also a deep affinity with it.

One might even go so far as to say that Muhammad was not great because he was a prophet, but that he was chosen as Prophet because he was great. This somewhat elliptical way of putting things must not, needless to say, obscure the fact that his pre-existing human greatness was raised to altogether cosmic dimensions by virtue of the graces attendant upon receiving the revealed message.

To love the Prophet, then, is to love the human embodiment and reflection of the Qur'an; it is to love that which is in perfect conformity with the highest truths in the holy book; and it is therefore to attract to oneself the graces issuing from these truths. In this light, one can better appreciate the following verse, in which the Prophet is told to proclaim to the believers: "If ye love God, follow me; and God will love you. . ." (III,1)

The Muslim, on the basis of his existing love of God, is told here that God will love him if he "follows" the Prophet; it is because the Prophet is himself *Habīb Allāh*—the beloved of God—that following him truly, with all one's heart, will make the believer himself more lovable unto God. Thus, according to a saying of the Prophet, whoever invokes blessings on the Prophet is given as reward a tenfold blessing from God.[5] In other words, God rewards the Muslim's love of the Prophet by bestowing His blessings upon the soul of the lover, the greatest of these blessings being His own love. This process of ever-deepening and mutually reinforcing love of the Prophet and God, far from being just an abstract theoretical possibility, constitutes a lived reality for truly pious Muslims: neither piety nor *a fortiori* sanctity is conceivable in Islam apart from the love of the Prophet.

To be a saint in Islam is to be a "friend" of God, walī Allāh; and there can be no "friendship" or proximity to God that is not also and at the same time proximity to the Prophet; this is expressed in the verse of the Qur'an which asserts:

Verily, the Prophet is closer to the believers than their own selves. (XXIII,6)

The actual experience of this closeness cannot be fully explained to one standing outside the tradition; it manifests itself in a mysterious way, such that many ordinary believers do not regard the Prophet just as an individual from another age, but as someone whose intimacy is deeply sensed. Another important fact which is commonly encountered within the Islamic tradition and can be easily grasped by religious people anywhere is that love of the Prophet grows deeper the further one advances along the path that leads to God. For the spiritual affinity between the inner being of the Muslim and the perfection of the Prophet is revealed in direct proportion to the deepening of piety, of consciousness of God.

To understand the deeper implications of the above-quoted verse, it is necessary to understand that within each human soul there is a hierarchy of degrees of being and consciousness; and that, at the outset, the outward self of the ordinary believer is far removed from that inner essence that is his true self, the immortal soul in its primordial purity, fashioned in the image of God; the Prophet, on the other hand, is one who has realized to the full this primordial nature, and is thus closer to the believer's essence than the believer himself in his actual state of alienation from his own primordial perfection. In a certain sense, the Prophet is like an exteriorized form of the primordial perfection of the soul, just as this innate perfection is like the Prophet of one's own being, a commonly encountered theme in Sufi speculation and esoteric hermeneutics of the Qur'an.

The Qur'an refers to this primordial nature as the *fitrah* (XXX,30): each soul was made in the "finest stature" (XCV,4), with innate knowledge both of God and of the vocation of man as His vice-regent on earth. This is expressed in the Qur'an by the "Covenant of Alast" at the dawn of time: prior to their birth in the world, God brought forth all the souls from the reins of Adam and asked them: *Am I not your Lord?* To which each soul replied in the affirmative. God then said: *This is lest on the Day of Judgment ye say: of this we had no knowledge.* (VII,172)

Now this positive testimony of the Lordship of God expresses the deepest ontological dimension of each human soul; in its essence, the soul is thus pure receptivity to God, a receptivity that has become clouded by the Fall, but which is always retrievable through the light of faith and the practice of virtue, and which is deepened by contact with the truth and the presence of the sacred. The Prophet is the embodiment of this pure receptivity that remains for most souls but a virtuality; the believer, then, in his quest for God, must re-discover within himself this *fitrah*, compounded of receptivity to God; and he has an awareness—intuitive and for the most part unarticulated—that the Prophet's state of being, his realized perfection, is closer to his own heart than he is himself in his actual state of imperfection. Thus one finds the Prophet saying: *He who has seen me has seen the truth.*[6]

What this signifies, among other possible meanings, is that whoever truly "sees" the Prophet sees his innermost nature, the *fitrah* which is pure knowledge of God, love of God and submission to God; and he likewise knows that within himself resides this same primordial nature which must be realized if he is to perfect his own relationship with God: one cannot "see" or come to know the Truth that is God without having first acquired that faculty of spiritual vision that is proper to the *fitrah*. In other words, restoring to man his primordial perfection is the indispensable condition for coming to know the Truth of the Divine Reality. In developing a relationship with God, there is, therefore, something absolute about the need to regain this primordiality, this inalienable birthright of all, that was realized fully by the Prophet.

This helps to account for that element of absoluteness in the Muslim's devotion to the Prophet; it is as if the pious Muslim knows in the depths of his heart that he loves the Prophet more than his own self, and that this love signifies an orientation towards that which he must himself realize; it is thus a mode of spiritual aspiration towards God, an expression with all one's being of the sincere desire to transcend one's faults and limitations, for the sake of God.

This reveals another of the principal spiritual dynamics engaged in Islam by the love of the Prophet: the inner warfare against the soul. To say that the Muslim is capable of loving the Prophet more than himself is to affirm implicitly the existence of an objective element in the soul that is capable of opposing the soul in its fallen state, mastering it, and, in the last analysis, transcending it. It is to this struggle for victory over oneself that the Prophet referred, after returning from a victorious battle against the disbelievers: *We have returned from the Lesser Holy War to the Greater Holy War.* Upon being asked by his companions what this Greater Holy War (*al-jihād al-akbar*) was, he replied: *The war against the soul.*[7]

The Qur'an likewise refers to the imperative of self-mastery in the following verse:

Whoso feareth the station of his Lord and restraineth his soul from its (base) inclinations, verily the Garden will be his home. (LXXX, 40-41)

This resistance to the soul's lower instincts and predispositions occurs at the stage of spiritual development referred to in the Qur'an as that of the *self-accusing soul* (LXXV,2); this stage marks a certain victory over the naturally fallen state of the soul which *inciteth to evil* (XII,5) in which hardly any trace of moral conscience is to be found. But it is only with the complete restoration of *fitrah* that final victory is attained, and this is the station of the *soul at peace* (LXXXIX,27) *al-nafs al-mutma'innah*—the word *itminān* comprising the combined meanings of serenity and certitude, virtues which, in their plenary nature, sum up the quality of the Prophet's soul.

Every Muslim longs to hear, at death, the words of God addressed to him:

O thou soul at peace
Return to thy Lord, pleased and well-pleasing to Him
Enter thou amongst my slaves
Enter thou my Paradise (LXXXIX, 27-30)

Now, the principal means of returning to God and attaining his good pleasure is at the same time the chief weapon in the war against the soul: that is, prayer, in the widest possible sense. It is this spiritual imperative to give oneself to God in worship that carries with it, as inevitable corollary, the spontaneous outpouring of love for the Prophet Muhammad, whose name means "the praised": he is praised precisely on account of his perfect realization of the whole purpose of creation, which is summed up in the following verse of the Qur'an:

I only created the jinn and mankind so that they might worship Me. (LI,56)

Thus, the spiritual return to God begins with an awareness of a movement of love towards the Prophet; to love God entails a love of the Prophet, for this love manifests, and by that very token helps to actualize, one's own deepest nature, which is not just blind faith but an absolute certitude of God—*imān* in its highest sense. It is for this reason that the Prophet affirmed:

No one has faith in God who has not faith in me.[8]

To have faith in the Prophet is not just to believe his message and to trust in his sincerity; it also involves a moral, psychological and spiritual orientation towards him, not as a redeemer or savior as is the case with the Christian devotion to Christ, but essentially as a "reminder": for the Prophet "re-minds" Muslims of God, that is, his message and his example puts them in mind of God, awakening in them their own innate knowledge of the Truth and their own capacity to respond to the call to salvation. Whereas Christ calls himself "the Truth, the Way and the Life," Muhammad is referred to in the Qur'an as *a witness, a bearer of good news and a warner* (XLVIII,8): he bears witness to the Truth, he conveys the ultimate good news by embodying the Way to Salvation and warns of the folly of turning away from the true Life in God and towards the false life of this world:

The life of this world is naught but sport and play; and verily the abode of the Hereafter, truly that is Life, if they but knew. (XXIX,64)

Whereas Christ is referred to as "true man, true God," Muhammad is the "perfect man" for Muslims in general, but for Sufis in particular.[9] That is, he stands as a moral ideal for all the faithful and the mystical guide for the spiritual seekers; in this latter respect there is a certain opening towards the role of Christ for Christians, but only up to a point: exoterically, Muhammad cannot be given any explicitly divine character, even if he be granted the powers to perform miracles. It is only esoterically that Muhammad is assimilated in terms of his *sirr*, that is, his "secret": his mysterious identity with God; but then, in the Sufi tradition, the realization of this identity is not the exclusive prerogative of the Prophet, but also of all the Prophets and even the saints, the *awliyā'*, those who give themselves up entirely to the spiritual life.

Islam, as noted at the beginning of this chapter, is primarily oriented towards the transcendence of God: before this transcendence all creatures are equally "slaves"; Christianity, on the other hand, is focused on the immanence of God in Christ, to the exclusion of all other creatures who are "sinners." But the difference in perspective narrows, even if it is never abolished, when account is taken of the mystical dimension of Islam; here, the "slavehood" of the Prophet is taken as the ultimate degree of self-effacement, *fanā'*; and when the slave is utterly effaced, God alone remains. This mystical appreciation of the meaning of slavehood finds support in a *hadīth qudsī*, a Divine utterance through the mouth of the Prophet:

> My slave ceaseth not to draw nigh unto Me through devotions of free-will until I love him; and when I love him, I am the Hearing Wherewith he heareth and the Sight Wherewith he seeth and the Hand Wherewith he fighteth and the Foot Wherewith he walketh.[10]

The gap between the perspectives of Islam and Christianity is also narrowed, in ordinary piety, by the intercessionary role accorded to the Prophet: he is regarded as the intercessor *par excellence*, one of his most important titles being precisely *al-shafī'*, the intercessor. Indeed the whole range of names and titles accorded to the Prophet illustrate vividly the extent to which veneration of the Prophet compensates, in a certain manner, for the inaccessibility of the transcendent Absolute; for the Prophet is called, among other things, *Rahīm*, the merciful, *Haqq*, the Truth, *Ra'ūf* the kind—names which pertain in the first instance to God. It is as if the pious imagination were given a certain leeway, within the framework of a rigorously transcendent conception of divine Unity, to identify with a more humanly accessible object of devotion, to fix itself on the immanence of the divine qualities such as they are reflected or refracted by the soul of the Prophet; in this manner, far from diminishing adherence to the Absolute as such, ordinary believers are afforded a more intimate knowledge or "taste" of the transcendent sources of all positive qualities in the divine nature, that is, the names and qualities of God Himself.

The Prophet, then, is at once a source of mystical inspiration, the object of pious veneration, and the model of ethical conduct, combining an other-worldly mystery with the enactment of a full life on earth. In this respect, his role again stands in contrast with that of Christ, the miracle of whose birth and the sublimity of whose actions eclipsed the modalities of his terrestrial existence. If Christ represented the humanization of the divine, the Prophet exemplified the sanctification of all that is integrally human. For all that is legitimately and naturally part of being human must be made holy through a conscious consecration to the divine. Through being the "perfect man" he restores to humanity as such its most profound meaning and purpose, reminding all of what it really means to be human: to worship God with all that one is, body and mind, soul and heart. It means offering up to God the totality of what one is and what one has, in accordance with the words spoken by Abraham in the Qur'an:

> Truly my prayer and my sacrifice, my living and my dying are for God, Lord of all creation. (VI,162)

NOTES

1. The most comprehensive appraisal of the forms taken by this veneration is undoubtedly to be found in Annemarie Schimmel's work, *And Muhammad is His Messenger—The Veneration of the Prophet in Islamic Piety* (Charlotte, SC: University of South Carolina Press, 1995). Here one can find detailed phenomenological descriptions of the celebrations associated with the Prophet, such as his mystical ascent into Heaven—the *mi'rāj*—and his birthday; and also a wide-ranging survey of the prayers, litanies, and poems devoted to him in Muslim piety, as well as the mystical speculations regarding his role.
2. A. Schimmel, *ibid.*, p. 96.
3. Ibn Hanbal, II, 281. See the excellent chapter on the virtues—ethical and spiritual—of the Prophet in F. Schuon, *Understanding Islam* (Bloomington, IN: World Wisdom Books, 1994).
4. Muslim, *Musafirin*, 139.
5. Darimi, XX, 58.
6. Bukhari, Ta'bir, 10.
7. Quoted on page 330 of the finest biography of the Prophet in any western

language, Martin Lings, *Muhammad—His Life Based on the Earliest Sources* (Cambridge, UK: Islamic Texts Society, 1991).

8. Ibn Hanbal, IV,70; V,372; VI,382.

9. For a concise exposition of the Sufi doctrine of *al-Insan al Kamil*—Perfect or Universal Man—see Chapter VI of Titus Burckhardt, *An Introduction to Sufi Doctrine* (Lahore: Ashraf Press, 1959).

10. Quoted in Abu Bakr Siraj ad-Din (Martin Lings), *The Book of Certainty—The Sufi Doctrine of Faith, Vision and Gnosis* (Cambridge, UK: The Islamic Texts Society, 1992), p. 3.

13

CAN THERE BE MUSLIM-CHRISTIAN DIALOGUE CONCERNING JESUS/ISA?

M. Darrol Bryant

I. Introduction

IN THE *GLOBE AND MAIL*, one of Canada's leading newspapers, on April 29, 1995, there was a special report on Islam written by its Middle East Bureau Correspondent, Patrick Martin, entitled "Islam: The Children of Allah." It opened by quoting the Secretary-General of NATO, Willy Claes, saying that "the radical Islamic movement" is "the greatest threat to the West since communism" and asking if NATO should "intervene to prevent it spreading any further." The article then went on to discuss "Islam, The Children of Allah" wholly in terms of some newer "radical" movements within the Muslim world. I found this alarming. This caricature of Islam-as-terrorism is not only inaccurate but also engenders hostility towards Islam. It does not reflect the truth of the Muslim world and its peoples who know that Islam is rooted in peace, that peace that comes from submission to Allah. But the appalling statement by the NATO Secretary-General is unfortunately all too characteristic of Western attitudes towards the great faith and tradition of Islam. It is rooted in a long history of perverse caricature of Islam within Christianity and the West and rests in a pervasive ignorance concerning Islam itself. Such statements only underline the necessity for new understandings of Islam in the West and the importance of inaugurating a new history in the relations of Muslims and Christians.

Something of a possibility of a new history of relations between Muslims and Christians is beginning to emerge in the post-World War II efforts of Muslims and Christians to enter into dialogue with one another. While misunderstanding and religious antagonism still persists and is at the root of many encounters between Muslims and Christians, we have also seen efforts at dialogue between these two communities. In 1989, for example, Stuart Brown edited a volume entitled *Meeting in Faith* that documented twenty years of Muslim-Christian dialogue sponsored by the World Council of Churches.[1] But this movement is still small.

There are a host of important topics that need to be addressed so that Muslims and Christians might better understand one another. These two traditions make up more than fifty percent of the world's religious population, but the relations between the traditions have seldom been positive. And it is imperative, as I have argued elsewhere, that the long history of mutual antagonism between Muslims and Christians, relieved by some wonderful moments of more positive relations, be overcome.[2]

In this essay I focus on an issue that has, surprisingly, not been much addressed in the meetings of Muslims and Christians. This is the issue of Jesus in Islam and Christianity. Indeed, this is a topic which will challenge the very limits of dialogue.

Our topic is fraught with unusual difficulties. Neal Robinson in his study of Christ in Islam and Christianity[3] indicates that this topic has been burdened by polemical—"you are wrong"—and apologetic—"I am right"—attitudes over the thirteen centuries of Christian-Muslim relations. Christians have impugned the Qur'an and its Prophet and disputed its portrait of Jesus, while Muslims have repeatedly charged that Christians betray the Oneness of God. And so there have been dramatic fireworks of antagonism between Muslims and Christians on this issue, but little of the warm glow of understanding between these "People of the Book."

Before turning to our topic, it is necessary to make clear something of the nature of interfaith encounter and dialogue.[4]

The possibility of a new meeting of Muslims and Christian will depend on our ability to meet in dialogue rather than debate. It will require a spirit of mutual openness and respect rather than one of defensiveness. It will require a willingness to hear each other as each bears witness to the experience of God in their own terms. Interfaith dialogue is a new, post World War II possibility/development in the history of relations between people of different faiths. The purpose of dialogue in the meeting of men and women of different faiths is mutual respect and understanding.[5] This principle must be clearly understood. The point is that in our dialogue, we should not make our first concern to prove that the Christian view of Jesus is the right one and that the Muslim view of Isa is wrong, or that the Muslim view is right and the Christian wrong. Our first task is to hear one another aright, to listen long and deeply. It is this listening that will allow us to move towards mutual understanding of one another's faith. In the encounter and dialogue between Islam and Christianity, there are many different things that will emerge. Sometimes that dialogue may lead to mutual agreement but at other times it may result in a deepened awareness of profound differences. In focusing on Jesus, we are entering an area of dialogue that will probably not lead to mutual agreement, since this is a matter on which there is a profound and probably unbridgeable difference. But, hopefully, it will issue in some increase in mutual understanding and erase some of the misunderstandings on this issue that too much cloud Muslim-Christian relations.

With these preliminary remarks, then, let me turn to our topic. And in doing so, I want to place over my discussion these words from the Holy Qur'an:

> Say: "O People of the Book! Come now to a word common between us and you, that we worship none but God, and that we associate no others with Him, and that some of us do not take others as lords, apart from God." (Surah 3:64)[6]

II. Jesus in Christianity

II. A. The Scriptures

Let me begin with Jesus in Christianity. This account will necessarily be brief and schematic given the limitations of space. But we want to look at Jesus in the Christian Scriptures, in early Christian literature, and in the Ecumenical Creeds.

The Christian Scriptures are not contemporaneous with the life and ministry of Jesus. They were written after Jesus' life, ministry, death and resurrection. The earliest books of the New Testament were the writings of Paul, followed by the Gospels. But these writings contained the conviction that was central to the early Christian community, namely, that Jesus was the Messiah, the "anointed of God." The term "messiah" means, in Hebrew, "anointed" and is the equivalent of the Greek "Christos." In the Jewish tradition, there were a variety of beliefs that surrounded the term "Messiah." The most common was to link the "Messiah" to a restoration of the Davidic kingship[7] Contemporary biblical scholarship points out that Jesus does not, in the synoptic gospels, use this word to describe himself. It is clear that Messiah comes to be used in a special way in the developing Christian tradition. But here, we want to begin with its more traditional meaning as, simply, "anointed."

In the Gospels, then, Jesus emerges as the one who stands in the synagogue in his home town of Nazareth and reads from the Prophet Isaiah:

"The Spirit of the Lord is upon me, because he has anointed me to preach good news to the poor. He has sent me to proclaim release to the captives and recovering of sight to the blind, to set at liberty those who are oppressed, to proclaim the acceptable year of the Lord." And he closed the book and gave it back to the attendant. . .And he began to say to them, "Today this scripture has been fulfilled in your hearing."[8] (Luke 4:18-21)

Thus, according to Luke, began Jesus' ministry. For the early Christians, then, Jesus was the long awaited Messiah and they heard and saw his ministry within the context of their Jewish world. He was "the anointed One."

Seen in this context, then, Jesus had a short ministry of one to three years. He gathered around himself a small group of disciples and followers, including Peter, James, John and Mary Magdalene. He spoke in words that often astounded; he spoke with authority. In Matthew's Gospel we find the "Sermon on the Mount" where Jesus said, "'You have heard that it was said, "You shall love your neighbor and hate your enemy." But I say to you, Love your enemies and pray for those who persecute you, so that you may be sons of your Father who is in heaven . . .'" (Matt. 5:43-45) He often spoke in parables. In Mark, we read Him saying, "'With what can we compare the kingdom of God, or what parable shall we use for it? It is like a grain of mustard seed, which, when sown upon the ground, is the smallest of all the seeds on earth; yet when it is sown it grows up and becomes the greatest of all shrubs. . .' With many such parables he spoke the word to them, as they were able to hear it. . ." (Mark 4:30-33) He prayed to God—often using the distinctive term "Abba" or "Father" to address God, as in the Lord's Prayer that begins "Our Father, who art in heaven. . ." And he sought continually to do God's Will.

This Jesus was also a healer. Many came to him and he healed many. Once, in a crowd, a woman touched Jesus' garment and he said to her, "Daughter, your faith has made you well; go in peace, and be healed of your disease." (Mark 5:34) He is a healer not only of physical illness, but also of spiritual affliction. To the Samaritan woman at the well, he offered "a spring of water welling up to eternal life." (John 4:14) He was a voice of wisdom.

According to the Christian scriptures, Jesus' life and ministry began to attract opposition. There were those who felt that Jesus had blasphemed against the Way of tradition and the prophets, others that he was fomenting rebellion against Roman authorities. And it was in this setting that Jesus comes to Jerusalem for the last time. After, according to the Christian scriptures, a triumphant entry into the city, he is betrayed by Judas, one of his disciples. Jesus is then put to death by the Roman authorities. According to the Christian scriptures, Jesus is raised from the dead by God, meets Mary Magdalene at the Tomb (John 20) and the disciples on the road to Emmaus who know Him "in the breaking of bread." (Luke 24) And after some time with his followers in his "Resurrected Body" (which is not a resuscitated corpse), Jesus then ascends into Heaven, is taken up into life with God.[9]

For the early Christians, the resurrection is a surprise and a confirmation of Jesus' messiahship. It is evidence that in Jesus Christ, a mighty work of God was being unfolded. Likewise, Jesus' miracles are not evidence of Jesus' divinity, but reveal that God was present to Jesus in a profound way. The Synoptic Gospels present Jesus as a wholly human Messiah, but the picture shifts in the Gospel of John. In John, we find the crucial passages that begin to link Jesus in a very special way to the Heavenly Father. Within the Christian scriptures themselves, we can see the emergence of the distinctive Christian convictions concerning Jesus. The Apostle Paul, for example, articulates this special work as follows: "God was in Christ reconciling the world to himself. . ." (II Cor. 5:19) And by the Resurrected Christ, the disciples are given the Great Commission in the Gospel of Matthew,

"Go therefore and make disciples of all nations, baptizing them in the name of the Father and of the Son and of the Holy Spirit. . ." (Mt. 28:19) Thus, for Christians, Jesus is not only a Teacher and a Messiah but he is also, as Peter writes, "our Lord and Savior Jesus Christ." (II Peter 1:11)

My point here is that Jesus in the Christian scriptures is presented as the Messiah who is related to God in some remarkably special way. What is the appropriate way to answer the question of who Jesus was? Should he be seen as a Jewish Rabbi or Teacher? a charismatic Healer? a first century Prophet? the incarnate Word of God? The answer to this question is not a straightforward historical one. It is, rather, always answered in relation to the religious and theological convictions that one holds.

II. B. Jesus in the Early Christian Writers

As I indicated before, the scripture of the first generation of Christians was the Jewish Bible. Though the letters of Paul and the Gospels circulated among the small communities of Christians, it was only in the late second century that the Christian Bible was in the form that we now know it. Thus in the early Christian writings (as well as Scripture) we can see how the Christian ways of speaking of Jesus were developing and growing. In, for example, the writings of Clement (c. 100) "Jesus" is spoken of as "our Lord Jesus Christ," and Clement affirms that we have "one God, one Christ, one Spirit of Grace." Ignatius of Antioch (c. 110) speaks of the "New Man Jesus Christ" and the "one physician —of flesh yet spiritual, born yet unbegotten, God incarnate, genuine life in the midst of death, sprung from Mary as well as God. . . Jesus Christ our Lord." Jesus Christ is, Ignatius writes, the one in whom "we shall get to God." Polycarp (c. 70-155) speaks of our destiny to "believe in our Lord Jesus Christ and in 'his Father who raised him from the dead.'" And Justin Martyr (c. 150) speaks of "that Christ" who "is the First-begotten of God" and "the Reason/Logos of which every race of man partakes."[10]

In these ways of speaking about Jesus, we see the development and growth of early gentile Christian understanding of Jesus as the Christ. Jesus as the Christ is emerging in Christian self-understanding and experience as more than, we might say, the historical Jesus. Increasingly, Christians are coming to see that Jesus is related to God in some special manner such that in Jesus Christ we meet, see, are led to encounter God. This is already signaled in John's Gospel when we read in John

1:1-4, "In the beginning was the Word, and the Word was with God, and the Word was God. He was in the beginning with God; all things were made through him, and without him was not anything made that was made. In him was life, and the life was the light of men." It was thus a process involving Christian experience of the Risen Christ and continued discernment of his life and message that led the majority of the early Christian community to the formulation, in the Ecumenical Creeds of Christianity, of the doctrines of the incarnation and the trinity, two doctrines that have been especially troubling in the relations between the Muslim and Christian worlds.

Thus the orthodox Christian Creeds that were to emerge are not a simple reflection of the historical life of Jesus of Nazareth; they are, rather, a symbol of the developing Christian belief that in Jesus a divine work unfolded that related Jesus to God in a special way.

II. C. Jesus in the Early Ecumenical Creeds

The Ecumenical Creeds of Christianity emerged after the social status of Christianity was dramatically transformed. Prior to 316, Christianity had been an outlaw religion and was subject to seasons of persecution. After 312, Christianity was tolerated and in 325, Constantine made Christianity the official religion of the Empire. And it was the Emperor who called the first Ecumenical Council at his summer palace at Nicea in 325. From this Council emerged the symbol that was to mark the orthodox Christian confession: "in one Lord Jesus Christ, the Son of God, begotten of the Father as only begotten, that is, from the essence of the Father, God from God, Light from Light. . ." And later in 381 at the Council Constantinople, came this formula: "the only-begotten Son of God, begotten from the Father before all time, Light from Light, true God from true God, begotten not created, of the same essence as the Father, through Whom all things came into Being." Then in 451, we have the Council of Chalcedon which affirmed that "the one and Only Son, our Lord Jesus Christ. . .is perfect both in deity (*theoteti*) and also in human-ness (*anthropoteti*). . . ."[11] These are the formulas that stand at the heart of the Christian doctrine of the Trinity, a doctrine that Muslims find compromises the absolute Singleness of God and that, it must be acknowledged, many Christians find incomprehensible. These doctrines were originally formulated in the language and assumptions of ancient Greek thought. And while they may be difficult to understand, they wish to affirm that Jesus as the Logos/Word is connected to God, is of God, in some very special way.

When these credal formulations are then used to re-read Scripture, they lead to much confusion. How can the Jesus who seeks to do God's will and prays to the Father that the cup of the crucifixion be removed, be "very God of very God"? Christians often gloss over this logical impossibility. They/we should acknowledge that the Christian witness to Jesus as the Incarnate Word is a religious/theological affirmation we have come to rather than a reflection of the historical ministry of Jesus.

This brief review of Jesus in scripture, early Christian writings and the early Creeds should make us aware that the orthodox Christian understanding of Jesus as the Christ is quite complex. The anointed One or Messiah of the Synoptic Gospels becomes the "begotten from the Father before all time" of the Council of Nicea. Yet Christians want to affirm the full humanity of Jesus and thus we get these paradoxical formulations of the Creeds. Early Christian thinkers believed that the doctrine of the Trinity was necessary precisely in order to preserve the Unity of God—not to compromise that conviction. But can that claim, difficult enough for Christians to grasp, even be heard within the Muslim world?

III. Isa in the Qur'an and Islam

It is important to be aware that our topic is not simply Jesus in Christianity but also Isa in the Qur'an and in Islam. This larger heading means that we should not restrict this dialogue to the Scriptural sources, but look more broadly within the Way of Islam as it has unfolded over the centuries. When the Prophet Muhammad burst onto the scene, Christianity was already more than 500 years old. It had moved through its formative stages and had come to its orthodox articulations in the early ecumenical Creeds of the Christian Church. The attempts of historians to determine if Muhammad had any links to the Christian community and how well he knew it have not been very successful, though there are some intriguing suggestions that Jewish Christians in the Arabian peninsula may have always resisted the "ecumenical formulations" and maintained beliefs more consonant with what we find in the Qur'an. But such historical investigations do not get us to the heart of the question; they are not necessary. Since the heart of the Prophet's Message is that "There is no God, but God" and since that belief is exemplified in the Qur'an, it is to the Qur'an that we must first look to see the Islamic Way.

For Muslims, the Qur'an is a sacred scripture unlike any other. It is the "standing miracle"; it is, Muslims believe, the direct communication of Allah to Muhammad through the angel Gabriel. It is not, as in the Christian scripture, a witness to God or to God's Word, but it is the very WORD OF GOD. The nature and status of the Qur'an is a question for the dialogue of Muslims and Christians, but it is not one we can pursue here. But we must at least note the difference between Muslims and Christians in regard to the status of their sacred scriptures. (And the differences among Muslims and among Christians too, but that is another story.) Christians, by and large, do not understand their scriptures as the Muslims, by and large, regard the Qur'an. While Christians affirm that Jesus is the Word of God, to which the scriptures bear witness, Muslims use this same formula—the Word of God—to describe the Qur'an.[12]

It comes as a surprise to most Christians to discover the honor given to Isa in Islam and the Qur'an. Most Christians are simply unaware that Muslims regard Isa as a Messenger and Prophet. The Qur'an accords Isa, within its perspective, the highest honor. Isa is a "Prophet" within the great tradition that now culminates in Muhammad. Isa's dignity lies in the fact that he was chosen by Allah to proclaim God's Message in his own time and to his people. Surah 2:136 reads, "We believe in God and that which is revealed to us; in what was revealed to Abraham, Ishmael, Isaac, Jacob, and the tribes; to Moses and Jesus and the other prophets by their Lord. We make no distinction among any of them and to God we have surrendered ourselves."[13] Sometimes this respect for Isa is combined with a criticism of certain teachings concerning Isa. For example, "People of the Book, do not transgress the bounds of your religion. Speak nothing but the truth about Allah. The Messiah, Jesus, the son of Mary, was no more than Allah's apostle and his Word. . . So believe in Allah and his apostles and do not say 'three.' Allah is but one God. Allah forbid that He should have a son!" (Surah 4:171 in Kung article)[14] (Or in Murata and Chittick's trans.: "The Messiah, Jesus son of Mary, was only the Messenger of God, and His Word that He committed to Mary, and a Spirit from Him. So have faith in God and His messengers, and do not say, 'Three.' Refrain; better it is for you. God is only One God."[15])

Sachiko Murata and William Chittick in their *Vision of Islam* make a crucial point when they write that "Muslims see other religions in terms of Islam, which in their eyes is the perfect religion. Of course, followers of other religions also look from their own perspective; this is not a quality unique to Muslims."[16] Indeed, it is not unique to Muslims, but this fact also helps us to pose the problem that Muslims

and Christians face at this point, namely, can we see the understanding
of Jesus/Isa that emerges in the sacred scriptures of the two traditions
in the other's terms?

Isa is, in the Qur'an, miraculously born of the Virgin Mary, and he
proclaims with the Prophets the eternal Message that there is "No God
but God." The Qur'an denies the crucifixion, but affirms that Isa is
taken directly into heaven by God. Kenneth Cragg summarizes the
Qur'anic picture of Jesus in the following words:

> I have come unto you with a sign from your Lord. I create for you out
> of clay the likeness of a bird, I breathe into it and by God's permission
> it is a bird. I heal the blind and the leper and I raise the dead by God's
> permission and I proclaim unto you what you may eat and what you may
> store up in your houses. (3:37 esp.). . . Christ is, then, a prophet, a
> teacher, a healer of the sick, a spirit from or of God. To him is given the
> Gospel—not the good news about God in Christ, but a book of words or
> preaching, which the Qur'an does not anywhere reproduce. . .[17]

Such a portrayal of Isa is in line with the Qur'anic view of the Prophet
as a Messenger of God but is very different from the salvific role of
Jesus that emerges in the Christian scriptures.

Dr. Badu Kateregga well summarizes the traditional Muslim view
when he says,

> Muslims have great respect and love for Jesus (Isa) the Messiah. He is
> one of the greatest prophets of Allah. To deny the prophethood of Jesus
> is to deny Islam. . . .On the other hand, Muslims are genuinely opposed
> to the belief by Christians that Isa (PBUH) was Divine or "Son of God."
> . . .This is the point where Muslims and Christians painfully part com-
> pany. The issue is deeply theological and anthropological. The Christian
> view of incarnation seems to compromise God's transcendence and
> sovereignty while at the same time exalting a mere man to God-like
> status. . . .The gulf between Christians and Muslims is further widened
> by the Christian silence on and non-recognition of Muhammad (PBUH)
> as the Seal of Prophets, and the final guidance (the Qur'an) that was
> revealed to him by God.[18]

We will have to let these few words on Isa in the Qur'an and the brief
summary by Kateregga stand.

Does the Qur'anic view of Isa mean that Muslims must automatically
reject Christian views of Jesus that relate Jesus as the Word of God to
the "Trinity"? While it would seem so, there are some Muslims who see
the issue in a more nuanced way. Seyyed H. Nasr, for example, allows

that "Islam would accept an interpretation of the Trinity which would not in any way compromise Divine Unity, one which would consider the persons of the Trinity to be 'Aspects' or 'Names' of God standing below His Essence. . ."[19] But this would lead us into a much longer discussion than is possible here. Here, our brief look at Isa in the Qur'an and Islam should lead us to see that Isa is perceived in profoundly different terms—those of prophet and messenger—than the Jesus of the Christian scriptures. And now we will turn briefly to some almost concluding points, beginning with the conflicts.

IV. Points of Conflict

Even from this brief review, it is obvious that the issue of Jesus/Isa in Islam and Christianity is a controversial, complex and troubling one, touching issues that are at the very heart of the respective faiths. From this brief presentation of Jesus in Christianity and Isa in Islam there emerges three areas of clear difference. Each is too big to handle here. So my comments will be brief.

First, the very accounts of Jesus/Isa that we find in the Christian Scriptures and in the Qur'an clearly differ from one another in terms of the very events of Jesus' life and ministry. At the heart of those differences is the issue, from the Christian side, of the death and resurrection of Jesus and, from the Muslim side, the issue of Isa's status as a Prophet and as fully human.

Second, we find clear and perhaps irreconcilable differences in the interpretations of Jesus/Isa in Christianity and Islam. Most Christians have affirmed that Jesus is the Incarnate Word of God, the second Person of the Trinity. But not all Christians, either historically or especially today, hold this faith. If there is going to be any mutual understanding, it will be imperative for Christians to clarify the meaning of the doctrines of the incarnation and trinity since Christians that hold these doctrines do not believe that they deny the Unity and Oneness of God. Muslims seem often to hear Christian talk of the "Son of God" in literal terms that Christians should also reject. Likewise, I often find myself agreeing with the Qur'an in its criticisms of certain Christian formulations. Christians do not teach, for example, that God is "Three." God is always and only One God. Nor, properly speaking, is it right to speak of "Jesus (the historical figure) as God" as many Christians do. And Muslims rightly see that the Christian way of speaking of Jesus as "Son of God" and of the Trinity is often more opaque than enlightening.

Muslims, on the other hand, interpret Isa as a "Prophet/Messenger."
This is an important witness to Jesus that Christians should, in my view,
take much more seriously than they have up until now. Christians
should be quick to agree that Jesus' intention was to bear witness to
God, the Creator of all. As the lawyer asked Jesus, "'Teacher, which
is the great commandment in the law?' And he said to him, 'You shall
love the Lord your God with all your heart, and with all your soul, and
with all your mind.'" (Matt. 22:36-37) It is God that we are called to
remember, to heed, to worship and none other. On this point, Muslims
and Christians should find themselves in agreement.

Third, in the midst of the conflict and difference over Jesus/Isa
stands the issue of the Qur'an as "the Word of God" and the Prophet
Muhammad (PBUH). While Muslims accept the Christian scriptures,
though with some theological qualifications, and accept Isa as a
Messenger of God, there is no reciprocity from Christians concerning
the Qur'an and the Prophet Muhammad. Christians have, by and large,
rejected the Qur'an as spurious and have caricatured the status of the
Prophet. We Christians have misnamed the faith of Islam as
Mohammadenism until recently, and even now only some Christians
have gotten it right. So, it is imperative, if we are to proceed in
dialogue, that Christians reexamine and reassess their views of the
Qur'an and the Prophet. I can only speak for myself when I say that I
have read the Qur'an and I have great respect for its clear witness to
God. I also respect the Prophet as a Messenger, though perhaps not in
the same way as Muslims do. But then it would be wrong to expect that
out of dialogue I would become a Muslim, any more than that I would
expect Muslims to become Christians.[20] That is not the point. But it is
to the point that we should advance through dialogue towards deepened
respect for one another and our respective Ways to Allah/God.

The story of Muslim-Christian encounter in relation to Jesus/Isa has
largely been one of missing one another. While Christians have sought
to witness to their belief that Jesus is the incarnate Word of God,
Muslims have witnessed to their conviction that Isa is a Prophet. When
these two beliefs concerning Jesus meet, they seldom produce mutual
understanding. We could, however, move in that direction if we were
to realize that while we may not agree, we can at least attempt to hear
one another in our witness to Jesus/Isa in our own terms.

We will perhaps begin to move in that direction when Christians and
Muslims meet in a spirit that reflects the text from the Qur'an that I
quoted at the outset: "Say: 'O People of the Book! Come now to a word

common between us and you, that we worship none but God. . .'" This we can do only as we move beyond the polemical and apologetic attitudes that have characterized Muslim-Christian meeting in the past and begin to meet each other anew in a spirit of dialogue. In that new attitude of dialogue we must seek to understand that faith that leads the Muslim to find the way to God through the Prophet and the Qur'an and the Christian to find the way to God in Jesus as the Christ.

NOTES

1. Stuart E. Brown, *Meeting in Faith* (Geneva: WCC Publications, 1989). According to this volume, the most troubling and divisive religious and theological differences between the two traditions have not, unfortunately, been addressed. See also *Issues in Christian-Muslim Relations, Ecumenical Considerations* (Geneva: Office on Inter-Religious Relations, 1992).
2. See M. Darrol Bryant, "Overcoming History: On the Possibilities of Muslim-Christian Dialogue," *Hamdard Islamicus*, Vol. XVII, No. 2., Summer, 1994, pp. 5-15. It also appears in this volume in a slightly revised form.
3. Neal Robinson, *Christ in Islam and Christianity* (London: Macmillan, 1991). Robinson notes that like Muhammad, "the Qur'anic Jesus is called a 'prophet' (*nabi*), a 'messenger' (*rasul*) and a 'servant' (*abd*) of God. Like him too he is to said to have been sent as a 'mercy' (*rahma*). He received a revelation called 'the Gospel' just as Muhammad subsequently received the Qur'an. . . .Its central thrust was identical with the central thrust of the Qur'an—the summons to serve and worship God." (p. 37) See also Kenneth Cragg, *Jesus and the Muslim* (London: George Allen and Unwin, 1985), who characterizes current Muslim attitudes in this way: "Through all we have reviewed there runs a great tenderness for Jesus, yet a sharp dissociation from his Christian dimensions. Islam registers a profound attraction but condemns its Christian interpretation. Jesus is the theme at once of acknowledgment and disavowal." (p. 278)
4. Two points need to be made at the outset. First, I participate in this dialogue as a Christian, and a student/scholar of religion and culture, who is deeply committed to dialogue with people of other faiths. I am not an expert on Islam. My knowledge of Islam is limited, but I have been able to meet many Muslims over the last twenty years. I have been a Visiting Scholar in the Indian Institute of Islamic Studies in New Delhi on two sabbaticals. And I have prayed in mosques in India and Turkey. I have met Muslims from Indonesia, Iraq, Pakistan, Egypt, Saudi Arabia, Kenya, Morocco, Iran, and the former Soviet Union as well as Canada and the USA. These experiences and conversations have supplemented and enriched my reading about, and understanding of, the faith and tradition of Islam. They have made me aware that not all Muslims speak in the same tone, nor do they all hold exactly the same beliefs. This is also true of Christianity.

    Second, I do not speak Arabic, nor Hebrew, nor Greek. Thus I am not an expert on the sacred text of Islam, the Holy Qur'an, nor am I an expert on the

Christian Scriptures either the Old or New Testaments. Thus I have been able to read and to study these scriptures only in translation. This is an especial problem in relation to Islam where, traditionally, there has been a pervasive conviction that the Qur'an is not to be translated, but only read in its original Arabic. And after pouring over different translations of the Qur'an, I know what a real problem translation is since different translators translate the same texts in widely different ways. I have mainly used the "new revised edition" of The Holy Qur'an translated by Abdullah Yusuf Ali. But I have also consulted the translations of N. J. Dawood, *The Koran* (Penguin), Pickthall's *The Meaning of the Glorious Koran*, and the excerpts translated in R. Zakaria, *Muhammad and the Qur'an*, and Sachiko Murata and William Chittick, *The Vision of Islam*.

5. See M. Darrol Bryant, *Religion in a New Key* (New Delhi: Wiley Eastern Ltd., 1992).

6. Ali translation.

7. See Alan Richardson, *A Theological Word Book of the Bible* (New York: Macmillan Co., 1964), p. 44.

8. The texts quoted from the New Testament are from the Revised Standard Version.

9. The new quest for the historical Jesus has resulted in some important perspectives on Jesus. See Marcus Borg, *Jesus: A New Vision* (San Francisco: Harper and Row, 1987).

10. These quotes are all from the writings gathered in the *Early Christian Fathers*, Library of Christian Classics, Vol. I (Philadelphia: Westminster Press, 1953).

11. See John Leith, ed., *Creeds of the Christian Churches* (Garden City, NY: Anchor/Doubleday, 1963), pp. 33, 35, 39.

12. This difference between Christians and Muslims in relation to the "Word of God" is explored in Daniel Sahas, "The Christological Morphology of the Doctrine of the Qur'an," in M. Darrol Bryant, ed., *Pluralism, Tolerance and Dialogue: Six Studies* (Waterloo: University of Waterloo Press, 1989), pp. 77-98. I am also aware that some fundamentalist Christians do speak of the Bible as the "Word of God" in ways very similar to how Muslims speak of the Qur'an as the "Word of God." But even here, the agency of revelation is, in the Christian case, the inspired writers rather than the direct transmission to the Prophet. For good introductions to Islam, see Sachiko Murata and William Chittick, *The Vision of Islam* (New York: Paragon, 1995). Also useful is Frederick Denny, *An Introduction to Islam* (New York: Macmillan, 1985). See also S.H. Nasr, *Ideals and Realities of Islam* (London: Allen and Unwin, 1966).

13. Dawood translation of the Qur'an, Surah 2:136

14. See article by Hans Kung, "Christianity and World Religions: Dialogue with Islam," in Leonard Swidler, *Toward a Universal Theology of Religion* (Maryknoll, NY: Orbis Books, 1987), pp. 192-209.

15. See S. Murata and W. Chittick, *op. cit.*, p. 175.

16. See S. Murata and W. Chittick, *The Vision of Islam, op. cit.*, p. 179.

17. Kenneth Cragg, *The Call of the Minaret*, 2nd edition (Maryknoll, NY: Orbis Books, 1985), pp. 233-234.

18. See B.D. Kataregga and D.W. Shenk, *Islam and Christianity, A Muslim and a Christian in Dialogue* (Nairobi: Uzima, 1980), pp. 131-132.

19. See Seyyed Hossein Nasr, "The Islamic View of Christianity," pp. 126-134 in Paul J. Griffiths, *Christianity Through Non-Christian Eyes* (Maryknoll, NY: Orbis Books, 1990), p. 128.

20. I discovered that my conclusions parallel those found in Kenneth Cragg in *Jesus and the Muslim, op. cit.* Cragg remarks that "it is fair to say that what divides Muslim and Christian—how to recognize revelation, what constitutes 'Scripture,' the measure of what humanity entails for God and God requires of man—can all be seen as implicit in the question of Jesus" p. 289.

14

JESUS OF NAZARETH:

A SCRIPTURAL THEME TO PROMOTE MUSLIM-CHRISTIAN DIALOGUE

Muhib. O. Opeloye

Introduction

JESUS (THE QUR'ANIC "ISA") is perhaps the most controversial of all the world religious figures. The controversy surrounding his personality has been largely responsible for the dividing line between Islam and Christianity as two separate religions. Jesus is to the Christians the expected Messiah whom some Jews denied and the Romans killed. He is to them the son of God and God Incarnate. To the Muslims he was no more than a prophet, a prophet sent to the children of Israel. This notwithstanding, the Qur'an is replete with views corroborating the Biblical account of Jesus. It is the aim of this paper to highlight the extent to which the Qur'anic views on Jesus are complementary to those of the Bible with a view to using them as a basis to promote Muslim-Christian dialogue.

The subject would be examined under four subheadings: concord in the Qur'anic and Biblical views of Jesus; narratives about Jesus peculiar to the Qur'an; areas of conflict in the Qur'anic and Biblical views and the Qur'anic salvation scheme for the Christians.

Concord in the Qur'anic and Biblical Accounts of Jesus

The Qur'an, unlike the Bible, does not contain a detailed account of Jesus' life. We are informed of how he was born, given an account of his prophetic mission, and a refutation of his divine nature and crucifixion. The first area of concord in the two scriptures' perception of Jesus is noticed in his birth account.

Surah 3: 45-47 of the Qur'an gives its account thus:

> Behold! the angels said: "O Mary! God gives thee glad tidings of a word from him: his name will be Christ Jesus, the son of Mary, held nn honour in this world and the hereafter and of (the company of) those nearest to God." She said: "O my Lord! how shall I have a son when no man has touched me?" He said: "Even so, God creates what He wills. When He has decreed a plan He says to it, 'be' and it is." (cf. Surah 19: 16-22)

This Qur'anic passage compares to some extent with the information contained in Lk. 1:26 - Lk. 2:7 and Mt. 1:18-25. The two scriptures agree on the miraculous birth of Jesus. They are both of the view that the conception of Jesus took place immediately after the angelic announcement without Mary (the Qur'anic Maryam) having any sexual dealing with a man. The exclamation "How can this be for I am still a virgin" recorded in Luke 1:34 re-echos in Surahs 3:47 and 19:20.

The authenticity of the virgin birth narrative cannot be undermined simply because the records are missing in the other New Testament books apart from Luke and Matthew, as E. T. Tinsley would want us to believe.[1]

In view of the charges levied against Mary by some Jews in consequence of her unnatural conception, the Qur'an sees the need to exonerate her with the reasoned arguments proceeding the birth narrative starting from Surah 3:33.

As a proof of her chastity, she is presented as a holy woman dedicated to God in conception and at birth. (Surah 3: 35-36) She was to grow in purity and beauty in the care of Zacharias. (Surah 3:37) Moreover, the story of Zacharias (the Qur'anic Zakariya) is related in Surah 3:38 to show that the power of God exercised in giving him and his barren wife John (Qur'anic Yahya) in their old age was still at work in the miraculous conception of Mary. The Qur'an would have no need of making reference to this if Jesus had been born the natural way.

The next area of concord is similarity in the Qur'anic and Biblical views on Jesus' employment of miracles to assert his authority in the course of his ministry. As we read in the Bible, the Qur'an informs us that Jesus was given the power to heal the sick, bring life to the dead, restore the sight of the blind and heal the leper. (Surah 3:49) According to Surah 5:113 he was able to do these because he was strengthened by God with a holy spirit. These miracles, as far as the Qur'an is concerned, were meant to convince the Israelites that Jesus' mission was divinely inspired.

Thirdly, despite the Qur'anic denial of Jesus' crucifixion on the cross, the scripture agrees with the Bible on his ascension into heaven as evident in Surah 4:158, which declares:

Nay, God raised him up unto Himself and God is exalted in power, wise. (cf. Surahs 3:55 and 5:120)

The ascension passages, Surahs 3:55; 4:158 and 5:120 as understood by commentators like Abul A'la Maududi and Yusuf Ali, hold that Jesus still lives in the body in heaven.[2] The other view, which appears to us less plausible, is the view held by commentators like M. M. Ali, asserting that Jesus did die but not when he was supposed to be crucified and that his being raised up unto God only meant his being exalted and honored by God.[3] If the Christians' belief in Jesus' ascension had been baseless, it would have been refuted by the Qur'an point blank, just as it refutes some Christians doctrines.

Fourth is the common belief of the two scriptures in the second coming of Jesus. This view derives from Surah 4:159, which reads:

And there is none of the people of the Book but must believe in him before his death; and on the day of Judgement He will be a witness against them.

Again, there is difference of opinion in the interpretation of the passage. Those who hold the view that Jesus did not die but lives in bodily form with God interpret the passage to mean that all the people of the book alive at the time of his second coming will eventually believe in him before his natural death.[4] Those who hold the view that

Jesus did die would rather assert that the pronoun "his" in the passage is in reference to the people of the book and not Jesus, arguing that the emphatic expression "must believe" denotes more a question of duty than of fact.[5] M. M. Ali[6] is of this school of thought and it is a less popular view.

It must be emphasized that the complementary teachings of the Qur'an and Bible on these important aspects of Jesus' life are to my mind an index of the common origin of the two scriptures.

Narratives about Jesus Peculiar to the Qur'an

The Qur'anic narrative that Jesus talked as a baby in the cradle is one of his miracles peculiar to the Qur'an. Verses 22-26 of Surah *Maryam* contains the accounts of Mary's conception, her withdrawal to a distant place, her painful experience at childbirth and the coming to her aid of an angel. In verses 27-28 we are informed that after delivery, she brought the baby to her people who accused her of unchastity, having brought forth a baby without marital attachment.

In response to this, Mary simply pointed at the infant, asking them to direct their questions to him. Their reply was: "How shall we talk with him who is an infant in the cradle?" (S.19:29) There and then the child spoke out, saying:

> I am indeed a servant of God, He has given me revelation and made me a prophet. He has made me blessed wheresoever I be and has enjoined on me prayer and chastity as long as l live. He has made me kind to my mother and He has not made me oppressive and hard-hearted. So peace be upon me on the day I was born and peace shall be on me on the day I am raised to life. (Surah 19:30-33, cf. Surah 3:46 and 5:110)

Jesus made this statement to rescue his helpless mother whose explanation could not be accepted in view of the people's censorious mood. The statement forms a summary of Jesus' mission.

What we have in the Bible that is close to this experience is Luke's account of Jesus' disputation with the teachers in the temple at the age of twelve. (Luke 2:46)

According to Luke's gospel, Jesus as a child was strong in spirit and was filled with wisdom. (Luke 2:40) Besides, some apocryphal gospels describe him as preaching from infancy.

The miracle of the clay bird contained in Surahs 3:49 and 5:113 is not found in the New Testament even though some apocryphal books relate it.[7] In the Qur'anic passage, Jesus is credited with the statement: "I have come to you with a sign from your Lord, in your very presence I make the likeness of a bird out of clay and breathe into it and it becomes by God's command a bird." Perhaps it is more appropriate to see this passage as a parable rather than as a statement of truth considering the fact that Jesus' dignity is much above such action as making toy birds. Moreover, the act of creation (*Khalq*) is God's prerogative.[8]

Conflicts in the Qur'anic and Biblical View about Jesus

Three principal areas of conflict are worthy of consideration, namely: Jesus' Godhead, Jesus' sonship and Jesus' crucifixion. The Qur'an is unequivocal in its rejection of the Christian belief that Jesus is God. Surah 5: 72-73 declares in this regard:

> They do blaspheme who say "Allah is Christ the son of Mary." But said Christ: "O children of Israel worship God my Lord and your Lord." Whoever joins other gods with Allah, God will forbid him the Garden and Fire will be his abode. . . They do blaspheme who say Allah is one of three in Trinity, for there is no god except one God.

Three principal reasons have been identified as being responsible for the prevalence of this belief in Jesus' divinity: the miraculous birth of Jesus, his concrete miracles, and his ascension into the heavens. Though the Qur'an confirms the three, it does not see in any of them reason to justify deification of Jesus. As for the first reason, the Qur'an makes it plain that the birth of Jesus without a father was only a manifestation of the infinite power of God who can create anybody in whatever manner He wills. This is why the scripture in Surah 3:59 compares the birth of Jesus to the creation of Adam. By so doing it tries to call attention of believers to the more miraculous manner by which Adam was brought to being.

With regard to the second reason, the Qur'an makes it clear that Jesus performed all his miracles through God's permission and not as an independent authority. And lastly, with regard to his ascension, the Qur'anic view is that he was recalled by the one who sent him only when his life was to be terminated without any just cause, and it was to that Being he directed his cry: "My God, my God why hast thou forsaken me?" recorded in Mark 15:34.

Also in Surah 9:30 we find the denunciation of the belief in the sonship of Jesus. The Muslims would argue that since the miraculous birth of John the Baptist (the Qur'anic Yahya) did not make him the son of God, so Jesus' miraculous birth could not make him the son of God. It is in recognition of the miracle that surrounded the birth of the two of them that they have been mentioned together in the same context in the gospel of Luke.

In Surah 4:157, the crucifixion of Jesus is emphatically refuted as we read:

> That they said (in boast) "We killed Christ Jesus the son of Mary, the apostle of God." But they killed him not nor crucified him, but so it was made to appear to them and those who differ therein are full of doubts with no (certain) knowledge, but only conjecture to follow, for surely they killed him not.

In the belief of the Muslims, God did not allow the fulfillment of the sinister plan to kill Jesus. According to Muslims, another person who was made to put on the appearance of Jesus was killed in his stead.[9] The rejection of the crucifixion doctrine is a logical consequence of Muslim's disbelief in the doctrines of original sin and its atonement with the blood of Jesus.

As far as the Muslims are concerned, Jesus was a prophet of God sent to the children of Israel. (Surah 3:49) According to Surah 4:171, he was God's word bestowed on Mary and a spirit proceeding from Him. This passage thus reveals another aspect of striking similarity in the Biblical and Qur'anic perception of Jesus which is the fact that he is God's "word" even though their interpretation differs. The Qur'anic presentation of Jesus as prophet is corroborated by Hebrews 3:1-3, which reads:

> Therefore holy brethren who share in a heavenly call, consider Jesus the apostle and high priest of our confession. He was faithful to Him who appointed him, just as Moses was faithful in God's house.

Apart from Jesus being referred to as apostle or prophet in this quotation, he is also compared with Moses who is generally acknowledged to be a prophet. The quotation asserts that Moses was faithful to God, thus demonstrating one of the traits of the prophets. What should interest any lover of dialogue among the Muslims and Christians is that in spite of the differences already identified, as fundmental as some of them are, the Qur'an does not exclude either Muslims or Christians from the people who may see salvation. This is the subject examined in the next section.

The Qur'anic Salvation Scheme for the Christians

Christians are included among the groups promised salvation, as evident in Surah 2:62 of the Qur'an. That that salvation does not depend on the special relation of any particular people with God is most explicit in the following passage as it declares:

> Those who believe in the Qur'an and those who follow the Jewish (scriptures) and the Christians and the Sabians, any who believe in God and the last day and work righteousness shall have the reward with their Lord, on them shall be no fear nor shall they grieve. (cf. Surah 5:72)

The requirements for salvation according to this passage are right belief and good deeds. One may then ask the question, what constitutes right belief?

This is the belief in and submission to one God without attributing to Him any associate, as enjoined in Deuteronomy 6:4 (cf. Exodus 20:3), Mark 12:29 and Surah 112:1-4. The issue of right belief is not irrelevant because even within each tradition there are groupings. For instance, among the Christians there are divisions between the "born again" and the "born once" just as among Muslims we have the "orthodox" and the "unorthodox" groups. Naturally, each of these groups would see itself as having the right belief. Whoever falls into wrong belief, whether he be Muslim or Christian, would be denied salvation.

It is in consequence of salvation promised the Christians that God in Surah 3:55 assures Jesus that his followers would be made superior to those who reject faith. It is interesting to note that some Christians in interpreting this passage have come up with the conjecture that Christians have a better claim to salvation than the Muslims. This is a wrong interpretation because Muslims neither reject faith nor reject Jesus. The people to whom reference is being made in the passage were the people who witnessed the mission of Jesus. It would be right, therefore, to say that Muslims are good Christians in view of their belief in Jesus, and Islam has incorporated Christianity within it because of its doctrine of progressive revelation.

Notwithstanding the Qur'anic criticisms of the Christians, Islam

still identifies Christianity as a branch of the Abrahamic faith.[10] This
is why Surah 29:46 declares:

> Say we (Muslims) believe in that which was revealed to us as well as
> that which was revealed to you. Our God and your God is one and the
> same we all submit to. (cf. Surah 2:136)

If the Qur'an identifies Christianity with Islam, it is because the
scriptures see mankind as one community of faith which later broke
into sects. Surah 25:52-53 testifies to this as it reads:

> And verily this brotherhood of yours is a single brotherhood and I am
> your Lord and cherisher, therefore fear me. But people have cut off their
> affair (of unity) between them into sects, each party rejoicing in that
> which is itself.

Even when the single community has broken into factions and each
faction sees itself as the chosen or the beloved of God, there are
guidelines in the scriptures to promote harmonious relations between
the different factions.[11]

Besides, the scriptures would like us to exercise caution against
condemning one another. This is the message of Paul in Romans
11:11-36 for the Gentile Christians, i.e., the message against an
attitude of conceit. A similar message can be derived from Surah
4:123-124 which makes it clear that God cannot be influenced by our
judgement of the others in passing His own judgement. This becomes
clearer when we notice that in spite of the Qur'anic criticism against
some Christians doctrines, Jesus in his pleading (see Surah 5:121) left
the decision to God in deciding the affairs of his people.

Allah could use His discretion to forgive or punish them. The
Muslims too are not exempted from this discretionary use of God's
power. It is a power that He exercises as He wishes in spite of the
assertion in Surah 3:49 that Islam is the only religion acceptable to
Allah. The lesson for us as Muslims and Christians is that we should
learn not to judge others.

Conclusion

The thesis of this study is that in spite of the fundamental
differences in the Qur'anic and Biblical conception of Jesus/Isa, there
are striking similarities in the two scriptures' views about him which
serve as an index of common origin of the two. This being the case,

there must be mutual acceptance of the legitimacy of one another's religion. To my mind, such a mutual acceptance is *sine qua non* to any meaningful dialogue between the Muslims and the Christians. As is evident in the foregoing, the Islamic identification with Christianity is not in doubt, but a similar recognition is not accorded to Islam by Christianity.

This is what Krister Stendahl, the former Harvard Divinity School Dean, decries when he accuses the Christian of presenting the New Testament as being superior to the Old Testament without granting Islam the logical status of being even newer.[12] Many Muslim scholars, including Ahmad Deedat[13] and Abdul Ahad Dawủd in their researches into the Bible have tried to identify passages of the scripture which might be interpreted as making allusion to Islam or Muhammad. This is part of an attempt to establish Biblical sanction for the legitimacy of Islam. Their search for such passages must have been motivated by such Qur'anic passages as Surah 61:6 in which Jesus is presented as foretelling the coming of Muhammad.

While it is not for us to prove or disprove the veracity of the Biblical passages cited as lending credence to the legitimacy of Islam, one is constrained to call attention to the indisputable common root of Islam and Christianity, which was Abraham. The divine promise made to the great patriarch to make great nations out of his offspring does not exclude Ishmael, as evident in Genesis 21, verses 13 and 18. The greatness of the Ishmaelite's descendants (the Arabs) does not rest on anything other than Islam. It follows, therefore, that Islam and Christianity as branches of Abrahamic faith are both legitimate, and they should recognize one another as such and leave judgment on the salvation of the adherents of the two traditions to God the Almighty.

NOTES

1. E.T. Tinsley, *The Cambridge Bible Commentary: The Gospel According to Luke* (Cambridge: Cambridge University Press, 1984), p. 30.
2. Abul A'la Maududi, *The Meaning of the Qur'an*, Vol. 1 (Delhi: Board of Islamic Publications), p. 243.
3. See M.M. Ali's Commentary on Surah 3:54 on p. 147 and his Translation of Surah 4:158 and Surah 5:117.
4. See Abul A'la Maududi (Vol. 1) and Yusuf Ali's interpretation of Surah 4:159.
5. Abdullah Yusuf Ali, *The Holy Qur'an, Text Translation and Commentary* (Brentwood: Amama Corporation, 1989), p. 231.
6. To appreciate the difference of opinion in the interpretation of the passage it

may be useful to compare Abdullah Yusuf Ali's translation and that of Maulana Muhhamed Ali. The former's translation of Surah 4:159 reads: "And there is none of the people of the book but must believe in him before his death." The latter's translation reads: "And there is none of the people of the book but will believe in this revelation before his death. . ."

7. Abdullah Yusuf Ali, *op. cit.*, p. 135.
8. M.M. Ali, *The Holy Qur'an, Text translation and Commentary*, 5th Edition (Lahore: The Ahmadiyyah Anjuman Isha'at Islam, 1963), p. 144.
9. Sayyid Qutb, *Fi Zilal al-Qur'an*, Vol. 2 (Dar ihya' at-Turath al-Arabi Bairat, 1967), p. 588.
10. Muhammed Abdul al-Rauf, "Judaism and Christianity in the Perspective of Islam," in Ismail Raji al-Faruqi (ed.), *Trialogue of the Abrahamic Faiths* (Riyadh: International Islamic Publishing House, 1991), p. 27.
11. M.O. Opeloye, "Guidelines in the Qur'an on Interreligious Relations: An Overview," in J.K. Olupona (ed.), *Religion and Peace in Multifaith Nigeria* (Ile-Ife: Obafemi Awolowo University Press, 1992), p. 82.
12. Krister Stendahl, "Judaism and Islam in the Perspective of Christianity," in Ismail Raji al-Faruqi, *op. cit.*, p. 20.
13. Ahmed Deedat, *What the Bible Says about Muhammed* (Nairobi: Lino Publishers, n.d.), p. 4.
14. Abdul Ahmad Dawud, *Muhammad in the Bible* (Kuala Lumpur: Pustaka Ankara, 1969), pp. 11ff.

15

WOMEN IN MUSLIM CULTURE:

SOME CRITICAL THEOLOGICAL REFLECTIONS

Riffat Hassan

WOMEN SUCH AS KHADIJAH and 'A'ishah (wives of the Prophet Muhammad) and Rabi'a al-Basri (the outstanding woman Sufi) figure significantly in early Islam. Nonetheless, the Islamic tradition has, by and large, remained strongly patriarchal until today. This means, amongst other things, that the sources on which the Islamic tradition is based, mainly, the Qur'an (which Muslims believe to be God's Word transmitted through the Angel Gabriel to the Prophet Muhammad), *Sunnah* (the practice of the Prophet Muhammad), *Hadith* (the oral traditions attributed to the Prophet Muhammad), and *Fiqh* (jurisprudence) have been interpreted only by Muslim men who have arrogated to themselves the task of defining the ontological, theological, sociological and eschatalogical status of Muslim women. It is hardly surprising that until now the majority of Muslim women, who have been kept for centuries in physical, mental and emotional bondage, have accepted this situation passively. Here it needs to be mentioned that while the rate of literacy is low in many Muslim countries, the rate of literacy of Muslim women, especially those who live in rural areas where most of the population live, is amongst the lowest in the world.

In recent years, largely due to the pressure of anti-women laws which have been promulgated under the cover of "islamization" in some parts of the Muslim world, women with some degree of education and awareness are beginning to realize that religion is being used as an instrument of oppression rather than as a means of liberation. To understand the powerful impetus to "islamize" Muslim societies, especially with regard to women-related norms and values, it is necessary to know that of all the challenges confronting the Muslim world, perhaps the greatest is that of modernity. Muslims, in general, tend to think of "modernity" in two ways: 1) as modernization which is associated with science, technology and material progress, and 2) as Westernization which is associated with promiscuity and all kinds of social problems ranging from latch-key kids to drug and alcohol abuse. While "modernization" is considered highly desirable, "Westernization" is considered equally undesirable. What is of importance to note here is that an emancipated Muslim woman is seen by many Muslims as a symbol not of "modernization" but of "Westernization." This is so because she appears to be in violation of what traditional societies consider to be a necessary barrier between "private space" where women belong and "public space" which belongs to men. The presence of women in men's space is considered to be highly dangerous for—as a popular *hadith* states—whenever a man and a woman are alone, ash-Shaitan (the Satan) is bound to be there. In today's Muslim world, due to the pressure of political and socio-economic realities, a significant number of women may be seen in "public space." Caretakers of Muslim traditionalism feel gravely threatened by this phenomenon which they consider to be an onslaught of "Westernization" under the guise of "modernization." They believe that it is necessary to put women back in their "space" (which also designates their "place") if "the integrity of the Islamic way of life" is to be preserved.

Though I had begun my study of theological issues pertaining to women in the Islamic tradition in 1974, it was not until 1983-84 when I spent almost two years in Pakistan that my career as an activist began. The enactment of the "Hadud Ordinance" (1979) according to which women's testimony was declared to be inadmissible in Hadd crimes, including the crime of rape, was accompanied by a wave of violence toward women and a deluge of anti-women literature which swept across the country. Many women in Pakistan were jolted out of their "dogmatic slumber" by the "islamization" of the legal system which, through the promulgation of laws such as the Hadud Ordinance and the Law of Evidence (1984) as well as the threat of other discriminatory legislation (such as the Law of *Qisas* and *Diyat* or "blood-money"), reduced their status systematically, virtually mathematically, to less than that of men. It soon became apparent that forces of religious conservatism were determined to cut women down to one-half or less of men, and that this attitude stemmed from a deep-rooted desire to keep women in their place, which means secondary, subordinate and inferior to men.

Reflecting upon the scene I witnessed with increasing alarm and anxiety, I asked myself how it was possible for manifestly unjust laws to be implemented in a country which professed a passionate commitment to both Islam and modernity. The answer to my question was so obvious that I was startled that it had not struck me before. Pakistani society (or other Muslim societies) could enact or accept laws which specified that women were less than men in fundamental ways because Muslims, in general, consider it a self-evident truth that women are not equal to men. Among the "arguments" used to overwhelm any proponent of gender equality, the following are perhaps the most popular: that according to the Qur'an, men are *qawwamun* (generally translated as "rulers" or "managers") in relation to women;[1] that according to the Qur'an, a man's share in inheritance is twice that of a woman;[2] that according to the Qur'an, the witness of one man is equal to that of two women;[3] that according to the Prophet, women are deficient both in prayer (due to menstruation) and in intellect (due to their witness counting for less than a man's).[4] [Elsewhere in my work I have shown how the first three among the statements referred to above are not warranted by an unbiased, accurate reading of the Qur'anic texts on which they are based.]

Since, in all probability, I was the only Muslim woman in the country who had been engaged in a study of women's issues from a nonpatriarchal, theological perspective, I was approached numerous times by women leaders (including the members of the Pakistan Commission on the Status of Women, before whom I gave my testimony in May 1984) to state what my findings were and if they could be used to improve the situation of Pakistani women. I was urged by women activists who were mobilizing and leading women's protests in a country under martial law, to help them refute the arguments which were being used against them, on a case-by-case or point-by-point basis. Though I felt eager to help, I was not sure if the best strategy was simply to respond to each argument which was being used to deprive women of their human (as well as Islamic) rights. What had to be done, first and foremost, in my opinion, was to examine the theological ground in which all the anti-women arguments were rooted to see if, indeed, a case could be made for asserting that from the point of view of normative Islam, men and women were *essentially* equal, despite biological and other differences.

As a result of further study and reflection I came to perceive that in the Islamic, as well as in the Jewish and the Christian tradition, there are three theological assumptions on which the superstructure of men's alleged superiority to women has been erected. These three assumptions are: 1) that God's primary creation is man, not woman, since woman is believed to have been created from man's rib, hence is derivative and secondary ontologically; 2) that woman, not man, was the primary agent of what is generally referred to as "Man's Fall" or man's expulsion from the Garden of Eden, hence "all daughters of Eve" are to be regarded with hatred, suspicion and contempt; and 3) that woman was created not only *from* man but also for man, which makes her existence merely instrumental and not fundamental. The three theological questions to which the above assumptions may appropriately be regarded as answers are: 1) How was woman created? 2) Was woman responsible for the "Fall" of man? and 3) Why was woman created?

It is not possible, within the scope of this short essay, to deal exhaustively with any of the above-mentioned questions. However, in the brief discussion of each question which follows, an effort has been made to highlight the way in which sources of normative Islam have been interpreted to show that women are inferior to men.

How Was Woman Created?

The ordinary Muslim believes, as seriously as the ordinary Jew or Christian, that Adam was God's primary creation and that Eve was made from Adam's rib. While this myth is obviously rooted in the Yahwist's account of creation in Genesis 2:18-24, it has no basis whatever in the Qur'an, which describes the creation of humanity in completely egalitarian terms. In the thirty or so passages pertaining to the subject of human creation, the Qur'an uses generic terms for humanity (*an-nas*, *al-insan*, *bashar*) and there is no mention in it of

Hawwa' or Eve. The word "Adam" occurs twenty-five times in the Qur'an but it is used in twenty-one cases as a symbol for self-conscious humanity. Here, it is pertinent to point out that the word "Adam" is a Hebrew word (from *adamah* meaning "the soil") and it functions generally as a collective noun referring to "the human" rather than to a male person. In the Qur'an, the word "Adam" (which Arabic borrowed from Hebrew) mostly does not refer to a particular human being. Rather, it refers to human beings in a particular way. As pointed out by Muhammad Iqbal:

> Indeed, in the verses which deal with the origin of man as a living being, the Qur'an uses the words "Bashar" or "Insan," not "Adam" which it reserves for man in his capacity of God's vicegerent on earth. The purpose of the Qur'an is further secured by the omission of proper names mentioned in the Biblical narration—Adam and Eve. The term "Adam" is retained and used more as a concept than as a name of a concrete human individual. The word is not without authority in the Qur'an itself.[5]

An analysis of the Qur'anic descriptions of human creation shows how the Qur'an evenhandedly uses both feminine and masculine terms and imagery to describe the creation of humanity from a single source. That God's original creation was undifferentiated humanity and not either man or woman (who appeared simultaneously at a subsequent time) is implicit in a number of Qur'anic passages. If the Qur'an makes no distinction between the creation of man and woman—as it clearly does not—why do Muslims believe that Hawwa' was created from Adam's rib? It is difficult to imagine that Muslims got this idea directly from Genesis 2 since very few Muslims read the Bible. It is much more likely that the rib story entered the Islamic tradition through being incorporated in the Hadith literature during the early centuries of Islam. In this context, the following six *ahadith* are particularly important since they are cited in *Sahih al-Bukhari* and *Sahih Muslim* which Sunni Muslims regard as the two most authoritative Hadith collections, whose authority is exceeded only by the Qur'an:

> 1. Treat women nicely, for a woman is created from a rib, and the most curved portion of the rib is its upper portion, so if you would try to straighten it, it will break, but if you leave it as it is, it will remain crooked. So treat women nicely.[6]

2. The woman is like a rib, if you try to straighten her, she will break. So if you want to get benefit from her, do so while she still has some crookedness.[7]

3. Whoever believes in Allah and the Last Day should not hurt (trouble) his neighbor. And I advise you to take care of the women, for they are created from a rib and the most crooked part of the rib is its upper part; if you try to straighten it, it will break, and it you leave it, it will remain crooked, so I urge you to take care of woman.[8]

4. Woman is like a rib. When you attempt to straighten it, you would break it. And if you leave her alone you would benefit by her, and crookedness will remain in her.[9]

5. Woman has been created from a rib and will in no way be straightened for you; so if you wish to benefit by her, benefit by her while crookedness remains in her. And if you attempt to straighten her, you will break her, and breaking her is divorcing her.[10]

6. He who believes in Allah and the Hereafter, if he witnesses any matter he should talk in good terms about it or keep quiet. Act kindly towards women, for woman is created from a rib, and the most crooked part of the rib is its top. If you attempt to straighten it, you will break it, and if you leave it, its crookedness will remain there so act kindly towards women.[11]

Elsewhere I have examined the above *ahadith* and shown them to be weak with regards to their formal aspect (i.e. with reference to their *isnad* or list of transmitters). As far as their content (*matn*) is concerned, it is obviously in opposition to the Qur'anic accounts about human creation. Since all Muslim scholars agree on the principle that any *hadith* which is in contradiction to the Qur'an cannot be accepted as authentic, the above-mentioned *ahadith* ought to be rejected on material grounds. However, they still continue to be a part of the Islamic tradition. This is due certainly, in significant measure, to the fact that they are included in the Hadith collections by Muhammad ibn Isma'il al'Bukhari (810-70) and Muslim bin al-Hallaj (817-75), collectively known as the *Sahihan* (from *sahih* meaning "sound" or "authentic") which "form an almost unassailable authority, subject indeed to criticism in details, yet deriving an indestructible influence from the 'ijma' or general consent of the community in custom and belief, which it is their function to authenticate."[12] But the continuing popularity of these *ahadith* amongst Muslims in general also indicates that they articulate something deeply embedded in Muslim culture, namely, the belief that women are derivative and secondary in the context of human creation.

Theologically, the history of women's inferior status in the Islamic (as well as the Jewish and Christian) tradition began with the story of Hawwa's creation from a (crooked) rib. Changing her status requires returning to the point of creation and setting the record straight. Given the way the rib story has been used, it is impossible to overemphasize its importance. The issue of woman's creation is more fundamental theologically than any other. This is so because if man and woman have been created equal by God who is the ultimate giver of value, then they cannot become unequal, essentially, at a subsequent time. On the other hand, if man and woman have been created unequal by God, then they cannot become equal, essentially, at a subsequent time. If one upholds the view that man and woman were created equal by God—which is the teaching of the Qur'an—then the existing inequality between men and women cannot be seen as having been mandated by God but must be seen as a subversion of God's original plan for humanity.

Was Woman Responsible for the "Fall" of Man?

Muslims, like Jews and Christians, generally answer the above question affirmatively, though such an answer is not warranted by the Qur'an. Here, it needs to be pointed out that the Qur'anic account of the "Fall" episode differs significantly from the Biblical account. To begin with, whereas in Genesis 3 no explanation is given as to why the serpent tempts either Eve alone or both Adam and Eve, in the Qur'an the reason why *ash-Shaitan* (or *Iblis*) sets out to beguile the human pair in the Garden is stated clearly in a number of passages.[13] The refusal of *ash-Shaitan* to obey God's command to bow in submission to Adam follows from his belief that being a creature of fire, he is elementally superior to Adam, who is an earth-creature. When condemned for his arrogance by God and ordered to depart in a state of abject disgrace, *ash-Shaitan* throws a challenge to God: he will prove to God that Adam and Adam's progeny are ungrateful, weak and easily lured by temptations and, thus, unworthy of the honor conferred on them by God. Not attempting to hide his intentions to come upon human beings from all sides, *ash-Shaitan* asks for—and is granted—a reprieve until "the Day of the Appointed Time." Not only is the reprieve granted, but God also tells *ash-Shaitan* to use all his wiles and forces to assault human beings and see if they would follow him. A cosmic drama now begins, involving the eternal opposition between the principles of good and evil which is lived out as human beings, exercising their moral autonomy, choose between "the straight path" and "the crooked path."

In terms of the Qur'anic narrative, what happens to the human pair in the Garden is a sequel to the interchange between God and *ash-Shaitan*. In the sequel we learn that the human pair have been commanded not to go near the Tree lest they become *zalimin*. Seduced by *ash-Shaitan*, they disobey God. However, in Surah 7: *Al-A'raf*:23 they acknowledge before God that they have done *zulm* to themselves and earnestly seek God's forgiveness and mercy. They are told to "go forth" and "descend" from the Garden, but in addressing them the Qur'an uses the dual form of address only once (in Surah 18: *Ta-Ha*:123); for the rest, the plural form is used which necessarily refers to more than two persons and is generally understood as referring to humanity as a whole.

In the framework of Qur'anic theology, the order to go forth from the Garden given to Adam or Children of Adam cannot be considered a punishment because Adam was always meant to be God's vicegerent on earth (Surah 2: *Al-Baqarah*:30). The earth is not a place of banishment but is declared by the Qur'an to be humanity's dwelling place and a source of profit to it.[14]

There is, strictly speaking, no "Fall" in the Qur'an. What the Qur'anic narration focuses upon is the moral choice that humanity is required to make when confronted by the alternatives presented by God and *ash-Shaitan*. This becomes clear if one reflects on Surah 2: *Al-Baqarah*:35 and Surah 7: *Al-A'raf*:19, in which it is stated: "You (dual) go not near this Tree, lest you (dual) become the 'zalimin.'" In other words, the human pair is being told that if they go near the Tree, then they will be counted among those who perpetrate *zulm*. Commenting on the root *zlm*, Toshihiko Izutsu says:

> The primary meaning of ZLM is, in the opinion of many authoritative lexicologists, that of "putting in a wrong place." In the moral sphere it seems to mean primarily "to act in such a way as to transgress the proper limit and encroach upon the right of some other person." Briefly and generally speaking, "zulm" is to do injustice in the sense of going beyond one's bounds and doing what one has no right to.[15]

By transgressing the limits set by God, the human pair become guilty of *zulm* toward themselves. This *zulm* consists in their taking on the responsibility for choosing between good and evil.

As pointed out by Iqbal, the

> Qur'anic legend of the Fall has nothing to do with the first appearance of man on this planet. Its purpose is rather to indicate man's rise from a primitive state of instinctive appetite to the conscious possession of a free self, capable of doubt and disobedience. The Fall does not mean any moral depravity; it is man's transition from simple consciousness to the first flash of self-consciousness. . . .Nor does the Qur'an regard the earth as a torture-hall where an elementally wicked humanity is imprisoned for an original act of sin. Man's first act of disobedience was also his first act of free choice; and that is why, according to the Qur'anic narration, Adam's first transgression was forgiven. . . .A being whose movements are wholly determined like a machine cannot produce goodness. Freedom is thus a condition of goodness. But to permit the emergence of a finite ego who has the power to choose . . . is really to take a great risk; for the freedom to choose good involves also the freedom to choose what is the opposite of good. That God has taken this risk shows his immense faith in man; it is now for man to justify this faith.[16]

Even though there is no "Fall" or Original Sin in the Qur'an, the association of the episode described in Genesis 3 with fallen humanity and illicit sexuality which has played such a massive role in perpetuating the myth of feminine evil in the Christian tradition, also exists in the minds of many Muslims and has had an extremely negative impact on the lives of millions of Muslim women. The following comment of A. A. Maududi—one of contemporary Islam's most influential scholars—is representative of the thinking of many, if not most, Muslims:

> The sex instinct is the greatest weakness of the human race. That is why Satan selected this weak spot for his attack on the adversary and devised the scheme to strike at their modesty. Therefore the first step he took in this direction was to expose their nakedness to them so as to open the door to indecency before them and beguile them into sexuality. Even to this day, Satan and his disciples are adopting the same scheme of depriving the woman of the feelings of modesty and shyness, and they cannot think of any scheme of "progress" unless they expose and exhibit the woman to all and sundry.[17]

Though the branding of women as "the devil's gateway"[18] is not at all the intent of the Qur'anic narration of the "Fall" story, Muslims, no less than Jews and Christians, have used the story to vent their misogynistic feelings. This is clear from the continuing popularity of *ahadith* such as the following:

> The Prophet said, "After me I have not left any affliction more harmful to men than women."[19]

> Ibn Abbas reported that Allah's Messenger said: "I had a chance to look into Paradise and I found that the majority of the people were poor and I looked into the Fire and there I found the majority constituted by women."[20]

> Abu Sai'id Khudri reported that Allah's Messenger said: "The world is sweet and green (alluring) and verily Allah is going to install you as viceregent in it in order to see how you act. So avoid the allurement of women: verily, the first trial for the people of Isra'il was caused by women."[21]

Why Was Woman Created?

The Qur'an, which does not discriminate against women in the context of creation or the "Fall" episode, does not support the view held by many Muslims, Christians and Jews that women were created not only *from man but also for* man. That God's creation as a whole is "for just ends" (Surah 15: *Al-Hijr*:85) and not "for idle sport" (Surah 21: *Al-Anbiya*:16) is one of the major themes of the Qur'an. Humanity, consisting of both men and women, is fashioned "in the best of moulds" (Surah 95: *At-Tin*:4) and is called to righteousness which requires the honoring of *Haquq Allah* (Rights of God) as well as *Haquq al-'ibad* (Rights of creatures). Not only does the Qur'an make it clear that man and woman stand absolutely equal in the sight of God, but also that they are "members" and "protectors" of each other. In other words, the Qur'an does not create a hierarchy in which men are placed above women nor does it pit men against women in an adversary relationship. They are created as equal creatures of a universal, just and merciful God whose pleasure it is that they live together in harmony and righteousness.

In spite of the Qur'anic affirmation of man-woman equality, Muslim societies, in general, have never regarded men and women as equal, particularly in the context of marriage. Fatima Mernissi has aptly observed:

One of the distinctive characteristics of Muslim sexuality is its territoriality, which reflects a specific division of labor and a specific conception of society and of power. The territoriality of Muslim sexuality sets ranks, tasks, and authority patterns. Spatially confined, the woman was taken care of materially by the man who possessed her, in return for her total obedience and her sexual and reproductive services. The whole system was organized so that the Muslim "ummah" was actually a society of male citizens who possessed among other things the female half of the population. . . .Muslim men have always had more rights and privileges than Muslim women, including even the right to kill their women. . . .The man imposed on the woman an artificially narrow existence, both physically and spiritually.[22]

Underlying the rejection in Muslim societies of the idea of man-woman equality is the deeply-rooted belief that women—who are inferior in creation (having been made from a crooked rib) and in righteousness (having helped *ash-Shaitan* in defeating God's plan for Adam)—have been created mainly to be of use to men who are superior to them. The alleged superiority of men to women which permeates the Islamic (as well as the Jewish and Christian) tradition is grounded not only in Hadith literature but also in popular interpretations of some Qur'anic passages. Two Qur'anic passages—Surah 4: *An-Nisa'*:34 and Surah 2: *Al-Baqarah*:288 in particular—are generally cited to support the contention that men have "a degree of advantage" over women. Of these, the first reads as follows in A. A. Maududi's translation of the Arabic text:

Men are the managers of the affairs of women because Allah has made the one superior to the other and because men spend of their wealth on women. Virtuous women are, therefore, obedient; they guard their rights carefully in their absence under the care and watch of Allah. As for those women whose defiance you have cause to fear; admonish them and keep them apart from your beds and beat them. Then, if they submit to you, do not look for excuses to punish them: note it well that there is Allah above you, who is Supreme and Great.[23]

It is difficult to overstate the negative impact which the popular Muslim understanding of the above verse has had on the lives of Muslim women. Analysis of this verse shows how it has been misinterpreted. For instance, the key word in the first sentence is *qawwamun*. This word is most often translated as *hakim* or "rulers." By making men "rulers" over women, a hierarchy akin to the one created by St. Paul and his followers in the Christian tradition, is set up in the Islamic *ummah*. Linguistically, the word *qawwamun* refers to those who provide a means of support or livelihood. In my exegesis of this verse, I have argued that the function of supporting women economically has been assigned to men in the context of child-bearing—a function which can only be performed by women. The intent of this verse is not to give men power over women but, rather, to ensure that while women are performing the important tasks of child-bearing and child-raising they do not have the additional responsibility of being breadwinners as well. The root word *daraba*, which has been generally translated as "beating," is one of the commonest root words in the Arabic language, with a large number of possible meanings. That the vast majority of translators—who happen to be all men—have chosen to translate this word as "beating" clearly indicates a bias in favor of a male-controlled, male-oriented society.

The second Qur'anic passage which is cited to support the idea that men are superior to women is in the specific context of *iddat*—a three-month waiting period prescribed for women between the pronouncement of divorce and remarriage. The "advantage" men have in this regard is that they do not have to observe this waiting period due to the fact that, unlike women, they do not become pregnant (the three-month waiting period is for making certain that the woman is not pregnant). That the intent of this verse is to ensure justice is made clear by its emphasis that "women shall have rights similar to the rights against them, according to what is equitable."

The reading of the Qur'an through the lens of the Hadith is, in my opinion, a major reason for the misreading and misinterpretation of many passages which have been used to deny women equality and justice. The following hadith is often cited to elevate man to the status os *majazi khuda* (god in earthly form):

> A man came . . . with his daughter and said, "This my daughter refuses to get married." The Prophet said, "Obey your father." She said, "by the name of Him Who sent you in truth, I will not marry until you inform me what is the right of the husband over his wife." He said, . . . "If it were permitted for one human being to bow down (*sajada*) to another I would have ordered the woman to bow down to her husband when he enters into her, because of God's grace on her." (The daughter answered,) "by the name of Him Who sent you, with truth I would never marry!"[24]

A faith as rigidly monotheistic as Islam which makes *shirk* or association of anyone with God the one unforgivable sin, cannot conceivably
permit any human being to worship anyone but God. However, this
hadith makes it appear that if not God's, it was the Prophet's wish to
make the wife prostrate herself before her husband. Since each word,
act or exhortation of the Prophet is held to be sacred by Muslims in
general, this *hadith* has had much impact on Muslim women. How
such a *hadith* could be attributed to the Prophet who regarded the
principle of *Tauhid* (Oneness of God) as the basis of Islam, is, of
course, utterly shocking.

In Summation

Reference has been made in the foregoing account to the fundamental theological assumptions which have colored the way in which
Muslim culture, in general, has viewed women. That these assumptions have had serious negative consequences and implications—both
theoretical and practical—for Muslim women throughout Muslim
history up until the present time needs to be emphasized. At the same
time, it needs to be borne in mind that the Qur'an, which to Muslims
in general is the most authoritative source of Islam, does not discriminate against women despite the sad and bitter fact of history that
the cumulative (Jewish, Christian, Hellenistic, Bedouin, and other)
biases which existed in the Arab-Islamic culture of the early centuries
of Islam infiltrated the Islamic tradition, largely through the Hadith
literature, and undermined the intent of the Qur'an to liberate women
from the status of *chattel* or inferior creatures, making them free and
equal to men. Not only does the Qur'an emphasize that righteousness
is identical in the case of man or woman, but it affirms, clearly and
consistently, women's equality with men and their fundamental right
to actualize the human potential that they share equally with men. In
fact, when seen through a non-patriarchal lens, the Qur'an goes beyond egalitarianism. It exhibits particular solicitude toward women as
also toward other classes of disadvantaged persons. Further, it provides particular safeguards for protecting women's special sexual/
biological functions such as carrying, delivering, suckling and rearing
of offspring.

God, who speaks through the Qur'an, is characterized by justice,
and it is stated clearly in the Qur'an that God can never be guilty of
zulm (unfairness, tyranny, oppression, or wrongdoing). Hence, the

Qur'an, as God's Word, cannot be made the source of human injustice, and the injustice to which Muslim women have been subjected cannot be regarded as God-derived. The goal of Qur'anic Islam is to establish peace which can only exist within a just environment. Here it is of importance to note that there is more Qur'anic legislation pertaining to the establishment of justice in the context of family relationships than on any other subject. This points to the assumption implicit in much Qur'anic legislation, namely, that if human beings can learn to order their homes justly so that the rights of all within it—children, women, men—are safeguarded, then they can also order their society and the world at large, justly. In other words, the Qur'an regards the home as a microcosm of the *ummah* and the world community, and emphasizes the importance of making it "the abode of peace" through just living.

In my judgment, the importance of developing what the West calls "feminist theology" in the context of the Islamic tradition is paramount today in order to liberate not only Muslim women, but also Muslim men, from unjust structures and systems of thought which make a peer relationship between men and women impossible. It is good to know that in the last hundred years there have been at least two significant Muslim men scholars and activists—Qasim Amin from Egypt and Mumtaz Ali from India—who have been staunch advocates of women's rights, though knowing this fact hardly lessens the pain of also knowing that even in this age characterized by an explosion of knowledge, all but a handful of Muslim women lack any knowledge of Islamic theology. It is profoundly discouraging to contemplate how few Muslim women there are in the world today who possess the competence, even if they have the courage and commitment, to engage in a scholarly study of Islam's primary sources in order to participate in the theological discussions on women-related issues which are taking place in most contemporary Muslim societies. Such participation is imperative if Qur'anic Islam is to emerge in Muslim societies and communities.

NOTES

1. Reference is made, here, to Surah 4: *An-Nisa'*:34.
2. Reference is made, here, to Surah 4: *An-Nisa'*:11.
3. Reference is made, here, to Surah 2: *Al-Baqarah*:282.
4. Reference is made, here, to *ahadith* (plural of *hadith*, meaning an oral tradition)

cited in *Sahih al-Bukhari* and *Sahih Muslim*.

5. Muhammad Iqbal, *The Reconstruction of Religious Thought in Islam* (Lahore: Shaikh Muhammad Ashraf, 1962), p. 83.
6. M.M. Khan, translation of *Sahih Al-Bukhari* (Lahore: Kazi Publications, 1971), p. 346.
7. *Ibid.*, p. 80.
8. *Ibid.*, p. 81.
9. A.H. Siddiqui, translation of *Sahih Muslim*, Vol. 2 (Lahore: Shaikh Muhammad Ashraf, 1972), p. 752.
10. *Ibid.*
11. *Ibid.*, pp. 752-753.
12. Alfred Guillaume, *The Traditions of Islam* (Beirut: Khayats, 1966), p. 37.
13. For instance, Surah 15: *Al-Hijr*:26-43; Surah 17: *Bani Isra'il*:61-64; Surah 18: *Al-Kahf*:50; and Surah 38: *Sad*:71-85.
14. Muhammad Iqbal, *op. cit.*, p. 84.
15. Toshihiko Izutsu, *The Structure of Ethical Terms in the Koran* (Mita, Siba, Mina-toku, Tokyo: Keio Institute of Philosophical Studies, 1959), pp. 152-153.
16. Muhammad Iqbal, *op. cit.*, p. 85.
17. A.A. Maududi, *The Meaning of the Qur'an*, Vol. 2 (Lahore: Islamic Publications Ltd., 1976), p. 16, n. 13.
18. This well-known expression comes from Tertullion, a North African Church Father.
19. M.M. Khan, *op. cit.*, p. 22.
20. A.H. Siddiqui, *op. cit.*, p. 1431.
21. *Ibid.*
22. Fatima Mernissi, *Beyond the Veil* (Cambridge: Schenkman Publishing Company, 1975), p. 103.
23. A.A. Maududi, *The Meaning of the Qur'an*, Vol. 2 (Lahore: Islamic Publications Ltd., 1971), p. 321.
24. Sadiq Hasan Khan, *Husn al-Uswa* (Publication details unavailable), p. 281.

16

A MUSLIM PERSPECTIVE ON ISLAMIC FUNDAMENTALISM

Raficq Abdullah

I CANNOT HOPE to address all the details of this complex and extremely important topic in a short essay. Therefore, I intend to limit myself to a few observations, which, while they may seem only to touch the edges of the subject, may help us to understand something about the assumptions and attitudes which make up the world of "Islamic Fundamentalism."

First, I want to clarify the issue of nomenclature. The term "fundamentalism," like the terms "blasphemy," "democracy" and "sovereignty," do not easily translate into an Islamic lexicon. They convey primarily Western notions and can be profoundly misleading. In a sense, all Muslims are fundamentalists insofar as they believe that the Qur'an is the literal word of God and therefore infallible; they agree on the basic rules, regulations and the universal values set out in the Holy Text, and in the religious law or *Shariah* which has developed from it. However, while it would be justifiable to call all Muslims "fundamentalists" as long as we so limit the meaning of the word, such a move would be unenlightening, since the word has developed wider resonances. Not all Muslims are "fundamentalists" in this broader sense where the word refers to the type of person who uses religion as an all-encompassing ideology with undertones of fanatical commitment and a tendency to the use of violence to achieve his or her dogmatic goals.

Now the word "fundamentalism" does not translate easily into Arabic. Muslim writers use a variety of expressions which carry very different connotations. For example they may use the word *islah* (reform) or *salafiyya* signifying a return to the prelapsarian practices of the founding figures of Islam who have a sacred, mythical status for all believers. Sometimes, the words *tajdid* (renewal) or *nahda* (renaissance) are used. With the more radical movements, new concepts have come into existence, such as *takfir* (the heralding of something or someone as un-Islamic) or *hijra* (the flight from unbelief). New vociferous radical groups, adopting these concepts as their slogans or programs, have come into prominence during the last decade in the Islamic world; they have, with some doctrinal plausibility, politicized religious belief by making Islam the blueprint of an ideal and completely sacred social order based on a set of rules which are divinely ordained, eternal and entirely independent of the will of mankind. However, a more appropriate term for these Muslim ideologues would be "Islamists" or "Radical Muslims" which distinguishes them from the mass of Muslim believers. I shall use the former term, always keeping in mind, however, that "Islamists," like "fundamentalists," are not in themselves sufficient explanatory notions or synecdoches for the complexity, fluidity and richness of the culture and civilization which goes by the name of "Islam" and which does not correspond to a stable entity existing as a natural fact. There is a continuous struggle over the definition and the representation of the culture involving not only the vagaries of the grand narratives of meaning and value about which there may be common assent in the communal imagination, but also translating into particular social issues on matters concerning orthodoxy, specific legislation, immigration, justification of violence and so on. Notwithstanding the assertions to the contrary of Western conservatives and the Islamists who enjoy unconscious affinities which, in spite of their overt hostility, unwittingly expose some common ground between themselves, Islam is not some mythically pure entity free from the contamination of history. Therefore, to talk portentously about a so-called "Clash of Civilizations" as Sam Huntington does in a recent edition of *Foreign Affairs* is a preposterous and dangerous proposition.[1] Huntington's thesis, which is that Islam is a civilization which basically rejects western values, creates false antithetical essences. He takes no account of the erosive effects of history or the hybridity of notions such as the "West" or "Islam." There are indeed different values in the Islamic world as there are also values, especially ethical values, which are shared with the West (not particularly surprising since Western and Islamic cultures are contiguous and are derived from common roots). However, difference does not automatically imply *rejection*. As I have indicated above, Huntington's view manifests a curious correspondence with the attitudes projected by the Islamists.

Edward Said is right when he observes, "So the real battle is not a clash of civilizations, but a clash of definitions."[2] And the main or most interesting battle of definitions is occurring *within* the world of Islam in which many voices are striving to be heard. This idea may be too subtle or nuanced for polemicists like Huntington who are more used to the hurly-burly of journalism and "policy making" which thrive on blanket condemnations or approvals, at least in public. However, the idea merits serious consideration, and the Islamic world deserves a more refined analysis of its condition than either the policy makers of the West or the Islamists are prepared to grant it.

Not only should we tread lightly with regard to cultural differences, but also constantly remind ourselves about the inherent shortcomings of language which never reflects the complex, mercurial nature of reality, of the "world-out-there," but at best, acts as a rough and ready short-hand for our representations of this reality. Therefore, "fundamentalism" or Islamic radicalism, like "Islam," is what we make of it, or, to be more accurate, what the media and the pundits or the intellectuals who help to construct information *make* it for us in their bid to influence public consciousness.

It has now become commonplace in the Western world to associate Islam with terrorism, fanatical militancy and vitriolic, anti-democratic, anti-Western sentiment. There is a growing belief among some Western opinion-formers who seem to be incapable of thinking other than in stereotypes, that the Islamic world has replaced the now defunct Soviet Union and Communism as the common enemy. There is, indeed, an underlying strata of latent racism in the plethora of lurid images of Islam spewed out daily by the Western media which inevitably produce a reductionist and inimical representation of Islam, suggesting an almost genetically inscribed difference between Western, secular culture and a more viscerally-compelled yet rule-bound Islamic world.

This negative attitude is reflected by an equally paranoid if perhaps more justified feeling in the Muslim world that the expansive, imperial power of the West is the "real" threat to their interests even where the threat may in fact derive from endemic flaws in their own societies. The oppressive facts of colonialism and imperialism are still a living legacy to the subaltern and disabled communities of third-world countries.

We can see that the representation of a distrusting West and vulnerable and materially deprived Muslim world which is resentful of Western hegemony and yet dependent upon it—antagonistic, fixed entities with battle lines drawn—leads to an unstable and divisive relationship between the two cultures which, as I have suggested, may have an empirical, if shifting, existence but also register a spectral imaginary penumbra. This strain of mutual antipathy encourages a racist rejection by Western conservatives of different cultures and plugs into the aggressive rhetoric and hyperbolic tirades of the Islamists. Both camps indulge in a self-fulfilling process of "mutual satanization" in which one side regards the other in terms of a totally alien and inimical essence; the world is dichotomized into dangerous and illusory oppositions.

Since fear of Islam is not new, the images of blood-thirsty Muslims, enraged with modernity, incapable of rational reflection, bent on fanatical destruction in the name of obscurantist and mediaeval notions of right and wrong, are easy to come by. However, the fixing of labels does not teach us to understand the reasons and causes for the actions of the Islamists. As John L. Esposito so succinctly puts it: "Selective and therefore biased analysis adds to our ignorance rather than our knowledge, narrows our perspective rather than broadening our understanding, reinforces the problem rather than opening the way to solutions.[3]

In order to at least open the way, if not quite to a solution, then to the beginnings of a better understanding of the Islamists, I want to bring out some of the assumptions implicit in their world-view. Certain key ideas form the basis of their philosophy and some of these ideas create a profound rift or theological, metaphysical and ideological dichotomy between Western cultural expectations and the values propounded by the Islamists.

These ideas have an immense attraction for the Muslim masses, especially the vast army of the young, dispossessed and unemployed. There is a potent thrust of support for Islamist actions and postures by those who suffer from the dire consequences of socio-cultural dislocation, pauperization, and the profoundly alienating effects of marginalization. These millions of men, women and children are left without hope in an increasingly uprooted modern world. Modernity has nothing to offer them. According to the Islamists, it embodies the virulent return of *jahilliyah* or ungodliness which now infests the entire world, including Muslim societies. The Islamists are obsessed by what they see to be the omnipresence of a perfidious corruption infecting humanity. It is justified by man-made laws which transgress God's legislative authority as enshrined in the religious law or *Shariah*. This comprehensive failure to abide by the only sovereign law which is God's exclusive attribute and prerogative, is, in the opinion of the Islamists, the cause of the moral decay and spiritual bankruptcy prevalent in modern societies. A true Muslim's only shield against this seemingly intractable threat to his or her sense of identity is a reversion to the authentic experience of Islam as it was practiced during the lives of the Prophet and the rightly-guided Caliphs who ruled the Muslim *umma* or community in the early years of the Faith. This was a golden age before the wear and tear of history had set in, when the One God's revelation was new and the hearts of Muslims were open to its divine influence; God was in direct communication with the *umma* and Islam was identical with its society. In this way the Islamists commit epistemological legerdemain by projecting their deeply nostalgic version of events of the founding moment of Islam as ahistorical categories, as givens which it would be sacrilegious, indeed blasphemous, to place under critical scrutiny.

As I have suggested earlier, Islam is not a monolithic entity "out-there" so to speak, nor in fact are the ideological constructions of radical Islam as propagated by the Islamists monolithic. In the first place, we need to recognize the initial divide in doctrine and spiritual alienation between *Sunnis* and *Shias*. Thus the Iranian revolution under the guidance of Ayatollah Khomeini has not had the ideological impact on *Sunni* radical thinking one might have expected. However, there are some remarkable similarities in the overall pattern of Islamist thinking across the *Sunni/Shia* divide. Both feel that "Islam" is threatened by modernity and by the "West" which epitomizes, indeed creates, the demoralizing notions of modernity and which wields overweening influence and power in the world today. For the Islamists, Muslim society, which was once so pure, is contaminated today by some western values which are inherently decadent and corrupt. The Islamists claim to provide a unique solution or cure for the pervasive, pestilential, virulent conditions of societies immersed in *jahilliya*. They have a formula for survival for the Muslim masses who are trapped in the several dystopias of which they are nominally citizens, states marked by disorderly development, the destruction of traditional values, urban congestion, unemployment, endemic corruption—all of which threaten to break over them like a tidal wave. Since it is perfect and the only way (*al-hal-wahid*), "Islam is the solution" is a slogan with which the Islamists intend to persuade (with some success) Muslims that they, the Islamists, as the vanguard of the pure, can lead them out of the shadows of the *jahilliya* into the light of Islam; back to the final eruption of the Truth or *'ilm*, the right knowledge revealed to the Holy Prophet Muhammad by God. An essential part of the process of re-sanctification of the *umma* is the removal of the apparatus of the modern state, by violence if necessary, and also the creation of a new no-nonsense self-image for people torn from their villages, clan, lineage, under the protective shadow of the Qur'an and the *shariah*.

The key to the battle against ungodliness is *hijra* or psychological and, whenever possible, physical withdrawal from those who have lost the True knowledge, from the new Pharaohs and their victims, in order to prepare for the inevitable struggle, or *jihad* against them. This course of action has a sacred precedent since the Holy Prophet Muhammad also withdrew from his native city of Mecca whose powerful citizens had become his enemies, to the city of Medina where he built a separate and potent community. So too, the Islamists are intent on building separate and distinct communities which prepare themselves for the inevitable conflict with their enemies and therefore the enemies of God. Withdrawal from *jahilliya* is absolutely necessary in order to create and preserve a pure identity fixed on carrying out God's Will and reinstating the Truth. Only then can the vanguard of true Muslims become strong enough to wage *jihad*, the projection of God's politics by other means. The Algerian scholar, Mohammed Arkoun, describes the Islamists' compulsion towards *jihad* when he comments: "This intolerable situation renders the divine promise irrelevant, annihilates the work of the Prophet, and necessitates, as a result, recourse to combat on behalf of God—that is to say, in order to stay within the Covenant (*mithaq*) established between God and His creatures."[4]

This sanctified combat or *jihad*, placed at the forefront of the Islamist armory of religious obligations and generally described by Muslims as "struggle," has taken on, in Islamicist discourse, a more aggressive connotation. The *jihad* of the Islamists is derived from the ideas of a mediaeval theologian, Ibn Taymiyya, who used the notion to invoke violent struggle against the Mongols. The Islamists regard the teachings of Ibn Taymiyya as valid today and argue that the solution of taking the battle to the enemy is prescribed by God himself in the verse of the sword which reads: "When the holy months are over, kill polytheists wherever you find them; capture them, besiege them, ambush them." (Qur'an 9.5) Thus the Islamists legitimize violence by an extremely selective, decontextualized reading of the holy text by way of a contrived system of abrogation which chooses to ignore 114 other verses in the Qur'an which preach tolerance, and by citing other texts (such as that of Ibn Taymiyya) which are regarded as touching on the status of the sacred through the ostensible assent of the *umma*. In this way, the Islamists gain a degree of legitimacy by apparently holding fast to sacred history and to holy text. Thus, according to al-Mawdudi, the Pakistani precursor of Sunni radicalism, Islam is "a revolutionary ideology," and its followers are, as a consequence, an "international revolutionary party" who are committed to the creation of a true Islamic polity, a nomocracy in which the *shariah* prevails. In order to carry out the will of God, the "revolutionary party" must seize political power and dismantle the state as presently constituted. The new elite, revitalized by the Qur'anic revelation and empowered by the complete implementation of the *shariah*, can proceed to put humanity upon the right path and purify the modern world of its chronic and godless barbarism. One can see how such a doctrine, which speaks in condemnatory and comforting generalities (Islamists are curiously shy of detailed political programs) can exercise an immense attraction for people who feel beleaguered by modernity and by the implacable impact of a rapacious and amoral global economy or New World Order.

Incapable of envisaging the Qur'an as a linguistic space which contains a multiplicity of discourses (including the prophetic, legislative, eschatological, narrative, metaphysical, spiritual), Islamists choose to ignore the fact that they are interpreting a mythical past and carrying out a partial, generally decontextualized, reading of the words of God.

As Arkoun comments: "The principle of return to founding texts is maintained, even rigidified, but the semantic and discursive manipulation of the texts is entirely subordinate to the ideological ends to the exclusion of all 'scientific' procedures (syntax, semantics, rhetoric, history, theology, even philosophy), that every legal expert (imam mujtahid) was supposed to master."[5]

Encased in a form of hardening of the epistemic arteries which attaches them to a mediaeval mode of thinking, and fixated on the rejection of modernity, Islamists do not recognize the possibility of practicing any form of natural theology which would compel them to acknowledge a system of problematics at work both with the texts they revere and against the cultural, political, ideological and anthropological contexts in which these texts were created in the first place. Such a course of action would be likely to reveal levels of significance unacceptable to their way of thinking. There is a sense in which fundamentalist thinking of any sort may be regarded as a form of respite care in which the fundamentalist wins permanent respite from personal accountability and from the responsibility of independent choice. Armed with the divinely-inspired weaponry of revelation, vulnerability does not come naturally to extremists, be they Jewish, Christian or Muslim. They invariably pound their followers with the ineffable righteousness of their cause. Dogmatism prevails and authoritarianism follows. There are no voices among this rampant brotherhood which are prepared to explore the limits of their vision, never mind the possibility of transgression. A pivotal trait in the Islamists' worldview is an abhorrence of innovation or *bid'a*. There is only one model, that is their version of the life of the Prophet and the ideal community which he established in Medina. Paradoxically, they have no sense of the Islamic notion of *hudud* or limits which is profoundly connected to compromise and tolerance. Unable to detect the hidden or implicit processes, contradictions and telling lacunae in all knowledge, including the knowledge received through revelation, they are imprisoned by their own construction of the Divine Law. Correct belief, and even more importantly, correct practice becomes the basis for a stable society and any alternative belief or value is regarded by the Islamists as apostasy, which is a capital offence akin to treason. In such a moral environment, the traditional values of mercy and compassion so emphatically enshrined in the Qur'an are disposed of in the quest for purity. Thus, as we have seen recently in Pakistan, the *Shariah*, or Islamic Law, is used to repress minorities who have different beliefs and to delegitimize any form of intellectual questioning. The Islamists dream of a pure, cleansed society modeled upon the archetypal community of the Holy Prophet in Medina. The danger, of course, is that in their zeal to create a sacred utopia, they in fact bring about a society which is based upon fixed and authoritarian structures, political and psychological. Any deviation from this dystopia of misguided religious zeal is considered by the Islamists as a sin deserving of the most severe penalties. They dream of a potent, orderly and God-fearing society which, if realized, is likely to be a society of fear and terrible moral blight.

NOTES

1. See Sam Huntingdon, "The Clash of Civilizations," *Foreign Affairs*, Vol. 72, No. 3, Summer, 1993.
2. Edward Said, "Interview with A. Coburn on 'What Is Islam,'" in *New Statesman & Society*, 10 February 1995, pp. 20-22.
3. John L. Esposito, *The Islamic Threat: Myth or Reality?* (New York: Oxford University Press, 1991), p. 173.
4. Mohammed Arkoun, *Rethinking Islam* (Denver, CO: Westview Press, 1994), pp. 96-97.
5. *Ibid.*, pp. 97-98.

17

THE ETHICS OF MARRIAGE AND FAMILY IN CHRISTIANITY AND ISLAM

Thomas G. Walsh

MY CONTRIBUTION to the dialogue of Muslims and Christians focuses on Muslim and Christian ethics concerning marriage and family. The attempt to summarize Christian and Muslim ethics on this topic can easily suffer from oversimplification. After all, both religions stand today on the foundation of many centuries of history, and both have as much diversity and complexity as they have unity and simplicity. Nevertheless, there seems merit in introducing this topic to explore both commonalities and differences between these two traditions on this important issue of Christian and Muslim perspectives on the ethics of marriage and family.

I believe that greater knowledge of each other may contribute to a more constructive and peaceful relationship in the future. In this respect, what follows has the practical purpose of promoting inter-religious understanding.

All peoples and cultures make moral judgments. That is, some actions, such as helping those in need, are judged to be good, right or obligatory; others, such as lying, are judged wrong or impermissible. Even the character of people is evaluated according to moral standards. One person may be judged self-indulgent and another self-controlled; one judged cowardly and another courageous. Religious ethics looks at moral obligations and moral ideals as they are understood within a religious framework. That is, in religious ethics, one judges actions or qualities of character in terms of the fundamental principles and teachings of a given religion.[1]

These fundamental principles and teachings, in turn, are most often derived by appeal to the authority of a sacred text or scripture which contains the revealed word of God. The New Testament and Hebrew Bible, for Christians, and the Qur'an for Muslims are authoritative texts that stand above all other human thoughts, for they represent the word of God on matters of right and wrong. The revelation contained in sacred texts, however, is seldom the sole criterion upon which moral judgments are based in a given religion. In addition to revelation there are other often complementary standards: 1) the lives of exemplary persons such as the founders, saints and sages of a given religious tradition; 2) human reason as it functions to interpret revelation and apply it in circumstances not directly mentioned in the revelation; 3) tradition or the consensus among authoritative voices or respected scholars within a given tradition. Each of these factors—revelation, exemplary lives, reason, and consensus—come into play in important ways in the ethics of both Islam and Christianity. In this sense, when we consider the ethics of Islam and Christianity, we find significant similarities. Neither understands the moral life independent of religion. Scripture is central to both. Each refers to the life and teaching of a central person as the model or paradigm of the moral life. In both traditions, in addition to scripture, reason and consensus function in important ways in the development of ethics. In effect, many commonalities exist, at least at the level of what might be called the general approach to ethics. We now turn to consider the ways in which marriage and family are understood within Islam and Christianity.

Marriage and Family in Christian Ethics

If we examine the Biblical foundations of the Christian view of marriage and family, we find a range of contrasting perspectives. Basic, though, is Jesus' teaching that there are but two great commandments, "You shall love the Lord your God with all your heart, and with all your soul, and with all your mind. This is the great and first commandment. And a second is like it, You shall love your neighbor as yourself. On these two commandments depend all the law and the prophets." (Matthew 22:37-40) Christian ethics, it can be said, is an ethics of love modeled on the life of Jesus, as the exemplary figure or model of the moral life. But let us look more closely at Jesus' teaching concerning marriage and family. On the one hand, Jesus, apart from forbidding divorce [the Gospel of Matthew 19:3-9 makes an exception in cases of sexual misconduct, usually interpreted as adultery], says little about marriage. Moreover, his comments on ordinary familial relations are not entirely positive in that such relations are generally depicted as potential impediments to a faithful relationship with God. In a passage from the Gospel of Mark, we read, "And a crowd was sitting about him; and they said to him, 'Your mother and your brothers are outside, asking for you.' And he replied, 'Who are my mother and my brothers?' And looking around on those who sat about him, he said, 'Here are my mother and my brothers. Whoever does the will of God is my brother, and sister, and mother.'" (Mark 3:31-35) In Matthew we read, "Do not think that I have come to bring peace on earth; I have not come to bring peace, but a sword. For I have come to set a man against his father, and a daughter against her mother, and a daughter-in-law against her mother-in-law; and a man's foes will be those of his own household." (Matthew 10:34-36)

In addition to Jesus' prohibition against divorce, interpretations of Jesus' affirmation of marriage are derived from his attendance and working of his first miracle at a marriage feast at Cana in Galilee, a story mentioned only in the Gospel of John 2:1-12. The story has no discussion of marriage, but focuses on Jesus' changing water into wine. Jesus' parable of the marriage feast in Matthew 22:1-14 is less a discussion of marriage than an allegory of those who are invited but resist the call to the Kingdom of God. Meanwhile, in another parable in Matthew, Jesus links faithfulness to the coming kingdom with virginity. (Matthew 25:1-13)

The Epistles of Paul reflect a generally mixed evaluation of the benefits of marriage. In I Corinthians 7:38 we read, "So that he who marries his betrothed does well; and he who refrains from marriage will do better." Paul advises against marriage "to promote good order and to secure your undivided devotion to the Lord." (I Corinthians 7:35) In a longer passage from the same epistle (7:1-8) we read:

> Now concerning the matters about which you wrote. It is well for a man not to touch a woman. But because of the temptation to immorality, each man should have his own wife and each woman her own husband. The husband should give to his wife her conjugal rights, and likewise the wife to her husband. For the wife does not rule over her own body, but the husband does; likewise the husband does not rule over his own body, but the wife does. Do not refuse one another except perhaps by agreement for a season, that you may devote yourself to prayer; but then come together again, lest Satan tempt you through lack of self-control. I say this by way of concession, not of command. I wish that all were as I myself am [unmarried]. But each has his own special gift from God, one of one kind and one of another. To the unmarried and the widows I say that it is well for them to remain single as I do. But if they cannot exercise self-control, they should marry. For it is better to marry than to be aflame with passion.

We see that Paul accepts marriage, but prefers celibacy.

In a later, and perhaps his last epistle, Ephesians 5:21-6:6, Paul seems to be more realistic in the assessment of marriage, and offers counsel for managing a Christian household, calling wives to be subject to their husbands, for husbands to love their wives as Christ loves the Church, children to obey parents. Some argue that this indicates the waning of Paul's eschatological enthusiasm and growing recognition that ordinary life may continue for some time before the Last Judgment.

Other New Testament references to marriage and family include a mention in Hebrews 13:4 that "marriage be held in honor," and in I Timothy 4:3 the author declares heretical those, such as Manicheans, who teach that marriage is forbidden.

For the most part, both Jesus and Paul seem to privilege the celibate life. According to most theorists, and for whatever it signifies, both Jesus and Paul practiced celibacy. Early Christian theologians almost universally preferred the celibate life. The two central models of the Christian faith, particularly in the medieval era, were Jesus and Mary, both understood to be lifelong virgins. Even Joseph, the husband of Jesus, was idealized by many as a celibate husband in an unconsummated marriage. There is disagreement among Christians as to whether, after Jesus' birth, Mary engaged in ordinary conjugal relations, even producing children, siblings of Jesus. Roman Catholics and the Orthodox assume Mary's perpetual virginity.[2] By and large, virginity was seen as a lifestyle much closer to perfection; hence the reasoning behind the requirement in Roman Catholicism to this day that clergy be celibate. According to Joseph Martos,

> A number of the fathers of the church, including Gregory of Nyssa and John Chrysostom, taught that intercourse and childbearing were the result of Adam and Eve's fall from grace, and that if they had not sinned God would have populated the earth in some other way. Virginity for both men and women was extolled as the way of perfection for those who sought first the kingdom of God and wished to devote themselves to the things of the Lord.[3]

For the Orthodox, only bishops need be celibate; and Protestants do not require and neither do they prefer a celibate clergy.

Early Christianity had no particular interest in the regulation of marriage, leaving that to civil authorities. There was even no official ecclesiastical, liturgical ceremony for marriage. Once married, however, Christians were expected to infuse their marriage with Christian virtue. The theology of marriage that emerged, particularly with Augustine, identified three major goods in marriage: children, fidelity or permanence, and its sacramental quality. However, it was not until the thirteenth century, when Peter Lombard treated it as such, that marriage came to be viewed as a sacrament on par with baptism or the eucharist.[4] Protestant reformers, a few hundred years later, rejected the claim that marriage was a sacrament, as that term was understood within Roman Catholicism.

Certainly Protestantism retained, and even elevated the sacred importance of marriage. Although the terminology of sacrament was rejected by Protestant reformers, the ideal of marriage as an "order of creation" or "vocation" ordained by God for companionship and procreation was affirmed and celebrated. Luther referred to marriage as an "order" or "estate" to which all men and women, with very few exceptions, were called. Expounding on Genesis 1:28 which calls Adam and Eve to "be fruitful and multiply," Luther says,

> From this passage we may be assured that man and woman should and must come together in order to multiply. Now this [ordinance] is just as inflexible as the first, and no more to be despised and made fun of than

the other, since God gives it his blessing and does something over and
above the act of creation. Hence as it is not within my power not to be
a man, so it is not my prerogative to be without a woman. Again, as it
is not in your power not to be a woman, so it is not your prerogative to
be without a man. For it is not a matter of free choice or decision but a
natural and necessary thing, that whatever is a man must have a woman
and whatever is a woman must have a man.[5]

Even the Puritans, often viewed as disinterested in sexuality and
marital love, were in reality strong advocates of a deeply loving
marriage and families dedicated to the service of God. Edmund
Morgan's research on the Puritan family illustrates this point. Morgan
states, "The Puritans recognized this fact in characterizing families as
'the root whence church and commonwealth cometh,' 'the seminaries
of church and commonwealth,' 'the foundation of all societies,' and
'the nurseries of all societies.'"[6]

Despite some differences within the Biblical texts, and divergent
opinions among theologians, there are points of general consensus.
Even in contexts where celibacy is affirmed, marriage and family are
viewed as extremely important and valuable dimensions of human
experience. Christianity has never affirmed polygamy, nor sexual
activity outside of marriage. Sexual intercourse was to be restricted to
a single set of marriage partners. Homosexuality was forbidden.
Children are one of the purposes of marriage; children were to respect
their parents; permanency is affirmed and divorce is seen as a serious
moral failure. Of course, in contemporary Christianity there is wide-
spread debate about many of these issues. There are voices advocating
divorce, extramarital activity, and homosexuality as morally legitimate, and wrongly proscribed in the past.

Marriage and Family in Islamic Ethics

Islam grounds its ethics in the Qur'an. The Qur'an serves as the
basis for Islamic law and ethics, known as Al-Sharia. The Holy
Qur'an, however, is supplemented by the other authorities. First, there
is al-Sunnah, or the ways, practices and sayings of the Prophet. Most
notably within al-Sunnah are the *hadith*, the sayings of the Prophet
Muhammad, which have been passed on reliably from first-hand
observers. In addition to the *hadith*, practical reason, or *ijtihad*, and
consensus, or *ijma*, play significant roles.

Islamic ethics places great emphasis on religious or theological virtue. The central virtue for a good Muslim is submission or surrender to the will of Allah. The word "Islam" means submission, surrender to God, for "There is no god but God." From the *hadith* of Umar we hear that, "The surrender is to testify that there is no god but God and that Muhammad is God's Messenger, to perform the prayer, bestow the alms, fast Ramadan and make, if thou canst, the pilgrimage to the Holy House."[7] One way to summarize the virtues of the faithful Muslim are to mention the virtues of *islam* (submission), *iman* (faith), and *ihsan* (doing what is beautiful). In *The Vision of Islam* we read, "one could say that 'submission' [*islam*] is religion as it pertains to acts, 'faith' (*iman*) is religion as it pertains to thoughts, and 'doing the beautiful' (*ihsan*)is religion as it pertains to intentions."[8] Islam is also a religion built upon revelation and scripture, a sacred text believers trust as the direct word of God. The word "Qur'an" means recitation. The Qur'an is the text transcribed from the angel Gabriel's revelation to Muhammad over a period of some twenty-three years. The Qur'an is understood as the final statement in a line of revelation that began with the Bible of the Hebrews, continued through the New Testament Gospel of Christianity, through to the final revelation given to Muhammad. Muhammad is in some respects the ideal and exemplary person, the moral paradigm for all Muslims. Jesus, for Muslims, is indeed a beloved prophet of God, born with no satanic taint, but he is not the "son of God" and not the messiah, as Christians understand that term. While Muhammad is understood very differently from the way Christians view Jesus, one can see what might be called functional equivalents within the respective traditions. For example, like Jesus, Muhammad is seen as the exemplar of human behavior, the model, the paradigm, the authoritative teacher.

Unlike Christianity, where the ideal of marriage emphasized in the Old Testament was less wholeheartedly affirmed in the New Testament, and where the central person of Christianity lived celibate, as did his mother and step-father (according to Roman Catholicism), Islam has no ambiguity in its treatment of the importance of marriage. Whereas throughout most of Christian history there was a division between married Christians, or laypersons, and celibate Christians or clergy, in Islam there is no basis for the affirmation of celibacy. First, like Abraham and Moses, the Prophet was married, and married more than once, first to Khadija, a widow fifteen years his senior who was his first and most loyal follower. Tradition reports that "God comforted him through her, for she made his burden light."[9]

In this respect there is similarity between Islam and both Judaism and Protestant Christianity. The Prophet Muhammad stated that "Marriage is my Sunnah. He who does not act according to my Sunna does not belong to me." Elsewhere he has said, "A person who marries achieves half his religion, so let him fear God in the other half." Ghazali says, "Most of the people of the *Fir* [Hell] are bachelors." Other quotes from Ghazali: "No building is built in Islam more beloved to God than marriage," and "A Muslim man can acquire no benefit after Islam greater than a Muslim wife who makes him happy when he looks upon her, obeys him when he commands her, and protects him when he is away from her in herself and his property."[10]

Some commentators have questioned Muhammad's own multiple marriages, suggesting that perhaps he had a weakness for women. On this point, Seyyed Hossein Nasr has commented,

> During the period of youth when the passions are most strong the Prophet lived with only one wife, who was much older than he, and he also underwent long periods of abstinence. And as a prophet many of his marriages were political ones, which, in the prevalent social structure of Arabia, guaranteed the consolidation of the newly founded community. . . .The multiple marriages of the Prophet, far from pointing to his weakness towards "the flesh," symbolize his patriarchal nature and his function, not as a saint who withdraws from the world, but as one who sanctifies the very life of the world by living in it and accepting it with the aim of integrating it into a higher order of reality.[11]

The Qur'an affirms marriage: "And He it is who has created man from water and, then he has made for him blood and marriage relationship." (25:54) Marriage is not altogether obligatory, for in cases where one cannot adequately support or care for a wife and children, one should not marry. In general, however, Islam is best counted among those religious traditions that strongly encourage marriage. The Qur'an states: "And among His signs is this, that He created mates for you from among Yourselves, that ye may dwell in tranquillity with them, and He has put love and mercy between your (hearts): Verily in that are signs for those who reflect." In Islam, marriage is part of God's original plan of creation. It is Sura IV (On Women) of the Holy Qur'an which treats marriage and family matters in most detail. The Sura begins, "O Mankind, reverence Your Guardian Lord, Who created you from a single Person, Created, of like nature, His mate, and from them twain scattered (like seeds) countless men and women;

Reverence God through whom you demand your mutual (rights) and (reverence) the wombs (that bore you): for God ever watches over you." (IV:1) Some interpreters point to the significance of speaking of marriage in the same passage which calls for reverence to God, the highest Islamic virtue; in this way, marriage is even more exalted. The passage speaks of the rights of husbands and wives in relation to each other and the value of motherhood.

This same Surah mentions the permissibility of multiple wives: "If ye fear that ye shall not be able to deal justly with the orphans, marry women of your choice, two or three or four. But if ye fear that ye may not be able to deal justly with them, then only one. . . ." (IV:3) The reference to orphans has to do with the number of widows and orphans that resulted from the war of Uhud. Most notable in this verse that approves, but does not require polygyny, are two things: polyandry is not mentioned; perhaps due to the lack of men after the war, and polygyny is acceptable only on the condition of "dealing justly." Interestingly, this verse has been interpreted in radically opposite ways. For some it legitimizes polygyny; for many more, perhaps, it is a prohibition, given the impossible requirement that wives be treated with perfect justice or equality.

Both men and women alike are to inherit property, as verse seven clarifies: "From what is left by parents and those nearest related, there is a share for men and a share for women, whether the property be small or large, a determinate share." Verse eleven further clarifies, however, that male heirs receive twice that of females: "God thus directs you as regards your children's (inheritance): to the male, a portion equal to that of two females."

This Surah also goes into some detail on matters related to who one is able to marry from among one's relatives: prohibited are wives of one's father, one's mother, daughter, sister, father's sister, mother's sister, brother's daughters, sister's daughters, foster-mothers, foster sisters, wife's mother, stepdaughters, wives of a son, and already married women. (IV:23, 24). Marriage to any other is lawful "provided ye seek them in marriage with gifts from your property, desiring chastity, not lust." (IV:24) Marriage between first cousins is acceptable.

The Qur'an does, like Paul in Ephesians, indicate a super-ordinate position for men in the household. We read, in IV:6, "Men are the protectors of women, because God has given the one more strength than the other, and because they support them from their means. Therefore, the righteous women are devoutly obedient, and guard in the husband's absence what God would have them guard." Riffat Hassan, a Muslim scholar, has argued the following point:

> Making men "rulers" over women, a hierarchy akin to the one created by St. Paul and his followers in the Christian tradition, is set up in the Islamic "*ummah*." Linguistically, the word "*qawwamun*" refers to those who provide a means of support or livelihood. In my exegesis of this verse I have argued that the foundation of supporting women economically has been assigned to men in the context of child-bearing and child-raising, a function which can only be performed by women. The intent of this verse is not to give men power over women but, rather, to ensure that while women are performing the important tasks of child-bearing and child-raising they do not have the additional responsibility of being breadwinners as well.[12]

Among the prohibitions in Islam are fornication, homosexuality, adultery, and polyandry. Divorce is seen as reprehensible, but not forbidden and the Qur'an is explicit about the conditions and terms of divorce. One *hadith* (Sunan Ali Daud) states that, according to the Prophet, "of all the permissible things divorce is the most disliked by God." It should be noted that the right to divorce was granted to man and woman alike. Marriage itself requires the consent of both man and woman. Interfaith marriage is permitted, between Muslim men and either a Christian or a Jewish women, although the woman forfeits her right to inherit the husband's wealth. Muslim women are not permitted to marry non-Muslims.

There is some suggestion in the Qur'an that a kind of "temporary" marriage is permitted to soldiers and those whose vocation takes them far from home for extended periods. Shiites uphold this as legitimate, though Sunnites are divided on the issue.

The ends of marriage in Islam, according to Kenneth Craig, are "procreation, unification of families, mutual cherishing, and purity of life."[13] Christianity, too, counts procreation among the ends of marriage, and affirms the value of mutual cherishing and purity of life; the unification of families is somewhat alien to the Christian perspective, especially the modern. Another distinction in Muslim marriage is the financial dimension or dowry which is paid to the bride; this practice has no legitimation in Christian scripture or tradition.

Conclusion

At the time of the 1994 Cairo Conference on Population and Development, Muslims and Roman Catholic Christians allied themselves, to some extent, against the secularist, sexual ideology represented by the United Nations sponsors and affiliates. Christians and Muslims alike were suspicious of a program which seemed to treat abortion cavalierly, and sexual activity as a normal expression of biological needs in no way requiring the sanctification of marriage. Issues of marriage and family thus may be seen as a place for some commonality and sense of shared values among Christians and Muslims.

Muslims and Christians both uphold monotheism. Both accept the authority of revelation. Christians and Muslims alike understand the moral life as fundamentally rooted in the religious life. Moral guidance is derived in both traditions from the following foundations: 1) scripture, i.e., the Bible and the Qur'an; 2) the moral ideal of the exemplary person; 3) reason; 4) consensus.

Both Christians and Muslims see the moral life as related to ultimate ends, personal happiness and ultimate salvation. In terms of marriage and family, the Qur'an seems to pay greater respect to family than does the New Testament. Still, both Christians and Muslims regard the family as a fundamental part of one's earthly and religious life. Islam is more conciliatory in terms of divorce, a factor which some would view as a concession to the legitimate interests of women. While New Testament language is severe, Protestantism has come to be tolerant of divorce, and while Catholics continue to prohibit divorce, they have permitted annulment.

Muslims and Christians, in theory, are against all forms of sexual activity outside of marriage. Within Christianity, however, these traditional views are being radically challenged by homosexuals and those who see a sexually permissive lifestyle as healthy and preferable to restraint. The issues of sexual morality, marriage, and family are emerging as pressing issues in both religious traditions. The rise of feminist theology, homosexual activism, and the call for equality between men and women are giving rise to fundamental debates within both traditions, though more so within Christianity, embedded as it is in Western civilization and its plethora of social and political movements. As such, it seems that the discussion of these issues among people of different faiths is useful, and provides an occasion for mutual benefit, not only in coming to a better understanding of another religion, but in coming to a better understanding of one's own.

NOTES

1. See David Little and Simner Twiss, *Comparative Religious Ethics* (San Francisco: Harper and Row, 1978).
2. See, for example, Dyan Elliott, *Spiritual Marriage: Sexual Abstinence in Medieval Wedlock* (Princeton: Princeton University Press, 1993) and Elaine Pagels, *Adam, Eve and the Serpent* (New York: Basic Books, 1991).
3. Joseph Martos,"Marriage," in Kieran Scott and Michael Warren, eds., *Perspectives on Marriage* (Oxford: Oxford University Press, 1993), p. 43.
4. Martos, p. 51.
5. Martin Luther, "The Estate of Marriage," in Herbert Richardson and Elizabeth Clark, eds., *Women and Religion: A Feminist Sourcebook of Christian Thought* (New York: Harper, 1977), p. 135.
6. See Edmund Morgan, *The Puritan Family* (New York: Harper and Row, 1996), p. 143.
7. Sachiko Murata and William Chittick, *The Vision of Islam* (New York: Paragon, 1994), p. 147.
8. Huston Smith, *The World's Religions* (San Francisco: Harper, 1991), p. 224.
9. These quotes are taken from Sachiko Murata, *The Tao of Islam* (Albany: SUNY Press, 1992), pp. 171-172.
10. S.H. Nasr quoted in C. Waddy, *The Muslim Mind* (New York: Longman, 1976), p. 61.
11. Riffat Hassan, "Women in Muslim Culture: Some Critical Theological Reflections," *Dialogue & Alliance* (Spring/Summer 1995), p. 134. It is reprinted in this volume on pp. 187-201.
12. Kenneth Craig, *The Call of the Minaret* (Oxford: Oxford University Press, 1964), p. 168.

PART IV

PROSPECTS

18

BOUNDARIES AND GATEWAYS IN THE SOCIAL, CULTURAL AND RELIGIOUS LANDSCAPES OF MUSLIM-CHRISTIAN RELATIONS

Frederick M. Denny

THE RELATIONSHIP between religious beliefs and doctrines and their expressions in everyday life is a fascinating subject. Concerning relations between Muslims and Christians, I have been continuously aware of a shared moral framework that includes truthfulness, a sensitive regard for the rights of others, common courtesy, tolerance and generosity. Gradually, over the years during which I have been professionally engaged in the study of Islam and Muslim societies, I have come to feel very much at home in Muslim contexts. In this essay I view several examples of what I call boundaries and gateways in

Muslim-Christian relations. Boundaries are beliefs, practices and socio-cultural patterns and customs that distinguish between religious communities, sometimes sharply, at other times subtly. Gateways are aspects of religions that welcome the outsider in some way or other, whether intentionally or not. At this point I have not developed these categories in great detail; I am just exploring a direction for understanding interreligious relations at the social, symbolic and behavioral levels more than at the level of doctrine. My reflections may well strike the reader as too personal and anecdotal but I do not know how else to address the subject at hand inasmuch as it relates to dialogue and not to detached scholarly discourse.

Worship and Creeds

When I have been present at *salat*, whether in a public *masjid* or a private residence, I have felt welcome and honored as a guest. When Muslims have visited my place of worship, a rare occurrence in my personal experience, I believe that they have experienced a similar welcome. But neither Muslim nor Christian is normally fully at home in the other's worship space and liturgical format. Yet they are usually able to carry on an intellectual discourse about the most central mysteries and doctrines of their respective faiths without feeling either out of place or compromised. Is this because doctrinal discourse is somehow less weighty than ritual engagement? Or is it because the act of worship completes and certifies in a public manner the otherwise interior and personal beliefs and opinions of the religious subject?

The *Shahada* (There is no God but God. . .) is a sort of performative utterance that goes well beyond indicating a Muslim's personal religious opinion. It is an affirmation and a commitment in public to lead a Muslim life. Its very utterance is an element in sustaining the Ummah. Similarly, the Apostle's and Nicene Creeds, for Christians who embrace them, are utterances that mean more than theological opinions. Both *Shahada* and Christian Creeds are forms of witnessing, and witnessing involves the whole person. A Muslim cannot hedge when it comes to the *Shahada*, because it is at its inception the gateway into Islam. And ever afterwards it serves as one of the defining boundaries of the community of submission. Not all Christians subscribe to a set creed, although the vast majority do regardless of whether they are Roman Catholic, Eastern Orthodox or Protestant. Set creeds have been of great importance in Christian tradition, but they have not been indispensable to following the Christian life. As Kenneth

Cragg once wrote, "It is more important to be alive to God than correct about Him."

In today's late modern and post-modern world, traditional Christian creeds seem to have less appeal than formerly, particularly in the West. Islam has no obligatory creed beyond the compact *Shahada*, although it is certainly possible to point out a consistent pattern of fundamental doctrines and duties agreed to by virtually every Muslim. In the 1960s, then Episcopal bishop of California, the Right Reverend James A. Pike, caused a furor when he announced that he could no longer recite the Nicene Creed. As I recall, he considered it to be too burdened with outgrown philosophical baggage about "substance" and "hypostases" and so forth. Bishop Pike did affirm, however, that he could still sing the Creed. So a metaphorical or symbolic or aesthetic assent to Christian doctrine could continue to serve and provide some coherence between that conscience-stricken priest's personal faith and his public duties as shepherd of the Episcopalians in the Golden State. The Nicene Creed, perhaps even more than the older Apostles' Creed, does have antique philosophical language that is difficult if not impossible for many modern Christians to embrace in a literal fashion. But it also continues to serve in some ways as a boundary of orthodoxy, separating those within the church from all others, as well as providing a consistent and coherent statement of faith, even if only sung and thus rendered in a poetic frame of mind and heart.

The *Shahada*, on the other hand, is a creed for all seasons. In the literal sense, it could be affirmed by Christians of a liberal cast. I have no difficulty affirming the Divine Unity and Muhammad's Apostlehood. Of course, it would be naive, even foolish, to imagine thereby that if I were publicly to utter the *Shahada* I could have my cake and eat it, too. Islamic tradition, as well as revealed doctrine, fairly clearly specify what embracing the *Shahada* entails. Seen this way, religion that is not "brand name" religion is not of any real consequence because it can be all things to all persons. So when I agree with the *Shahada*, I must also come clean about my qualifications regarding its application. The same applies to a Muslim or Jew, who can generally assent to the opening clause of the Nicene Creed, although a Muslim would bracket out "Father." Most of the remaining content of the creed would be unacceptable to a Muslim or Jew, thus constituting a boundary. And the boundary was erected in the first place not to exclude people of other religions—they already followed their own beliefs—but people within the church who had deviated from the

Apostolic faith, as it had come to be articulated and defined, not to mention enforced, by the mainstream.

In my own experience as a visitor at Islamic worship, I have on occasion wanted to participate. But I have held back from doing so because I did not want to mislead my hosts into thinking that I had converted to Islam. I have no disagreement with much of Islamic doctrine, although my liberal reading of scripture would probably not be equivalent to a pious Muslim's. Indeed the matters that I would not be able to sign off on probably do not exceed the doctrinal elements in other Christian confessions that would be outside my circle of affirmation. But I am willing to worship in practically any church that will have me without fearing that my intentions have been misinterpreted by their adherents. If Roman Catholics or Southern Baptists view this visiting Congregationalist as coming over to their side when I join them for worship, I am unconcerned. But if my Muslim hosts were to interpret—as they are entitled to do—my *ruku'* and *sujud* as a witness of conversion to Islam, then I should be greatly concerned. Christians are, or ought to be, used to denominational differences within the Body of Christ, even if, as H. Richard Niebuhr insisted, they are due to an ethical failure (*The Social Sources of Denominationalism*, 1929). Muslims do not have, for the greater part, the types of differences among themselves that produced Christian denominations. As Sunnis and Shi'ites are fond of saying, regardless of the political and cultural matters that sometimes divide them, "The *din* (basic beliefs and practices) is one."

I see a pattern of civic worship emerging, if not from interreligious dialogue then from just living together in our pluralistic societies. Will we have portions of a prayerbook reserved for such occasions, like the passages in the Book of Common Prayer that have appropriate prayers both for rain in time of drought and for the ending of torrential rains? Interreligious worship moments occur at public functions in North America where members of Muslim, Christian, and Jewish communities are present. Usually it is a liturgically simple matter of someone providing a generic invocation or other prayer. An example in America was the first prayer offered by a Muslim imam to open a session of the U.S. Congress in 1991, when Imam Siraj Wahhaj, of Brooklyn, New York's Masjid al-Taqwa served as prayer leader for the occasion. (Of course, the Senate has had a Christian chaplain for many years.) In 1995, a Muslim scholar for the first time delivered Stanford University's baccalaureate sermon.

Ritual Purity

A couple of years ago, in a graduate seminar I taught during spring semester on the liturgies of Judaism, Christianity, and Islam, the class visited a major Islamic center in Denver for Friday *salat*. The three male students were warmly welcomed into the main *masjid* area and provided places to sit against the back wall even though the crowd was overwhelming. The four female students were ushered to the women's area upstairs. However, upon being questioned regarding their state of ritual purity, three of the four were quickly told to leave the worship area because of their menses. Only an older female student was spared such questioning and permitted to remain with the female worshipers. During the discussion at the next meeting of the seminar, the younger women expressed disappointment and frustration. And even though we had gone over the laws and procedures concerning ritual purity in Islam (and Judaism as well), reading a *fiqh* discussion is a different matter than encountering an actual socio-religious boundary of exclusion. My female students knew that their exclusion was not based on personal reasons, and that it applied equally to Muslims as well as guests. And they understood also that ritual impurity is not an ontological condition but a temporary state, whether for males or females. But they still have had to "bracket out"—as it were—their personal experience as distinct from the object of their study. The young women probably did not enjoy a religious experience during their visit to the *masjid*, although they surely had an experience of religion. One of those students later presented before the seminar a perceptive paper on female purity and impurity rules in Islam and Orthodox Judaism.

The ritual purification required of Muslims before the *salat* is absent from Christian worship. (Perhaps an echo is in Eastern Orthodoxy, which has traditionally excluded women—whether menstruating or not—from going behind the iconostasis in the sanctuary, whereas there is no such restriction for males.) There have been and continue to be, in some denominations, certain requirements for being in a fit state to receive the sacrament of communion. Likewise, some Christian bodies—e.g. individual Southern Baptist congregations—practice "closed" communion, barring everyone not belonging to the local congregation (even members of the same denomination).

I have noticed when visiting Arab countries that when my hosts learn that I speak some Arabic, they tend to treat me differently. They know that I am a Christian, or at least that I am not a Muslim, but somehow knowledge of the language of the Qur'an confers a mediating quality on my person and presence. Once I was ritually challenged when riding on horseback in Petra by some boys who were having fun hearing me speak Cairene dialect. When one of the boys asked if I knew any of the Qur'an by heart, I started reciting an *aya*. At first the youth smiled with satisfaction but then he turned in his saddle and, with furrowed brow, queried: "Are you pure?" (i.e. *mutahhar*). It is permissible to listen to the recitation of the Qur'an in an impure state, but not to recite it, whether from memory or from the written copy. In any case, one should not even handle a copy in such a state. I answered, "Of course, young fellow!" And that settled the matter, at least so far as my amigo's conscience was concerned.

Well, I was not pure in the Islamic ritual sense, because I had not performed *wudu'*, whether that morning or at any other time. Had I performed *wudu'* in order technically to remove impurity, what effect would it have had in view of my not being a Muslim to start with? If I am not a Muslim, then I cannot be in an impure state, although surely I can carry impurity to Muslims. In Anthony Burgess's occasionally hilarious novel about Malaysia on the eve of independence—*The Long Day Wanes: A Malayan Trilogy*—ethnic Malays, who are Muslim, avoid physical contact with Chinese at all costs when in a crowd, because the non-natives have touched pork and alcohol and are thus agents of impurity. Interestingly, being a Malay is an ethnic boundary marker for being Muslim, to the extent that one Malay expression for becoming a Muslim means "becoming a Malay."

Names and Naming

Another strong boundary marker, which curiously can also be a gateway, is personal naming. It did not take me long, when I first resided in Egypt for an extended period, to discern who was Muslim and who was Christian just by knowing their names. Butrus, Boulos, Girgis, Abdel-Masih, and Makarios were definitely Christian names. Nadia, Salwa and Maryam were often, though not always, names of Christian women. On the other hand, Muhammad, 'Ali, Fatima, Khadija and Husayn were invariably Muslim names. I think that Muslims like to imagine their Christian friends as Muslims in some way. A longstanding acquaintance, a distinguished Shi'ite theologian, likes to call me Farid al-Din. (He takes my short name "Fred" and converts it into the Arabic root letters fa', ra', and dal, from which he

then derives "Farid.") Once, in a small Javanese village I was introduced to a gathering of social and agricultural welfare workers as Dr.
Frederick Muhammad Denny (my host, a distinguished educational
administrator, said he didn't know what my middle initial "m" stood
for, so he decided to bestow an appropriate name for someone in my
profession). In my graduate school Arabic classes, I was given the
name "'Umar" and that has continued to serve as a tag to my cohorts
from those days long ago. Christian naming practices have been extremely diverse and inconsistent through history, much more so than
Islamic naming. A modern historical account of Muslim conversion
in caliphal times was done through a quantitative method of discerning
the name changes that accompanied the spread of Islam, as recorded
in deeds and other official documents.[1] African-American Muslim
athletes are making Islamic names familiar and respected, a sort of
boundary marking that is also a gateway to new socio-religious understandings.[2]

Sacred Spaces

Muslims have always been extremely protective of their two holiest
shrines, Mecca and Medina, so that non-Muslims are forbidden access.
The fact that certain non-Muslim westerners have gained entry and
lived to tell—and in the cases of Burton and Snouck-Hurgronje—to
write about it, attests to the efficacy of knowing both the Arabic language and the "manners and customs" of the godfearing inhabitants of
the Dar al-Islam.[3] The concepts of Dar al-Islam and Dar al-Harb are
themselves strong boundary ideas. In today's world, such medieval
notions—which have their counterparts in Christendom and heathendom
—are rather outmoded and unrealistic. The growth of Muslim communities in Europe and the Americas requires a new manner of
boundary-setting, most probably, as do modern nation states around
the globe.

Social Boundaries

According to the strictest practice, Muslims are not permitted to
mix socially with members of the opposite sex outside the bonds of
legal consanguinity. When I visit strictly observant Muslim friends, I
expect to converse and eat only with males, both hosts and guests, and
to have little or no opportunity to exchange words with the females
present in the household. Perhaps the woman of the house will offer

a personal greeting before retiring to the women's space in another sector of the home. I accept this separation as normal and proper. When Muslim guests visit my home, they generally expect to be in a mixed social group, conversing and eating with people of both sexes who are non-mahram to each other. I am aware that this is sometimes a strain on my Muslim guests, who nevertheless suspend their usual habit for the time being.

My wife and I would never serve anything that is not *halal* to Muslim guests. But in some ways our home is not quite right for Muslims, because we have a dog that stays inside. We keep our pet enclosed in her wire cage when Muslims visit, so that they do not have to experience having their hands licked. But we do not usually remove our shoes when we enter our living room, because our home is not a *masjid*, as a proper Muslim home must be.

In professional circles, particularly in academe, Muslims and non-Muslims of both sexes often meet for social reasons in restaurants or private homes. And not just in the West. There is a kind of status identity that makes it acceptable for some non-mahrams freely to mix in secular public settings like hotel lobbies and dining rooms, scientific conferences, and airline terminals. Of course, this would not apply to an airline terminal in Saudi Arabia. But the Wahhabi social boundaries collapse when one boards there a foreign carrier, for example Thai Airways, for a flight to Bangkok. As soon as the aircraft doors are sealed shut, the Hijabs come off, women display stylish international fashions, people start partying, and no one seems to be overly worried about mahram/non-mahram status distinctions in the airliner cabin. Clothing and dress codes are important boundaries, with complex webs of meaning.

Greetings and Conversation

Social greetings are both boundaries and gateways. It is common for Muslims to greet a caller on the phone or a person encountered in the street with *Al-Salaamu 'alaykum*. In strict practice, that greeting is reserved for fellow Muslims. Several years ago I was enjoying a visit to Pakistan. After delivering a public lecture at a policy thinktank, I entertained questions and comments. A retired admiral asked me whether I knew what the proper answer for a Muslim was when greeted with *"Salaamu alaykum"* by a non-Muslim. My host, a retired army general (and of course a Muslim), said something under his breath like "What is going on here?" Because of my silence, the questioner in the audience informed me that the correct reply is: *"wa alaykum."* And he was quite right. But my genial host expressed extreme annoyance at what he apparently considered to be a breach of hospitality in raising an issue of boundary marking in Muslim/ non-Muslim social relations. A guest is a guest, after all, and entitled to the dignity and indeed protection of that status.

I have thought about that incident occasionally, not with sadness or resentment, but with curious fascination. It somehow reminds me of a quite different occasion, in East Java, when I was traveling with my Muslim hosts to a distant Qur'anic recitation boarding school—a *pondok pesantren*—on the north coast. I had met my colleagues—a professor at an Islamic university, a graduate student who served as my research assistant, an administrator from the same university, and a blind *muqri'* who would introduce me to the *kiai* of the Qur'anic school and show me about. My jeep had that morning expired at the point, some kilometers outside Surabaya, where I left it when meeting the others. On the longish trip, crowded into a small car, the blind *muqri'* proceeded to describe for me the advantages of being a Muslim. He recited numerous passages of the Qur'an and tied them together in a consistent and rather impressive *da'wa* message. A captive listener, I grunted in a non-committal but friendly manner to his points, and assured my guide that I understood what he was saying, mostly. After a while he fell silent for a bit. Then he grasped my arm, turned toward me and said: "You're worried about your jeep, aren't you?" I said that I was, a little, but that even more I was looking forward to our visit at the Qur'anic boarding school. He then dropped the *da' wa* business and became an ordinary guy.

Of course, we discussed Qur'anic education and related matters like the specialists we were. But he did not idealize anything. At one point he demonstrated his rapid method of chanting, *b'il-hadr*, as it is technically known. I asked him why in the world he wanted to recite so fast. He said that it helped him retain the text in memory. He added that he could recite the whole Qur'an on the train trip between Surabaya and Yogyakarta. I was doubtful and observed that the trip was only some three hundred kilometers, whereupon he specified that he rode the cheap train that stopped at every village. After that day, we remained on excellent terms. Somehow, beyond my scholarship and his valuable additions to it, we realized that we could not only trust and respect each other, but be friends, too. Our mutual but different interest in the Qur'an was a gateway and not a barrier type of boundary.

Scriptures

The Bible and the Qur'an may also be viewed within a discourse about boundaries and gateways. It may be that the Bible is a gateway in most respects, but that in Muslim-Christian relations it is often a boundary. The Qur'an is both a boundary and a gateway. For non-religious people, it is an invitation to ponder ultimate matters. For Christians, it provides an opportunity to see how monotheistic ideas have developed in culturally exotic contexts. The experience of discovering familiar names and narratives—such as the Joseph saga, Moses's encounter with Pharaoh, the birth of Jesus—however different as to details nevertheless invites closer examination and encourages dialogue. But access to an understanding of the Qur'an requires hard work and time. And the Qur'an cannot really be appreciated without experiencing it in the original Arabic. Arabic, for most people, is a formidable boundary, really a barrier. But once one learns enough of the language to read and speak it some, then the Arabic itself becomes a gateway to treasures of scripture and culture.

It is quite possible for Christians to see in the Qur'an God's continuing providence at work and to incorporate the message somehow into their own economy of commitment. The Christian may be able to read the Qur'an as an edifying and empowering message, incorporating it into her or his general understanding of religion like some outlying addendum, an apocrypha after the canon. There may be in this attitude, if it exists at all outside my own experience and opinions, a suggestion of imperialism in the sense that the greater can encompass the lesser scripture and domesticate it for Christian consumption. On the other hand, many Christians don't consider much of the Bible to be more than a collection of diverse religious, historical and moral opinions—a kind of source book for the spiritual journey and in no way a textbook of doctrine and ritual. If a Christian reader of Leviticus, Chronicles, Ecclesiastes, the Fourth Gospel, and the Epistle to James, for example, is able to rank them below the Psalms, Isaiah, Job, Luke-Acts, and Paul's Epistles, what is to keep such a reader from selecting from the Qur'an the cafeteria menu that best suits her?

Muslims, for their part, are obliged to regard the Qur'an as the very Criterion (*al-Furqan*) of truth and the scriptures of the Jews and Christians as corrupted by their communities over time. So, when the Bible is offered to Muslims, it is viewed often as a tainted canon, written by human beings, and full of errors, inconsistencies and contradictions. To be sure, the informed Muslim reader of the Bible knows that there are many good, true and beautiful passages in it. But the Bible is probably often more of a barrier than a gateway for the Muslim who sets about contemplating Christianity. The Qur'an—even though it is not easy to become acquainted with it—is, on the other hand, a gateway to understanding Islam and Muslims and can be read with profit and enjoyed without guilt by some types of Christians, at least. Probably literalist Muslim and Christian readers of their scriptures view the other and their holy books as rivals if not opponents. For each, the other's scriptures constitute barriers.

My first visit to Sumatra was to meet a respected *muqri'* (specialist in the variant readings of the Qur'anic text) who resided there. After my visit I was scheduled to fly to Malaysia across the Straits from Medan. When I approached the check-in counter for my flight, I was informed that my papers were not in order and that I could not depart. I truly do not to this day understand what the matter was. My host, a physician who had endowed a Qur'anic training school for children and actually teaches there part of the time himself, calmly interceded. He explained that I was in Sumatra studying Qur'anic education and that I needed to get across the Straits to Malaysia to see how they learn and follow the Qur'an there. My passport and visa were rechecked by the official who then waved me on to the boarding area for my flight to Penang. The good doctor bade me farewell by saying that my way had been opened because of the blessings of the Qur'an, and he was right.

Conclusions

We have seen in this discussion that there are both boundaries and gateways in Muslim-Christian relations. The former tend to be the specific habits of the heart and body, as well as the community, that set one religion apart from others. For Muslims this includes diet, social relations and separations, purity regulations, a general disinclination to read the Bible, names, forms of address, and space taboos, to mention a few. For Christians, boundaries include membership requirements, creeds, sacraments, denominational differences and the Bible. In both religions, ritual also acts to mark boundaries. The postures and gestures of the Muslim *salat* are as distinctive and unchangeable as are the words which accompany them, and they can be seen at a distance as clear Islamic acts. And only Christians will genuflect before the Cross, make the sign of the Cross, or submit to the kind of ritual separation that is baptism by immersion. I hope that my use of the category boundary in this essay is not interpreted in a negative sense, because my intention has been descriptive and functional analysis, not value judgment.

But there are also significant gateways that provide access to an outsider. Islam's sacred customs of hospitality are one such gateway, as is the Qur'an. Christians also are a welcoming people and their Bible has been made available in many of the world's languages. The denominational differences that divide Christians also provide a variety of dispositions, temperaments and cultures that serve as gateways to diversity.

Certain rituals are mutual gateways shared in by Muslims and Christians at the level of folk beliefs. In Egypt, for example, are saint cults that attract members of both religions, even though the saint may be either Muslim or Christian. Generally, women are most visible in such practices. In India are similar sharings of saint veneration between Muslims and Hindus. Saint veneration thus serves sometimes as a gateway between peoples of otherwise very distinct religious identity.

Much of what I have included in this essay is well enough known to scholars. Much more could be included, for example clothing and dress codes. A discussion of the ways in which Muslims and Christians follow and imitate Muhammad and Jesus would be a worthwhile addition, too. But I think that some of what I have provided could be of value for Muslim-Christian dialogue, especially at the level where people of the two faiths are meeting in such contexts as schools, community organizations, the workplace, prison inmate services, and politics.

NOTES

1. Richard W. Bulliet, *Conversion to Islam in the Medieval Period: An Essay in Quantitative History* (Cambridge: Harvard University Press, 1979).
2. For name choices of African-American converts to Islam, see Warithu-Deen Umar, *The Name Game: The Book of Lost Names—What Every African-American Should Know about Their Names* (Glenmont, NY: Muslim Broadcasting Syndicate, 1991).
3. Sir Richard Francis Burton, *Personal Narrative of a Pilgrimage to al-Madinah and Meccah*, 2 vols. (repr. of 1893 ed., New York: Dover Publications, 1964); C. Snouck Hurgronje, *Mekka in the Latter Part of the 19th Century* (Leyden: E.J. Brill, 1931).

19

THE SERMON ON THE MOUNT AND THE FAREWELL MESSAGE:

THE COMMON CONTENT AS THE BASIS FOR MUSLIM-CHRISTIAN DIALOGUE

Abdul Rashid

Introduction

ACCORDING TO THE TEACHING of Islam, when Allah created Adam as his vicegerent on earth, He also undertook to send unto him His guidance so that he may live a healthy, happy, harmonious and successful life on earth; he also warned that whosoever would follow the Divine guidelines would have neither fear nor sorrow. "We said 'Get ye down all from there; And if, as is sure, there comes to you Guidance from Me, whosoever Follows My Guidance, on them shall be no fear nor shall they grieve.'"[1] The promised divine guidance was given to man through divinely selected men, His ordained Messengers, from time to time.

Today Christianity and Islam are numerically the two major revealed religions, with followers numbering billions. Given the present human condition, it devolves upon the followers of both Jesus Christ and Muhammad (peace be upon them both!) to strive jointly for the betterment of humanity and the solution of its problems.

Consequently, I have selected to present the common elements of the Sermon on the Mount of Jesus Christ (P.B.U.H.) and the Farewell Message of Muhammad (S.A.W.S.) which can form the basis of a Muslim-Christian dialogue and the evolution of a joint action plan.

Sermon on the Mount

I would begin with the Sermon on the Mount, and take up the moral values mentioned therein.

> Blessed are the poor in spirit, for theirs is the kingdom of heaven. Blessed are those who mourn, for they will be comforted. Blessed are the meek, for they will inherit the earth. Blessed are those who hunger and thirst for righteousness, for they will be filled. Blessed are the merciful, for they will be shown mercy. Blessed are the pure in heart, for they will see God. Blessed are the peacemakers, for they will be called sons of God. Blessed are those who are persecuted because of righteousness, for theirs is the kingdom of heaven.[2]

Thus has Jesus Christ elevated the status of the downtrodden, laying a moral basis for what is to come later.

The sanctity of human life and its value has been underscored in the following words:

> You have heard that it was said to the people long ago, "Do not murder, and anyone who murders will be subject to judgments." But I tell you that anyone who is angry with his brother will be subject to judgment.[3]

Nothing can be more eloquent on the subject of brotherhood of man.

Modern humanity is covetous and greedy, always trying to grab what belongs to others. This is manifested at both the individual and collective levels, giving rise to social strife and wars of aggression and acquisition. Humanity's increasing rapacity has eroded the faculty of distinguishing between ethical and unethical, honest and dishonest ways of gaining wealth. Regarding this, the Holy Jesus Christ has this to say:

> Settle matters quickly with your adversary who is taking you to court.
> Do it while you are still with him on the way, or he may hand you over
> to the judge, and the judge may hand you over to the officer, and you
> may be thrown into prison. I tell you the truth, you will not get out until
> you have paid the last penny.[4]

Free, unfettered and irresponsible pursuit of carnal pleasure has
almost destroyed the social fabric and sundered the ties that bind the
family together. Sexual promiscuity has begotten AIDS for which there
is no cure. Jesus has warned his flock against it and admonished them
from even thinking about it.

> You have heard that it was said, "Do not commit adultery." But I tell
> you that anyone who looks at a woman lustfully has already committed
> adultery with her in his heart. If your right eye causes you to sin, gouge
> it out and throw it away. It is better for you to lose one part of your
> body than for your whole body to be thrown into hell. And if your right
> hand causes you to sin, cut it off and throw it away. It is better for you
> to lose one part of your body than for your whole body to go into hell.[5]

Such vehement emphasis speaks for itself.

The status of women is a major issue today. Women have been and
are being ruthlessly exploited physically, emotionally and spiritually
in the name of freedom. Some have been debased to the status of a
prostitute. Marriage too does not ensure for her security, love, happiness and fulfillment anymore. Divorce, which is flaunted as a symbol of freedom, is on the increase, with calamitous effects on the
young generation. Drugs, delinquency crime and mental sicknesses
have resulted directly form the breakup of families. On this, the Bible
says this:

> It has been said, "Anyone who divorces his wife must give her a certi-
> ficate of divorce." But I tell you that anyone who divorces his wife, ex-
> cept for marital unfaithfulness, causes her to become an adulteress.[6]

Lack of tolerance in a society creates civil strife and suffering of
which there are many instances to be seen in the present-day world,
for instance in South and South Eastern Asia, and in some parts of
Africa. Linguistic, ethnic, tribal and religious differences have led to
terrible carnage and taken a horrible toll in human life. The Bible is
very specific in its teaching of tolerance.

You have heard that it was said, "Eye for eye, and tooth for tooth." But I tell you, do not resist an evil person. If someone strikes you on the right cheek, turn to him the other also. And if someone wants to sue you and take your tunic, let him have your cloak as well. If someone forces you to go one mile, go with him two miles. Give to the one who asks you, and do not turn away from the one who wants to borrow from you.[7]

Love for fellow-man and striving for each other's good has been beautifully enjoined thus:

You have heard that it was said, "Love your neighbour and hate your enemy." But I tell you: Love your enemies and pray for those who persecute you, that you may be sons of your Father in heaven. He causes his sun to rise on the evil and the good, and sends rain on the righteous and the unrighteous. If you love those who love you, what reward will you get? Are not even the tax collectors doing that? And if you greet only your brothers, what are you doing more than others? Do not even pagans do that? Be perfect, therefore, as your heavenly Father is perfect.[8]

Self-projection is a characteristic of the modern life style. Today's person hardly ever does a good deed without publicizing it. This too has done much to erode the social structure; good *per se* is no longer a driving force but publicity is. According to Christian teachings, good is to be done only to earn divine pleasure and grace. The relevant passage from the Sermon on the Mount is as follows:

Be careful not to do your "acts of righteousness" before men, to be seen by them. If you do, you will have no reward from your Father in heaven. So when you give to the needy, do not announce it with trumpets, as the hypocrites do in the synagogues and on the streets, to be honored by men. I tell you the truth, they have received their reward in full. But when you give to the needy, do not let your left hand know what your right hand is doing, so that your giving may be in secret. Then your Father, who sees what is done is secret, will reward you.[9]

The glitter of gold has blinded people to the widespread misery around them. On the individual level, humanity is prepared to go to all lengths to make money, no matter what the cost to other fellow humans. On the collective level, the covetousness of big corporations and rich countries is well-known; trade in arms, destruction of the environment through pollution by irresponsible industrialization,

continued marketing—mainly in the Third World—of harmful medi-
cines long banned in the West are a few examples of this. Jesus Christ
has admonished his followers not to love wealth:

> Do not store up for yourselves treasures on earth, where moth and rust
> destroy, and where thieves break in and steal. But store up for your-
> selves treasures in heaven, where moth and rust do not destroy, and
> where thieves do not break in and steal. For where your treasure is,
> there your heart will be also.[10]

Conceit is a besetting sin of humans; each thinks too highly of
himself or herself and denigrates and criticizes others. Jesus Christ has
clearly warned against this tendency:

> Do not judge, or you too will be judged. For in the same way you judge
> others, you will be judged, and with the measure you use, it will be
> measured to you. Why do you look at the speck of sawdust in your
> brother's eye and pay no attention to the plank in your own eye? How
> can you say to your brother, "Let me take the speck out of your eye,"
> when all the time there is a plank in your own eye? You hypocrite, first
> take the plank out of your own eye, and then you will see clearly to
> remove the speck from your brother's eye.[11]

Man undoubtedly needs food and drink and these are the prime
movers of all that man does. The Holy Jesus has clearly stated that
Allah is the Sustainer and He shall grant sustenance. His actual words
are these:

> Therefore I tell you, do not worry about your life, what you will eat or
> drink; or about your body, what you will wear. Is not life more impor-
> tant than food, and the body; more important than clothes? Look at the
> birds of the air; they do not sow or reap or store away in barns, and yet
> your heavenly Father feeds them. Are you not much more valuable than
> they? Who of you by worrying can add a single hour to his life? And
> why do you worry about clothes? See how the lilies of the field grow.
> They do not labor or spin. Yet I tell you that not even Solomon in all his
> splendor was dressed like one of these. If that is how God clothes the
> grass of the field, which is here today and tomorrow is thrown into the
> fire, will He not clothe you, O you of little faith? So do not worry, say-
> ing, "What shall we eat?" or "What shall we drink?" or "What shall we
> wear?" For the pagans run after all these things, and your heavenly
> Father knows that you need them. But seek first His kingdom and His
> righteousness, and all these things will be given to you as well.[12]

The Sermon on the Mount explicitly directs humankind to have faith in God and do good to others so that good is done unto him or her:

> Ask and it will be given to you; seek and you will find; knock and the door will be opened to you. For everyone who asks receives; he who seeks finds; and to him who knocks, the door will be opened. Which of you, if his son asks for bread, will give him a stone? Or if he asks for a fish, will give him a snake? If you, then, though you are evil, know how to give good gifts to your children, how much more will your Father in heaven give good gifts to those who ask Him! So in everything, do to others what you would have them do to you, for this sums up the Law and the Prophets.[13]

One important aspect of this Sermon is that it warns against belief in pseudo-prophets, i.e. self-styled ones, and says that they shall be recognized by their deeds. The relevant passage is illuminating. The relevance of this passage to modern times is obvious. False self-seeking religious leaders and reformers of various sects have led humanity astray; they have contributed more to the drug culture and AIDS than anyone else.

> Watch out for false prophets. They come to you in sheep's clothing but inwardly they are ferocious wolves. By their fruit you will recognize them. Do people pick grapes from thornbushes, or figs from thistles? Likewise every good tree bears good fruit, but a bad tree bears bad fruit. A good tree cannot bear bad fruit, and a bad tree cannot bear good fruit. Every tree that does not bear good fruit is cut down and thrown into the fire. Thus, by their fruit you will recognize them.[14]

The Sermon ends on a golden principle: only active following of the guidance and teachings of the divinely ordained messengers can ensure the welfare of humans in this world and their salvation in the Hereafter. It is a clarion call for action.

The general irreligious attitude of today is directly attributable to the religious guides of today; their deeds belie their call and their way of life belies their calling. They are ever ready to change with the times, with the result that they have no firm ground to stand upon.

> Therefore everyone who hears these words of mine and puts them into practice is like a wise man who built his house on the rock. The rain came down, the streams rose, and the winds blew and beat against that house; yet it did not fall because it had its foundation on the rock. But everyone who hears these words of mine and does not put them into

practice is like a foolish man who built his house on sand. The rain came down, the streams rose, and the winds blew and beat against that house, and it fell with a great crash.[15]

The high morality preached in this sermon is undoubtedly universal and timeless, and its observance in word and deed can lead to human progress and to the solution of human problems.

The Farewell Message

Let us now consider the Farewell Message of Prophet Muhammad (S.A.W.S.). It should be noted that this Message was given shortly before his death and so it can be justifiably considered as Messenger Muhammad's last will and testament.

I believe that the Muslims and the Christians—all sects of them—can open a dialogue on the basis of the salient common points of these Sermons, and notwithstanding the theological differences, can reshape the world on the basis of the moral principles preached therein. Only thus can peace, prosperity and pleasure prevail and humans can live on earth as true Vicegerents of Allah or God or Jehovah or Rama should live.

The Farewell Message delivered by Muhammad (S.A.W.S.) on the occasion of his last Hajj pilgrimage is succinct and included all points that are relevant to present-day problems.

In 10 A.H. the Holy Prophet (PBUH) resolved to perform the Hajj Pilgrimage. The news spread throughout Arabia and thousands of Muslims travelled to Medina to accompany the Holy Prophet (PBUH) for the Hajj Pilgrimage. On 26th of Zi-Qad, he left Medina, reaching Makkah on the 5th Zil-Hajjah. He circumambulated the Holy Ka' aba and offered two Rak'at of Prayer. Then he went up Mount Safa and, facing the Holy Ka'aba, said:

> There is no deity worthy of worship except Allah who has no partner. He alone is worthy of all praise. He is omnipotent and there is no else worthy of worship. He has fulfilled His promise, helped His servant and has Himself defeated all the opposing hordes.

Then the Holy Prophet (PBUH) was engaged in the performance of the rites connected with the Hajj Pilgrimage. He reached Arafaat on the ninth day of Zil-Hajjah. After mid-day he mounted Qaswa, his famous she-camel, and came out of his tent to deliver the Hajj sermon which is reproduced below.

(i) The Arafaat Sermon

All glorifications belong to Allah, we sing His praises and Him alone we call for help. We seek from Him the forgiveness of our sins and express before Him our deep sense of remorse and repentance. We seek his protection from the mischief of our seditious hearts and the evil of our bad deeds. Whosoever finds the support of Allah to lead a straightforward life, no one can misguide him. And whosoever finds no support of Allah, no one else can put him on the right path. I declare the great reality that there is no deity worthy of worship except Allah. He is all Alone and has no partner. I further declare the reality that Muhammad (peace be on him) is His servant and His messenger. O servants of Allah! I exhort you to worship Him alone and this is my counsel of love for you. I begin talk with what is good for you. Then I say:

"Be attentive to me, O people! I lucidly explain to you things which are important because I may not be meeting you in a gathering like this next year. O people! your life-blood and your properties have been made unlawful for one another till you appear in the august presence of your great Lord Creator. Your lives and your properties are as much unlawful and sacred for one another as this day of Hajj is in this sacred month and in this sacred city (of Makkah). Be aware that I have done my duty in communicating to you the counsel and the guidance. O Allah! you also be a witness. If any one of you holds any thing in trust, he must return it to its rightful owner. I write off all moneys of interest earned during the pre-Islamic days of Jahiliyyah. All feuds and all claims of life-blood standing out since the pre-Islamic days are written off. First of all I forego the demand for the blood of Aamir bin Rabiyya bin Harith bin Abdul Muttalib (who was kinsman of Quraish). All honours and privileges connected with the Hajj Pilgrimage are declared to be null and void except guardianship of the Ka'aba and supply of water for the pilgrims. Willful and deliberate murder shall be avenged. Culpable homicide not amounting to deliberate murder which has occurred with a stroke of a stick or a stone shall be compensated with one hundred camels. The number exceeding one hundred will have no value in Islam and will be reminiscent of Jahiliyyah."

"O people! The Satan (devil) is disappointed that he cannot be worshiped in this country where the Divine way of life has been established. Short of his worship as a deity, the devil will rejoice at your indulgence in sins which you consider to be light and insignificant."

"O people! Change and alteration in the order of Sacred months (in which fighting is forbidden) is an addition in the anti-Islamic behaviour

of infidels. Through such behaviour the unbelievers fall into greater mis-
guidance. In one year they discard the sanctity to another month which
Allah, Almighty made sacred. Similarly, they accord sanctity to another
month at their own will, to complete the number (four) of the sacred
months (in which fighting is forbidden). The number of months fixed by
Allah since the creation of heavens and earth has been twelve always.
Among those the months of Zii-qadah, Zil-Hajjah and Moharram—all
three, are sacred in their natural continuity and the month of Rajab
standing aloof from the three—also sacred like them."

"Take notice O people! I have communicated to you all the truth (from
Allah). O Allah! you stand witness to my assertion.

"O people! your women folk have been granted certain privileges and
you too have given certain rights vis-à-vis your mutual relationship. It
is incumbent on them not to allow any one to enter your private bed-
room and not to allow any one disliked by you to enter your house without your permission. This is also proper for your womenfolk to avoid
immodesty in all forms and colours. If they indulge in any of the forbidden things, you are allowed to let them alone in their beds and, if
necessary, may also resort to physical punishment not causing injury. If
they repent and obey your wishes, you should discharge your obligations
regarding their sustenance. Certainly the womenfolk depend on you entirely and are under your command and control. You have taken them
as your companions as a trust from Almighty Allah and have taken their
physical bodies in use under the laws determined by Allah. So you
should fear Allah with regard to the women and discharge your obligations of sustenance in a beautiful way. Beware! I have communicated to
you the orders of Allah and Allah is also the witness."

"Beware of discord among yourselves, lest after I am no more among
you, you may not revert to conduct and behaviour countrary to fraternity
and start killing one another. All Muslims are brothers among themselves and the wealth of any one is unlawful and may not be taken without proper and willing consent of the owner. You will not go astray if
you adhere to the Book of Allah which I am leaving among you."

"Your Lord sustainer is one and your forefather, Adam, is the forefather
of all human beings and he was created from dust. The most honourable
of you in the sight of Allah is one who fears Allah most. No Arab has
any superiority over a non-Arab, nor does a non-Arab have any superiority over an Arab. Personal merit of any human being is dependent on
his fear of Allah. I have delivered to you the message of Allah and you
will be asked by Allah about me. May I ask you what will be your
reply? The people said: "We bear witness that you have faithfully

conveyed the message of Allah to us; you have unveiled the realities and delivered to us safely the great trust of Allah." Then he (peace be on him) said: "O Allah! Be witness! O Allah! Be witness! O Allah witness (to what people have deposed about my mission)."

Then he addressed the audience again:

Those who are present here, they may communicate the message to those who are absent because many who are absent may have greater capacity to guard the message and pass it on to others.

Allah has a fixed share for each heir in the legacy of every faithful person and it is unlawful to make a will about the wealth and property of a person except one third of it. The child shall belong to the man on whose bed he is born and the punishment for rape shall be stones. Any one who acknowledges as his father a man who is not his father, shall be cursed by Allah, His angels and all human beings. No ransom shall be accepted from him on the Day of Judgment. Peace and blessings from Allah may dwell on you all.

(ii) The Minna Sermon
This discourse was delivered at Minna and constitutes the international Magna Carta of Islam.
The Holy Prophet (PBUH) said:

O people!

1. No prophet will ever come after me and there will be no Ummah after you. (Ummah is the people who distinctly follow a particular prophet—as Christians are the Ummah of Jesus Christ and Jews are the Ummah of Moses.)

2. Listen to me with care and attention. Keep engaged in the worship of your one Lord Sustainer—Allah.

3. Guard and keep offering regularly the five times of prayers.

4. Guard and regularly observe the fast in the month of Ramadhan.

5. Pay gracefully and cheerfully the poor due (Zakat) from your wealth regularly every year.

6. Keep performing the Hajj Pilgrimage of the Holy Ka'aba regularly every year.

7. Keep obeying your rulers from among yourselves so that you deserve entry into the heaven of your Lord.

The above discourses of the Holy Prophet (PBUH) contain an ideal constitution and code of conduct for all human beings. The oneness and uniqueness of Allah as the only lawful, acceptable deity worthy of worship by mankind has been emphasized.

- The worship of one Allah has been laid down as the base and foundation of human social life.

- The lives and property of believers have been granted sanctity against any violation.

- Vengeance of an unlawful murder has been made the compulsory penal law for believers in Islam.

- The age-long social evil of usury had been abolished.

- The feuds of the pre-Islamic days of ignorance have been written off.

- The positions and ranks enjoyed by those with vested interest were totally abolished.

- The mutual rights and duties of married couples have been clearly defined.

- Firm and unshakable foundations have been provided for family life as the basic unit of human society.

- Women of all ranks have been declared to be the sacred trust of Allah, and their liberal treatment has been emphasized as a divine obligation.

- Fraternity and brotherhood has been made a compulsory article of faith among believers in the teachings of Islam.

- The Book of Allah (The Holy Qur'an) has been declared as an accepted code for all human conduct and relationship.

- One Allah and one forefather of mankind have been declared to be the one sure foundation for the oneness of the human race, and all prejudices based on color, race and motherland have been dismissed as irrational and baseless.

- Piety and godliness have been accepted as the only criterion for respect and love of human beings.

Whenever and wherever any social movement is started for the welfare of human beings, it will certainly follow the broad principles of Islamic social justice enunciated by the Holy Prophet of Islam (PBUH) in this marvelous discourse. This is the fundamental constitution of the Islamic social order to which the entire human race has been invited. If these broad principles are ignored by any so-called social reformer, the edifice built shall be un-Islamic and not acceptable to any group of Muslims. This constitution is the touchstone by which we can judge the efforts and achievements of any leadership, as well as all Muslim governments in various Islamic lands. This constitution indeed is the mirror wherein we can look in our own faces as well the faces of anti-Islamic cultures and civilizations, however high their claims may be.

These Discourses are the final message of our beloved Prophet and we Muslims are his real addressees. These sermons, therefore, have assumed the nature and character of the will of our Holy Prophet (PBUH). Every word uttered by our Holy Prophet (PBUH) has an inspiration and a pathos in it and our souls should be stirred into action at the clarion call of our beloved prophet. We must shake off the bondage of un-Islamic values and systems which have hitherto captivated our spirit and bodies and capture with firm hands the valuable system of Islamic life taught by our beloved prophet (PBUH) who underwent untold and prolonged persecution and oppression. His patience and forbearance were unprecedented in the history of mankind.

The sermons delivered at various stages of the Hajj rituals point towards his impending departure from the world and his separation from his followers. His address to a select gathering of his companions near a pond assumed the character of a parting message, touching the noblest sentiments of the listeners. After the usual praise of Almighty Allah, he said: "O people! I am after all a human being. May be that before long I will receive a message from my Lord Allah, calling me back to His audience and I will respond to His call. I am leaving behind for you two heavy things—the book of Allah (the Holy Qur'an) which contains light and guidance, wisdom and knowledge for you. If you catch hold of this book with firmness and devotion, you will never go astray. The second thing I am leaving under your care is my progeny (or my way of conduct and behavior)."

After elucidating the principal points of his teachings, Muhammad (S.A.W.S.) clearly announced that what he had said was not only for those who were present there but for others too; he enjoined upon his audience the duty of conveying this message to those who were absent. He said:

> Ye who are present, preach unto those who are not present as perchance some of those to whom you preach might be more able to remember it and safeguard it than those who are present here.[16]

Conclusion

The above brief treatment of the two key orations of Christianity and Islam clearly shows that both world religions have many teachings in common which can form the basis of a dialogue between the Christians and the Muslims. These essentially moral teachings encompass both individual and collective life and, therefore, if observed and obeyed in word and deed would lead to change in this world and salvation in the Hereafter.

NOTES

1. The Holy Qur'an 2:38.
2. The Holy Bible (New International Version - The New Testament) (Michigan: The Zondervan Corporation, 1984), Matthew 5:3-10.
3. *Ibid.*, 5:21-22.
4. *Ibid.*, 5:25-26.
5. *Ibid.*, 5:27-30.
6. *Ibid.*, 5:32.
7. *Ibid.*, 5:38-42.
8. *Ibid.*, 5:43-48.
9. *Ibid.*, 6:1-4.
10. *Ibid.*, 6:19-21.
11. *Ibid.*, 7:1-5.
12. *Ibid.*, 6:25-34.
13. *Ibid.*, 7:7-12.
14. *Ibid.*, 7:15-20.
15. *Ibid.*, 7:24-27.
16. Farewell message is found in various places in books of *hadith* and history. Here it has been given in one place only. The following references may be consulted in this connection:
    (i) Abi Yaqoob, Ahmed Ibn *Tarikh-i-Yaqoobi* (Beirut: Dar Sadir, n.d.), Vol. II, pp. 109-112.
    (ii) Ibn Hisham, *Al Seerah al Nabwiyyah* (Egypt: Mustafa Al Babi, 1355 AH), Vol. IV, pp.248-53.
    (iii) Ibn Baz, Abdul Aziz bin Abdullah, *Fath al Bari* (annotated edition of

Bukhari *Sahih*) (Riyadh: Jamia Imam Muhammad bin Saud Al-Islamiyyah), Vol.III, p. 573.

(iv) A. Guillaume, *The Life of Muhammad*, Translation Ibn Ishaq's Sirat Rasul Allah (New York: Oxford University Press, 1955), pp. 651-52.

20

CHRISTIAN-MUSLIM-JEWISH DIALOGUE IN DENVER, COLORADO

Jane I. Smith

FOR NEARLY SEVEN YEARS, a group of men and women representing the Abrahamic faiths met in Denver to share information,
discuss political concerns and faith commitments, and get to know each
other as individuals. Nearly a year ago the group ceased meeting,
apparently having lost its focus and its sense of purpose. In preparation
for this report I have talked with almost all of the members of the
group. It is clear that nearly everyone feels a keen sense of loss, and
hopes that the leadership will emerge to get it back on track. Following
is an attempt to describe, according to my own observations and those
of other group members, what worked well for us ("Signs of Promise"),
what was less successful, and some of the issues that need to be
addressed if we attempt to reconstitute ourselves and proceed with the
business of dialogue.

In May of 1988, a representative of the U.S. Interreligious Committee for Peace in the Middle East met with the Executive Director of
the Colorado Council of Churches about the possibility of establishing
a Denver chapter of the Committee in consultation with Muslim,
Jewish and Christian leadership in the greater Denver area. By the fall

of 1988, the group was constituted and began meeting formally. In the beginning, Jewish leaders in Denver were nervous about the possibility of such an association, fearing that it might turn into a forum for "beating up" on Israel. We never actually became the kind of chapter of the Committee for Peace in the Middle East that was originally anticipated, forming instead an independent interfaith dialogue[1] group under the general aegis of the Colorado Council of Churches. It is important to note, however, that the original impetus for the formation of the group, i.e. discussion of issues related to peace in the Middle East, remained a significant focus of our continuing conversations.

The group initially determined several "ground rules": (a) We would remain small and as constant as possible, with no more than five representatives from each of the respective communities. (b) The membership would be both male and female from each faith group. (c) We would rotate our meeting places, creating the opportunity to visit each other in our homes and in our places of worship. (d) Responsibility for coordinating the meetings would lie with the Colorado Council of Churches, and for chairing them with its Executive Director.

The "principle of selection" of the membership was casual; no one now is quite certain exactly how we were initially gathered. The result, however, was generally a happy one insofar as we represented a range of laypeople and religious professionals, some with quite detailed knowledge about their own faith as well (on occasion) as the faith of others, and some with only the kind of information garnered through personal experience within their own communities. Certain difficulties did arise as a result of this constituency, but they did not feel overwhelming. The lone Muslim woman, a convert from Christianity, felt that she was too inexperienced to say much and, I suspect, was slightly intimidated by the loquaciousness of the males in the group. The religious professionals sometimes tended to dominate the conversation or at least to feel that their word was definitive for their community. The fact that none of the Muslims was a religious professional may have been problematic, although one was president of the Colorado Muslim Society and an articulate and well-informed spokesperson. Those who knew quite a bit about the other traditions sometimes had to sit through long explanations of rather elementary materials on beliefs and practices. I personally was in the somewhat odd position as a Christian scholar of Islamic studies of occasionally knowing that a statement made by a Muslims in the group was not historically or

Qur'anically accurate, and not feeling comfortable in challenging that. Despite these problems, I think the mix was a good and helpful one.

The group, while experiencing a few substitutions of membership, remained fairly constant, with about five women and ten males. Some feel that the fact that there was any turnover at all was detrimental, and that the presence of a new person inevitably set us back or changed the course of the discussion. If the group *is* reconstituted, several issues related to membership will need to be addressed. Should we more consciously try to balance the males and females in the group, making sure that if we stay with fifteen members, at least two from each community are female? Should efforts be made to include African American Muslims? Do we want to have persons of color representing the Christian community, specifically African American, Asian, Hispanic? Would it be helpful to include orthodox Jews? Or, does the conscious attempt to be inclusive in these ways preclude the kind of diversity that the rather random selection of the original members actually provided?

There is little doubt that the greatest benefit for all of us in the group has been the opportunity to get to know members of other religious traditions in deep and personal ways. As we struggled over the years to keep ourselves on track—indeed to try to determine just what "on track" even meant—we continued to meet once a month whenever possible because we came to care too much about each other to stop. We were friends who shared each other homes, meals (on occasion), and places of worship. To state the obvious, we became real people to each other and not simply "representatives" of certain religious traditions. That bond saw us through some hard times, and I think continues to be strong enough that the group will be revived.

We began, then, as a forum for discussion of international concerns and hopes for peace, and continued to return to that theme over the years. Our political conversations focussed mainly on the Middle East, although we also discussed North Africa, Bosnia and other parts of the Muslim world. These conversations were painful but extremely important insofar as we were able to experience the degree of personal investment others in the group had in hoping for resolve of hard issues. The exchanges between Palestinians and Jews were difficult for each other, and perhaps even more difficult for the Christians in the group to watch. But we all learned from the experience. One member believes that it was only because the Christians were present as "mediators" that the Jews and Muslims were able to talk to each other. (A

Jew told me he was convinced that a Palestinian participant had quit because the group would not allow him to use the forum as a place to "rant and rave.") It was over political positions, however, that the group experienced its most serious difficulties, and indeed nearly collapsed after a few years. The most problematic moment came when a number of the members signed a petition to the U.S. government protesting loan guarantees to Israel. Members who participated in this signing did so *not* as representatives of the dialogue group but as individuals objecting to U.S. policy. The Jewish members of the group, however, in particular a rabbi whose participation in the dialogue was already suspect by many in his congregation, found this to be unbearably hurtful.[2] He resigned the group in protest, and only through much personal intervention by other members and indeed after a session in which we used outside mediation were we able to continue. We also had some painful moments during the Gulf War when Muslims were put in the position, or felt that they were, of explaining the actions of both Saddam Hussein and the rich Gulf elite. One Muslim felt that his co-religionists were trying too hard to sound "politically correct" (however that was defined) to the other members of the group to be able to sort out their own feelings appropriately.

Some participants have expressed their opinion that we were ill advised to even try to discuss issues such as the Palestinian-Israeli conflict since it is clear that we would never be able to reach agreement. Indeed, our repeated efforts to come up with a statement to which all of us—Christians, Muslims and Jews—could agree came to naught. We ran into similar difficulties when we tried to construct a statement condemning Serbian action in Bosnia. Almost unanimous, we were again thwarted because of the painful response of a Greek Orthodox woman in the group who felt we were unfair to the Serbs. Other participants in the dialogue, however, are absolutely convinced that unless a group such as this devotes itself to political conversations (what one Palestinian member calls "the search for reality") there is little ongoing reason for our existence. Our most important task, they feel, is trying to figure out how Muslims, Christians and Jews can coexist in America and in the world. We talked about the fact that for many western Christians, dialogue is an interesting and attractive exercise, while for others in different parts of the world, and even in some ways in America, it relates to basic issues of survival.

Despite our struggles, it is clear that several concrete and very important things happened as a result of these kinds of political conversations. In 1989 in his Kol Nidre sermon, one rabbi in the group called for negotiations without preconditions between Israelis and the Palestinian Liberation Organization. Subsequently he spoke in his synagogue about the need to exchange land for peace. While he paid the high price of the extreme anger of many of the members of his congregation, expressing their strong opposition to his even participating in our dialogue group,[3] it is clear that in fact he was a pioneer in the kind of thinking that moved the peace process to the signing of the Oslo Accords.[4] He has stated on several public occasions that it is only because of our group that he has been able to take such a position. In a kind of second step in that same process, this rabbi invited a Palestinian Muslim member to speak in his synagogue at the time of the signing of the Accords, a first in the Denver community. The Muslim talked about a new kind of nationalism, one not of exclusion but of the recognition of each other's rights to sovereignty. The same congregation that heard the Kol Nidre sermon with the greatest reluctance responded to this Palestinian Muslim with a standing ovation, an event much publicized in the Denver press. It would not have happened had it not been for our dialogue group.[5] As a follow-up to this visit, a Christian member of the group who hosts a religious radio program invited the Rabbi and the Palestinian to present a three-part public conversation which was very well received in the community.

The other major learning of our meetings came through explanations of what we believe and how we practice. We began by looking at passages in our respective scriptures in which we treat common themes. In a very engaging session, for example, Muslims talked about Qur'anic descriptions of Mary and the birth of Jesus, discussing the importance of the prophethood of Jesus. The group tried to sort out what we actually do have in common in our understanding of prophecy, what the term al-messih (messiah) means for Muslims, and why Christian beliefs about incarnation and trinity are so unacceptable in Islam.[6] The Jews raised the issue of what scripture is, moving from Torah through the range of sacred Jewish writings, and Muslims discussed whether or not hadith can be considered scripture by any definition. An interesting issue arose when it became clear that Muslims believed that they knew Christianity and Judaism quite well because of what the Qur'an has to say about these communities. They found it difficult to accept that in fact Jews and Christians have a quite different understanding of themselves than that portrayed in Muslim scripture.

A project about which all members of the group were excited, but which never came to fruition before we stopped meeting, was one which was designed to connect belief and practice. We decided that it would be extremely helpful if we were to spend one or two sessions per faith tradition talking about a particular holy day or ceremony, explaining what is done and what theological preconceptions underlie the ritual. Then the group was to attend a service or celebration in the respective mosque, church or synagogue. We identified the observance of Eid al-Fitr, the Jewish Seder meal and Easter as the three occasions we would try to share. I am personally extremely disappointed that we were never able to follow through on this project.

Although we never made the issue of preconceptions and prejudices a specific item on our discussion agenda, it is certainly the case that those of us who are American-born Christians learned about the pain of prejudice experienced by others in this country. In particular, we heard of the difficulties that Muslims have as the American press continues to highlight Islamic extremism and terrorism both here and abroad. Several Palestinians shared the responses that they made on public television to the airing of Steven Emerson's "Jihad in America." Most recently, members of the three faith traditions who have been involved in the group participated in a service of commemoration for the bombing victims in Oklahoma. A prominent theme of the service, sponsored by the Colorado Council of Churches and building on the friendships formed through the dialogue group, was public acknowledgment of the pain that Muslims experienced as Americans immediately assigned guilt for the bombing to members of the Arab/Muslim community. Conversations held in the dialogue group in which concerns over prejudice were aired were not without some tension and suspicion of undue exaggeration, but again we learned.

A North African Muslim male suggested that he felt pressure within the group to "conform" to the spirit of harmony and cooperation within the group to the point where he was uncomfortable expressing his real religiously-based opinions. This, he said, worked against one of our agreed-upon purposes for meeting, which was to understand and respect each other's differing views. A case in point was the issue of homosexuality raised by the passage in Colorado of Amendment Two, prohibiting "special privilege" for gays and lesbians. The general sympathy of the group was opposition to the amendment to the point where several Muslims felt that they could not express freely their conviction that homosexuality is wrong. Other Muslims with whom I have spoken, however, did not feel any such pressure to hide their own opinions or emotions.

To some degree this may reflect what some Muslims described as their occasional discomfort with the more generally "liberal" stance of most of the Christians and Jews in the group. They felt that they might have been more comfortable sharing their beliefs and concerns with members of the Christian and Jewish communities who are more theologically conservative. Another dimension of this may be the feeling of some members of the group, Muslim and non-Muslim, that it was harder for the Muslims to express their own theological differences than it was for the particular Christians and Jews who participated in these discussions. It is one of the better publicized observations of much of the recent reflection on Christian-Muslim dialogue that often the issues are more clearly defined along "liberal-conservative" lines than according to membership in one tradition or another. It is also the case that many Muslims with whom I have been in dialogue profess themselves as having more "respect" for Christians who hold firmly to their doctrinal beliefs than they do for those who while open to the insights of other faiths can affirm only rather watered-down versions of the beliefs of their own traditions. Our small group provides one microcosm of what it means to think in terms of "we-they" and whether or not our more traditional categories can continue to hold.

As I talked with members of the group recently about their perceptions of why we have (at least temporarily) stopped meeting, I heard a number of different responses. Most feel that we spent far too much time trying to figure out our agenda. As a Christian pastor put it, "We just kept spinning our wheels and couldn't get out of the rut." Some wanted more political discussion, some more theological exchange, and some thought we should be working together on issues of social concern to religious people in the greater Denver area. Occasional voices called for us to forget theology and politics and talk about what we can *do* together. To some extent these differences seemed to fall along gender lines. Men appeared to prefer the political/theological exchanges, while women generally favored more attention to social issues of common concern. Had we been more successful in organizing these priorities, and figuring out whether and how to attend to them all, the level of frustration would have been considerably lower. Members are unsure if having the head of the Colorado Council of Churches continue as moderator was wise. Several even feel that it would be best to dissociate the group entirely from the CCC, which by definition is a Christian organization.

A number of specific suggestions have been put forth by members of the group as to what a reorganization might look like. Some think that rotating leadership would be helpful and others favor the establishment of a steering group of three, one from each community, to determine agenda and lead the discussion. The question of commitment is a significant one for many; the suggestion was made that participants sign a written agreement of obligation to attend, with meetings scheduled at least a half year in advance. Some think that the group should be more attuned to local politics, and that whenever possible we take part in legislative hearings and make specific proposals as representatives of religious communities. One member feels that the group as such should work for its own dissolution, not by a kind of default as seems currently to be the case but by design, spinning off into a number of other groups so that the whole conversation can be enlarged. The theme of friendship was reiterated in the affirmation that whatever form it takes, the group (or groups) should meet at least once a year for a purely social occasion in which members of the participants' families can join and get to know one another.

Even if this group is not to continue in anything like its present form, it is clear that the benefit to the members and to the Denver community as a whole is substantial. One of the most exciting things to have come out of our dialogue was the impetus to construct an interfaith chapel in the new Denver International Airport. The project, as yet uncompleted, has official corporate sponsorship through the Colorado Council of Churches, the Colorado Muslim Society, the Denver Archdiocese and the Rabbinical Council. It is generally agreed, however, that this cooperative effort was a direct result of the interfaith exchange begun by our dialogue group. This will be the first airport chapel in the country to have a separate prayer room (which will be identified as a *masjid*) for Muslims.[7]

Such concrete results in terms of reaching into the larger Denver community certainly justify for the members of the group the efforts they made over a number of years to stay in contact. In addition to what we personally gained, the spinoff has gone in two directions— Denver as a whole has benefitted and so do our own individual faith communities. Those forces are in place and will continue. One Christian pastor who has been a faithful participant in the dialogue reports that he met recently with a conservative group of his parishioners doing Bible study. The religion of Islam began to be discussed, and one man remarked that he thinks Islam is a horrible and violent religion. The pastor simply asked him if he knew any Muslims personally. . . .

NOTES

1. While the term trialogue has occasionally been used for such a three-way conversation, I will continue to refer to it as a dialogue group, the terminology by which we have recognized ourselves.
2. Members of his congregation were quick to remind him that they always knew such a dialogue venture would be of no avail.
3. He even received "hate mail" from some of the members of his congregation. One holocaust survivor spat in his face and said he was as bad as the Nazis.
4. That the process is currently in grave difficulties, inevitable in the opinion of many because of the inequalities apparent in the provisions of the Accords themselves, does not detract from the importance of this rabbi's conviction that Jewish recognition of Palestinian rights is essential.
5. Another example of action coming as a result of our association was the assistance provided by an Algerian Muslim member to me as Dean of Iliff in my efforts to help a student married to an Algerian man who had taken their child back to Algeria.
6. Other topics that we talked about pursuing, but did so only in fairly peripheral ways, were roles of women in the respective traditions, our expectations for an afterlife and judgment, prayer, and the integrity of religious traditions. "Islam is not a supermarket," remarked one Muslim member, "where some items can be selected and others rejected."
7. The Colorado Council of Churches has received calls from members of all three religious communities expressing disappointment that the chapel is not yet available for persons wishing to find solace from the fear of the Oklahoma bombings. One of the issues currently under discussion is whether calling the combined worship spaces a "chapel" carries overly strong Christian connotations.

Contributors

Raficq Abdullah is a Muslim lawyer in London, United Kingdom.

S. A. Ali is the founder and former Director of the Indian Institute of Islamic Studies, Hamdard University in New Delhi, India.

M. Darrol Bryant is Professor of Religion and Culture at Renison College, University of Waterloo, Waterloo, Ontario, Canada.

Frederick M. Denny is Professor of Islamic Studies and the History of Religions, University of Colorado at Boulder, Colorado, USA.

Abdullah Durkee was Head of the Dar al-Islam Foundation in Alexandria, Egypt and now resides at Green Mountain, Virginia, USA.

Martin Forward was the Director of Interfaith Relations for the Methodist Church in the United Kingdom and is now Tutor at Wesley House, Cambridge University, Cambridge, England.

Paulos Mar Gregorios was Bishop of Delhi and the North, Syrian Orthodox Church, New Delhi, India and a Former President of the World Council of Churches. He founded and was the Director of Sarva Dharma Nilaya when he died in 1996.

Riffat Hassan is Professor of Religion, University of Louisville, Louisville, Kentucky, USA.

'Izz al-din Ibrahim is the former President of the University of the Emirates. He is at present Cultural Counsellor and Director of the Shaykh Zayed bin Sultan al-Nahayan Charitable Foundation, Abu Dhabi, UAE.

Badru D. Kateregga was a Professor of Religious Studies, Kenyatta University, Nairobi, Kenya and is now the Ambassador of the Republic of Uganda in Riyadh, Saudi Arabia.

Habibur Rahman Khan is President of Idara-E-Fikr-E-Eslami in Karachi, Pakistan.

Abdelmoneim M. Khattab is Imam and Director of the Islamic Center of Greater Toledo, Ohio, USA.

Muhib. O. Opeloye is an Associate Professor of Islamic Studies, Department of Religions, Lagos State University and the National Vice President of the Nigerian Association of Teachers of Arabic and Islamic Studies.

Abdul Rashid is the Chair of the Department of Islamic Learning, University of Karachi, Karachi, Pakistan.

Saba Risaluddin is the founder and Director of the Calamus Foundation, London, United Kingdom.

Reza Shah-Kazemi is the Editor of *Islamic World Report* and resides in London, United Kingdom.

Abdullah Siddiqui is a Research Fellow at the Islamic Foundation, Markfield Dawah Center, Leicester, United Kingdom and the Joint-Editor of *Encounters: Journal of Inter-Cultural Perspectives*.

Jane I. Smith was the Dean of the Iliff School of Theology in Denver, Colorado, and is currently at the Hartford Foundation in Hartford, Connecticut, USA.

Thomas G. Walsh is the Executive Director of the International Religious Foundation, New York, New York, USA.

Index